*For Gary, Theresa, and David*

# CONTENTS

# ILLUSTRATIONS

# ABBREVIATIONS AND A NOTE ON TEXTS

MILTON's poetry will be cited from Merritt Hughes, ed., *Complete Poems and Major Prose of John Milton*. Biblical quotations are from the Authorized (King James) version. I have modernized u, v, i, and j, and shortened some long titles in my seventeenth-century sources, but left the original spelling and punctuation unchanged.

The following abbreviations are used in my text for editions frequently cited. Full documentation is given under Works Cited.

Burnet, *History* (Gilbert Burnet, *Bishop Burnet's History of His Own Time*).

*CPW* (*Complete Prose Works of John Milton*, ed. Don M. Wolfe).

*CSPD* (*Calendar of State Papers, Domestic Series, of the Reign of Charles II*).

*CSPV* (*Calendar of State Papers, Venetian*).

Dryden, *Works* (*The Works of John Dryden*, ed. Edward Niles Hooker and H. T. Swedenberg, Jr.).

Evelyn, *Diary* (*The Diary of John Evelyn*, ed. E. S. de Beer).

*LR* (*The Life Records of John Milton*, ed. J. Milton French).

*MCR* (*Middlesex County Records*, ed. John Cordy Jeaffreson).

Mundy, *Travels* (*The Travels of Peter Mundy in Europe and Asia, 1608–1667*, eds. Richard C. Temple and Lavinia Mary Anstey).

Pepys, *Diary* (*The Diary of Samuel Pepys*, ed. Robert Latham and William Matthews).

Rugg, *Diurnal* (*The Diurnal of Thomas Rugg, 1659–1661*, ed. William L Sachse).

*State Trials* (*A Complete Collection of State Trials*, ed. Thomas Bayly Howell).

# ACKNOWLEDGMENTS

THIS project was generously supported by grants from the Pennsylvania State University Institute for the Arts and Humanistic Studies, the Folger Shakespeare Library, the National Endowment for the Humanities, and the Office of Research and Graduate Studies, College of Liberal Arts, Penn State.

I have entailed various other debts in completing this study. My graduate work on Milton was ably guided by Barbara K. Lewalski, upon whose advice and example I continue to draw. I am grateful for the encouragement and valuable suggestions on parts or all of the manuscript received from Arthur Kinney, Janel Mueller, Emily Bartels, and Mary Thomas Crane. My revisions were greatly aided by the trenchant comments from the University of Georgia Press readers, Martine Watson Brownley and Joseph Wittreich. My colleagues at Penn State provided intellectual and personal support, and I especially want to thank Deborah Clarke, Christopher Clausen, John Harwood, Sanford Schwartz, Robert Secor, and Paul Youngquist. It has been a pleasure to work with Nancy Grayson Holmes, my editor at the University of Georgia Press. Finally, I thank my husband, Gary, for helpful criticism, much patience, and ongoing support.

AN EARLIER version of chapter 1 appeared as "*Paradise Regained* and the Politics of Martyrdom" in *Modern Philology* 90. An earlier version of chapter 2 appeared as "'This So Horrid Spectacle': *Samson Agonistes* and the Execution of the Regicides" in *English Literary Renaissance* 20.

# HISTORICIZING MILTON

# INTRODUCTION

> This day came in his Majestie *Charles* the 2d to London after a sad, & long Exile, and Calamitous Suffering both of the King & Church: being 17 yeares: This was also his Birthday, and with a Triumph of above 20000 horse & foote, brandishing their swords and shouting with unexpressable joy: The wayes straw'd with flowers, the bells ringing, the streetes hung with Tapissry, fountaines running with wine. . . . I stood in the strand, & beheld it, & blessed God.
>
> John Evelyn, *Diary*

THE TRIUMPHAL entry of Charles II into London on May 29, 1660, restored not only the person of the king, but also the theatrical spectacle of divinely approved monarchical power. The entry, like the coronation to follow almost a year later, was a display of lavish magnificence and loyalty that involved the king as viewer and viewed, the people as spectators and participants. The Restoration triumph evinced the theatrical nature of restored monarchy, the particular iconography by which royal power was both constituted and celebrated.[1]

Charles II, like his predecessors, was acclaimed and fashioned by public spectacle—ceremonies that deployed pageantry, splendor, and ritual. But the nation had seen eleven years without a king. Restoration spectacle was marked by self-consciousness, anxiety, and ambivalence, by internal fissures as well as by dependence upon the theater of punishment as dark twin to the celebratory pomp.

The Restoration monarchy thus depended upon the dual display of praise and execration, the spectacle of punished treason that threatened and yet served as raison d'être for monarchical power. From the beginning, lavish celebration of the imminent and actual return of Charles II was doubled by the abuse of symbols of the old regime. The stress on the previous regime mediated the power of the returning monarchy; certainly the people knew less about the once-despised young man whom they were restoring to the throne than about the chaos and confusion that had preceded him. Indeed the acclaim that greeted the returning Charles II may have been largely the unanimity of discontent with the old.[2]

The lavish entry in May 1660 and coronation entertainment in April 1661 idealized Charles as returning the joys of the golden age, new Roman conqueror triumphant over hearts. But even the coronation triumph included images of the severed heads of Charles's enemies. Between the king's arrival and coronation, Parliament tried, hung, and quartered ten surviving regicides and ordered the exhuming and desecration of the bodies of Oliver Cromwell, Henry Ireton, and John Bradshaw. When fifth monarchist Thomas Venner staged a violent insurrection in January 1661, civic officials not only executed him but also widely publicized the rebellion, tarring nonconformity with the brush of political subversion. Theatrical monarchy was twinned with the drama of the scaffold.



Yet the spectacles of punishment and power, once put into circulation, could have unintended effects, and various discourses competed to control, reinterpret, or even to subvert the displays. Like the public execution of the king eleven years earlier, the hangings, beheadings, and quarterings of the regicides were reinterpreted as a display of martyrdom. The coronation triumph itself and the responses it evoked may have been less uniform and less joyful than it appeared. Venner's uprising was a forceful rejection of state spectacle—he and his men, fighting for King Jesus, were directly inspired by the courage with which the regicides met their grisly deaths. By 1665 and 1666, the natural catastrophes of plague and fire were similarly contested sites, read as divine punishment for rebellion—or for restoration—in terms strikingly evocative of the penal displays of state. And finally, the pope burnings of the 1670s showed the deployment of spectacle to challenge and curtail monarchical prerogative.

When the Independents took power in 1649, they tried in various ways to attack or appropriate the spectacles that had proven a great source of monarchical power. The public execution of Charles I, however, proved to be a tragic blunder without consideration that the audience response might not be uniform. With the Restoration, the Puritan sects were once again confronted with a powerful tool for marshalling public opinion in displays of punishment and ceremonies of state. Yet the execution of Charles had provided the opposition with a hermeneutic paradigm in the languages of scripture by which the spectacle could be contested, even destabilized. If Puritans attempted, with mixed results, to imitate royalists in their Interregnum displays, they also (ironically) followed them in their oppositional mode after the Restoration.[3]

Spectacles of the 1660s and 1670s complicate the current views of spectacle and power in Renaissance England established by new historicist criticism and largely based on the work of Michel Foucault. Foucault begins *Discipline and Punish*, his powerful and controversial study of modes of punishment in eighteenth- and nineteenth-century France, by envisioning a time when power worked more through theatrical display than through the mode of writing. In the scene on the scaffold, the law inscribes punishment on the body of the condemned; the site reflects the power of the king whose law has been violated.[4]



In discussing the reception of the spectacles of punishment, Foucault gestures toward resistance without making this a genuine factor in his analysis. Rather than delineating the ambiguities of power on display, or the heterogeneity and possible resistance of the people who view and then circulate the spectacle through image and printed word, Foucault tends to essentialize both monarch and people. Separating the historical moments of violent, excessive spectacle and more efficient discipline through surveillance and training of the body, Foucault underestimates both subjectivity and resistance. Discipline for Foucault can be only the product of civil authorities, not the grounds for resistance.[5]

New historicist work in the English Renaissance has relied heavily on a Foucauldian paradigm of spectacle and power. In important and influential studies, Stephen Orgel, Stephen Greenblatt, Louis Montrose, Jonathan Goldberg, and Leonard Tennenhouse have traced the semiotics of spectacle in Elizabethan, Jacobean, and Caroline England. In the earliest of these studies, Stephen Orgel argues for the power of the Caroline masque to idealize an increasingly autocratic monarchy under Charles I in the 1630s.[6] Stephen Greenblatt, in a representative and dazzling essay on Thomas Harriot, the Algonquian Indians, and Shakespeare's *Henriad*, suggests that "the subversive doubts [that *Henry V*] continually awakens originate paradoxically in an effort to intensify the power of the king and his war." Through the play's very ambiguities and tensions, Greenblatt argues, "the spectators are induced to make up the difference, to invest in the illusion of magnificence, to be dazzled by their own imaginary identification with the conqueror." Hence he reaches a Foucauldian conclusion: "This apparent production of subversion is . . . the very condition of power."[7] Greenblatt elsewhere makes a similar argument for the power of display in the opulent court of Henry VIII.[8]

More attentive to fractures within the display, Louis Montrose has shown how ambivalently gendered Elizabethan displays are represented in such plays as *A Midsummer Night's Dream* that empower the queen by reaffirming patriarchy.[9] Similarly, in tracing the Jacobean Roman style through James I's own discourse and the artists who represented it, Jonathan Goldberg cogently points out the contradictions of self-authorizing power, although he does not note the unique ambivalences of the Roman mode, nor attend to competing biblical models.[10] Leonard Tennenhouse acutely argues (against Foucault) for the spectacle as contested site, but does not extend such contestation to the drama he sees as idealizing, authorizing, or mythologizing royalty.[11] Even in analysis of spectacles of punishment and power under a stable monarchy, the Foucauldian model understates complexity, dissonance, and the possibilities for resistance.[12]



In practice, new historicists have been able to work with largely monolithic, effective displays by concentrating on classical rather than religious modes, as Deborah Shuger argues, and by not extending their analyses, as James Holstun and Caroline Porter contend, to genuinely oppositional voices.[13] Orgel's account of Puritans such as William Prynne, who opposed the theater as both dangerous and powerful, is instructive for analysis of what happens to spectacle after 1649.[14] Yet one does not find in the Interregnum and Restoration an absolute opposition between "Puritan" iconoclasm and royalist spectacle.

Greenblatt and other new historicists have given almost no attention to the poetry of John Milton, written and published after his personal and political defeat in Restoration England. New historicist (Foucauldian) models of spectacle, power, and poetry can be extended and revised by attention to the 1660s and 1670s and to the oppositional poetics of John Milton. But at the same time, the contextualizing, synchronic analyses of new historicist readings can address central problems and lacunae in Milton studies hitherto not adequately resolved.[15] One major issue thus addressed is the dominant literary history that sees Milton as a relic in the Restoration. A related lacuna is the dual nature of the canonical Milton, Puritan and humanist. Historicizing Milton in the 1660s and 1670s brings together the aspects of his poetry that have led to those divergent and finally unsatisfactory designations; it also helps account for the radical, complex, and distinctive nature of his three long poems.

If in 1915 Sir Walter Raleigh dismissed Milton's poetry as a "monument to dead ideas," literary histories and anthologies inform us that those ideas were already more or less dead upon arrival.[16] Although Milton's *Paradise Lost* (1667), *Paradise Regained* (1671), and *Samson Agonistes* (1671) appeared well into the Restoration period, in literary histories, anthologies, and even course syllabi, he is relegated to the earlier seventeenth century and viewed as a relic in the Restoration. In the fourth edition of *The Norton Anthology* (1979), Milton's poems are placed under the time period 1600–60 and referred to in Restoration section as "relics of an earlier age."[17] In the fifth edition of the *Norton*, the same point is made less directly: "Milton's major poems, a culmination of Renaissance art, appeared at the same time that John Dryden was establishing himself as the laureate of a new age of elegance."[18] *The Oxford Anthology of English Literature* (1973) states that "the fact that Milton's *Paradise Lost* or Bunyan's *Pilgrim's Progress* was published after the Restoration seems incongruous." Milton's poems are placed before 1660.[19]

Literary histories similarly move Milton back in time. Albert Baugh's classic *A Literary History of England* (1948) tells us that "Milton's renewed but unreconstructed genius projected itself like a Gulf Stream through the incongruous currents of the Restoration."[20] The Oxford and Cambridge histories place Milton in the earlier seventeenth century. Douglas Bush writes in the Oxford volume that "Milton's major poems were less typical of the thought and feeling of a large part of the nation [in the Restoration] than, say, the popular *Satire against Hypocrites* (1655) by his nephew John Phillips."[21] More recently, *The Oxford Companion to English Literature* (1985) has under the entry "Restoration" the following: "The re-establishment of monarchy in England, with the return of Charles II (1660); also the period marked by this event of which the chief literary figures are Dryden, Rochester, Bunyan, Pepys, Locke, and the Restoration dramatists."[22] Milton is nowhere to be found.



Underlying this nearly universal view of Milton as relic, there are really two canonical "authors"—the belated Puritan and the belated humanist.[23] Milton the Puritan, constructed by early biographers such as David Masson and by literary historians such as Arthur Barker and Don Wolfe, is a political reformer who participates in the revolution of the 1640s.[24] Active in the civil war and Interregnum, defeated and disillusioned in the Restoration, this Milton turns in his poetry from politics to a "paradise within." Douglas Bush asserts, "[Milton's] earlier pamphlets had been largely directed towards militant action; the decline and collapse of that external hope left him feeling the need of a closer walk with God. In his late poems, in place of the old ardent confidence in public reform, we find an 'un-Miltonic' emphasis on private experience, on humility, obedience, faith, and divine grace."[25] With the apparent collapse of Puritanism, Milton the Puritan turns from outward political and social reform to inner spirituality.

The humanist Milton was largely an answer to the perceived liabilities of the Puritan Milton. In 1966, James Holly Hanford argued that "we have insisted too long on the supposed austerity of [Milton's] temper and on the narrowness of his Puritan thought" and proposed to replace Milton the Puritan with Milton the "poet of humanity." For Hanford, recovering Milton's central concern with "the authentic humanist formula" of freedom links past with present: "These profound convictions put Milton clearly on the side of contemporary humanism, a humanism which, however 'new,' is not without its essential community with the old."[26]

Milton as humanist (or Christian humanist) is defined not only by what are seen as enduring individualist values, a kind of humanist ethos, but also by his classicism.[27] Yet according to the literary histories, this classicist Milton does not belong in the Restoration either but is rather the culmination of the Renaissance. David Daiches comments in *A Critical History of English Literature* (1970) that "*Paradise Lost* shows Milton as Christian Humanist using all the resources of the European literary tradition that had come down to him—biblical, classical, medieval, Renaissance," only to reach "the full flower of his poetic achievement in the midst of a civilization in which he had completely lost faith."[28] Such an approach separates Milton from the politics of his own time, particularly from Restoration politics. Indeed, the humanist Milton is one central figure on which the still-dominant idealist concept of literature is based, implicit in which is the separation of the political from the aesthetic.[29]

Yet in the last decades, since the seminal work of Christopher Hill, Milton as political radical (or Puritan) has been making a comeback. Critiquing previous critical bias toward literary sources, Hill links Milton with the radical third-culture thinkers of his own day in richly documented historical accounts. But Hill sees the effect of the Restoration as the defeat of Milton's politics, making it necessary for him to allude to those defeated politics in his poetry. In Hill's analysis, the poems look backward, acknowledging defeat, asking what went wrong and proposing solutions—in *Paradise Lost* the paradise within, in *Paradise Regained* to become a Son of God, and in *Samson Agonistes* to prepare for future action when God gives the signal.[30]

The Restoration ambiance for Hill thus seems a fairly simple model of domination versus defeat and disempowerment. Yet this model limits what can be done with Milton's poetry. Attentive to the conditions of censorship, Hill reads the "political" meanings of the poems through allegory and allusion, linking events and characters in the poem with events and characters in real life. Hill does not see the writing and stance of the political losers as an oppositional discourse that has its own power as a competing source of authority. Linked with the 1640s and almost exclusively with kingship, the poems remain anachronistic; they look back or within, retreating from the contemporary scene.

In critical studies linking poetry with prose, Milton's poems again retreat from the Restoration scene, to look back at a 1640s revolutionary context.[31] Such studies are often compelling and insightful; yet until the import of Restoration—as well as revolutionary—politics is recognized, the full political resonances of the poems cannot be appreciated. The dominant model of rejection and defeat fails to account, I would argue, for the complexities of Milton's poetic discourse and its multivalent responses to contemporary politics. This focus on the 1640s and 1650s needs to be supplemented and revised by attention to how the Restoration milieu produces and shapes as well as limits discourse—including literary discourse. The synchronic analyses of recent historicist work offer a model by which Milton can be not only politicized but also fully historicized.

Such a historicizing, the situating of Milton's poetry in relation to Restoration discourses and events, can more adequately account for those qualities that create an apparent disjunction between Puritan and humanist. Failure to situate Milton fully in the Restoration has kept the two sides at bay. But I would argue that it is precisely in his unique conjunction of "Puritan" and "humanist," iconoclastic reformer and erudite literary artist, that Milton responds to his Restoration milieu, and in particular to the ongoing spectacles of state.



Several recent discussions have begun to place Milton's poetry in its Restoration context; yet because these discussions have tended to focus on only one side of the Puritan-humanist divide, they have repeated, or not fully countered, the charge of anachronism. Nigel Keeble's seminal study traces the historical milieu, preoccupations, themes, and cultural achievements of nonconformity in Milton, John Bunyan, George Fox, John Owen, Richard Baxter, and others, whose writings, he persuasively argues, have been marginalized by a Whiggish literary canon.[32] Yet Keeble's focus and greatest contribution lies in the historical milieu. His analysis of the literature itself is very brief, usually only a paragraph or two for each work; hence crucial differences between Milton and the other nonconformists, in particular because of Milton's classicism, are obscured. In rightly redressing the previous critical failure to recognize the cultural achievements of nonconformists and Milton's place among them, Keeble understates the "humanist" and public side of Milton.

In another important discussion of Milton and the Restoration, Earl Miner places him in the emergence of a public mode that articulates not private psyche but the poet defined in relation to the world around him. Miner thus recognizes the classicizing, public side of Milton's poetry obscured by Keeble's analysis. While he focuses on Milton as "Christian humanist," Miner recognizes the crucial ambivalence of Milton's combination of classical and Christian: "But Milton gives us a great paradox. He is the best classical scholar of all our great poets and a neoclassicist in critical utterance as well as choice of literary kinds in his mature work. At the same time, however, he alters the classical epic and classical tragedy so far by giving them a Christian soul that their temper and meanings have been entirely altered."[33] This crucial insight is nonetheless not used to explore Milton's responses to the 1660s because Miner, inexplicably, stops at 1660 in his account of Milton's life and times. As if time stood still after May 1660, Miner sees Milton, Dryden, and Butler as poets "whose vision of the world and of [themselves] in it was shaped by experience before 1660."[34]

In another recent essay, Steven Zwicker cogently argues that Milton's very use of the epic genre appropriates and deploys cultural authority in the face of political and social disenfranchisement. Zwicker presents Milton's classicism as a polemical rebuttal: "The learning of this poem is assembled, Milton claims, to instruct and to console; it serves also to humiliate, to silence, to baffle, even to insult."[35] But Zwicker wants to show how Milton's classicism can "exalt Puritan scripturalism" because he apparently views that scripturalism as anachronistic. In his introduction (with Kevin Sharpe) Zwicker argues that "we cannot fail to discern in Milton's verse a tone which by the 1660s often rang with anachronism." Milton the relic once again returns, as Zwicker and Sharpe write: "Milton's anachronism was not merely a matter of personal tone. Though Dryden's near contemporary, in his religiosity Milton seems to speak to us from within the civil war and, in his insistent moralizing of politics, from even earlier decades."[36] But such a stance underestimates both Restoration nonconformity and the complex and responsive nature of Milton's poetry in Restoration England.

In his informative and detailed study of the Restoration, Nicholas Jose, like Zwicker, focuses on the Roman mode; but he places Milton very differently, concentrating on not the erudite classicist but the iconoclastic, anti-Roman author of *Samson Agonistes*, the "Puritan" Milton.[37] Jose sets *Samson Agonistes* in a rich historical context, countering critical tendencies to depoliticize the play. But he does not take fully into account the embedment of that iconoclasm in a literary text, or iconoclasm itself as counter-spectacle. Alternatively attending to the Puritan or the humanist Milton, these studies fail to account for the complex, even conflicting, responses of Milton's poetry to his Restoration milieu as he challenges, undercuts, and yet also appropriates the spectacles of state.

In 1649, the first spectacle of the Interregnum was an act of iconoclasm, the public destruction of an idol of state.[38] Iconoclasm and icon, Puritan reform and the ceremonies of church and state, were not absolutely opposed in 1649 or the years to follow.[39] The spectacle of execution, the displays of state under Cromwell, and the attempts to reinterpret royalist displays in the 1660s and 1670s were marked by ambivalence, an unstable combination of iconoclasm and spectacle that also distinguishes Milton's poetry as a unique mode of art against art.

This private spectacle that challenges the public mode complicates what others have pointed to as quietism or withdrawal in Milton's poetry, another means by which the poetry becomes anachronistic or apolitical. Joseph Wittreich, Michael Wilding, Andrew Milner, and others have argued that Milton rejects contemporary politics—partially in *Paradise Lost*, more fully in *Paradise Regained* and *Samson Agonistes*.[40] The pacifist arguments that point to the inner paradise and a withdrawal from or even repudiation of earthly politics only superficially resituate Milton in the Restoration, because the poems retreat from the contemporary scene, looking inward. But as David Quint has pointed out, even the rejection of earthly politics in *Paradise Regained* has political force.[41] And in *Samson Agonistes*, radical iconoclasm both precedes and constitutes divine spectacle.



While panegyric and pageantry undoubtedly took a classicizing turn after 1660, religious models remained forceful and unsettling; it is in his combination of two discourses that Milton provides a distinctively literary, sometimes conflicted response to the contested and ambivalent spectacles of state. Milton's iconoclastic impulse is manifested in a public, classical mode in order to redefine true martyrdom, true glory, true joy, true conquest, true prophecy. Suspicious of the human icon, whether of Cromwell, the regicides, Charles I, or Charles II, Milton nonetheless wants to imagine a divine spectacle, and he paradoxically creates that spectacle through classicizing human art.

For the blind Milton, who just weeks before the king's arrival had defiantly published an impassioned tract against monarchy, the Restoration was undeniably a personal and political defeat.[42] Milton himself was notorious as an advocate of divorce and, as Cromwell's Latin secretary, the author of widely read justifications of the regicide, including two officially commissioned Latin *Defenses*. When the king returned, Milton went into hiding, first leaving his house and then moving a second time to obscure his whereabouts. Milton's nephew Edward Phillips writes, "His next removal was, by the advice of those that wisht him well, and had a concern for his preservation, into a place of retirement and abscondence, till such time as the current of affairs for the future should instruct him what farther course to take: it was a Friend's house in *Bartholomew Close*, where he liv'd till the Act of Oblivion came forth."[43] Blind and financially reduced, Milton nonetheless secured royal pardon under the August 1660 Act of Oblivion.

Contemporaries differed on why Milton was not further punished. The Act of Oblivion, after all, specified a number of exceptions from pardon, including not only the actual signers of the death warrant for Charles I but also other supporters of the commonwealth considered dangerous. Phillips speculates that Andrew Marvell, member of Parliament from Hull, acted vigorously on Milton's behalf, keeping his name off the dreaded list of exceptions to pardon.[44] There was certainly some feeling that Milton had already been punished—with blindness, by a divine hand. A July 1660 broadside, *The Picture of the Good Old Cause*, is typical in listing under "Several Examples of Gods Judgements on some Eminent Engagers against Kingly Government" the instance of "Milton, that writ two Books against the Kings, and Salmasius his Defence of Kings, struck totally blind, he being not much above 40 years old" (*LR* 4:326). Still others pointed to the king's clemency—or forgetfulness: Bishop Burnet later writes "it was thought a strange omission if [Milton] was forgot, and an odd strain of clemency, if it was intended he should be forgiven" (*History*, 107). Milton was, however, imprisoned for a time. December 1660 finds him being released: "The celebrated Mr. John Milton having now laid long in custody of the sergeant at arms, was released by order of the house," but when Andrew Marvell complained regarding the exorbitant fee the sergeant had exacted from Milton, one Sir Heneage Finch ominously observed that "Milton was Latin Secretary to Cromwell and deserved hanging" (*LR* 4:353).





But for Milton the experience of defeat, writing in a heavily censored environment, was, as Annabel Patterson has argued more broadly in her study of writing and censorship, the very condition of writing poetry.[45] The broad, satiric, harsh analogies of Milton's prose become subtle, multivalent metaphor in his poetry, and in the stories of the fall, the Son of God in the wilderness, and the blind and suffering Samson, Milton figures other stories, other falls, other sufferings. Nigel Keeble has broadly shown how for Puritanism "political defeat was the condition of cultural achievement."[46] I want to delineate more precisely than has been done not only how Milton makes history but also how history makes Milton.

Both drawing on and revising synchronic new historicist analyses of spectacle, power, and the politics of literature, I argue that Milton's poems not only register the power and problematics of monarchical spectacle in the Restoration, but also go one step further to reconstitute spectacle as witness before a divine audience. In my reading, Milton's articulation of a "paradise within" does not withdraw from politics but both challenges and replaces the spectacles of state. In his three Restoration poems, Milton moves from spectacle to discipline, countering strategies of state by constituting an inwardness or conscience that can counter both the spectacle and the surveillance of civil and ecclesiastical authorities. And such discipline is not the end product but the precondition for divine apocalypse in which Milton never wholly lost faith.

Juxtaposing accounts of spectacle with literary texts, I place Milton's poetry within the discourses that arise around contested displays of power and punishment in Restoration England. I reconstruct these discourses from a range of contemporary sources—letters, diaries, newspaper accounts, occasional verse, sermons, royal proclamations, parliamentary records, contemporary travel accounts, and the correspondence of foreign ambassadors. I look at not only the written texts, but also the fascinating visual renderings, the iconography by which spectacles of punishment and power were circulated and interpreted. That first iconoclastic display—the execution of Charles I—was the defining act of the Interregnum government, the implications of which were felt for the rest of the century.[47] Four of the spectacles I examine—the execution of the regicides, the exhuming of Cromwell, the uprising and punishment of Thomas Venner, and the coronation triumph—occurred within a year of the Restoration. My next spectacles—the plague and fire of London—were similarly defining events, variously viewed as reinforcing or challenging restored church and monarchy. And finally I turn to the pope burnings of the 1670s to show how spectacle was turned against the monarchy, and the mode of display shifted from the tragic and sublime to the grotesque. Delineating the ongoing political discourses in which Milton's poetry participates, this book shows how Milton not only challenges but also redefines and appropriates the spectacles of state in Restoration England.



My first two chapters trace the opposing discourses of treason and martyrdom that competed to interpret the spectacles of punishment in civil war, Interregnum and Restoration England. I begin chapter 1 in 1649, with the execution of Charles I. The cult of the royal martyr, challenging the display of justice, kept opposition alive and helped to reestablish the Stuart monarchy in 1660. Turning to Milton's *Paradise Regained*, I argue that Milton's private, unemotional Son of God is in many ways a response and challenge to the Stuart deployment of Christic martyrology. Chapter 2 shows how the grisly hangings and quarterings of the regicides and the exhuming of Cromwell symbolically undid the earlier regicide. But the displays of punishment became, as with the beheading of the king eleven years earlier, a contested site, diversely interpreted as treason or martyrdom. In its Restoration context, Milton's *Samson Agonistes*, with its unique focus on punishment, treason, and apocalyptic violence, questions the martyrdoms of the regicides by pointing to the tendencies for idolatry in God's chosen people.

Chapters 3 and 4 shift from punishment to positive spectacles of state, showing how Milton's three major poems respond to and challenge the pageantry and panegyric of 1660 and beyond. In chapter 3, I discuss the motif of the golden age restored and the joy that characterized the lavish celebrations upon the king's return. *Paradise Lost* provides a forceful counterstatement in the loss of paradise and redefinition of bacchic joy as linked with human sin and Satanic perversion. Chapter 4 traces the glories of royalist Roman triumph said to surpass all predecessors. In *Paradise Lost* Milton rebukes the gaudy, vainglorious triumph in the figure of Satan, but goes further to depict a heavenly, truly glorious triumph that outdoes all earthly models. The glorious display linked with conquest is a temptation in *Paradise Regained* and a sign of impenitence in *Samson Agonistes.*

Chapters 5 and 6 move to more direct challenges by dissenters to the spectacles of state. Chapter 5 looks at how Thomas Venner's violent response to the execution of the regicides enabled an official discourse of treason used to legitimate intolerance and repression. In response to such issues, *Paradise Regained* rejects the use of immediate force as a Satanic temptation, but it does so by reinscribing millenarian prophecies to counter both the spectacles and the surveillance of an increasingly repressive state. Chapter 6 looks at the plague and fire as contested spectacles, variously interpreted through the jeremiad mode to challenge or reinforce restored church and state. *Samson Agonistes* problematizes the jeremiad; Samson achieves an uneven recognition of divine chastisement, but the Chorus remains marked by pride, blaming only the Philistines. Milton's last prose, *Of True Religion*, moves beyond the jeremiad to warn a nation verging on hardness of heart and the idolatry of popery. *Of True Religion* and *Samson Agonistes* nonetheless resist the demonization of the pope burnings of the 1670s. For Milton the true threat was always the Philistine—or the papist—within.

In the context of contested and contradictory audience responses to spectacle, Milton both foregrounds the issues and makes them more problematic. Milton's attempt to create a mode of antispectacle questions the very nature of human spectacle itself. Puritans (later, dissenters) struggle with how to enter into or contest the monarchical spectacle as a source of power. Milton's poetry participates in the contested spectacles but also goes a step further, exploring the problematics of spectacle itself and true and false appropriations of punishment, conquest, martyrdom, joy, and prophecy. In Milton the turn inward does not eschew politics but evinces a complex internalization of Puritan discipline that can carry on the Good Old Cause in the very theater of the Stuart monarchy.

# I

# *Paradise Regained* and Royal Martyrdom

> At the later end of the year 1648 I had leave given mee to goe to london to see my Father & during my stay there at that time at Whitehal it was that I saw the Beheading of King Charles the first. . . . On the day of his execution, which was Tuesday, Jan. 30, I stood amongst the crowd in the street before Whitehal gate, where the scaffold was erected, and saw what was done, but was not so near as to hear any thing. The Blow I saw given, & can truly say with a sad heart; at the instant whereof, I remember wel, there was such a Grone by the Thousands then present, as I never heard before & desire I may never hear again.
>
> Philip Henry, *Diaries and Letters*

THE EXECUTION of Charles I followed nearly a decade of fighting in print and with arms over the nature and limits of kingship.[1] The revolutionary Independents had, with the support of the army, purged parliament and set up the Court of High Commission that tried, condemned, and sentenced Charles. Both the trial and execution were public displays, designed to persuade the people that Charles was being justly punished for capital offenses against them. But the groan of the crowd as the king's head was severed from his body might have warned the revolutionaries of an audience not quite as tractable or convinced as they had hoped. In its response the audience demonstrated that the effects of punishment could not be fully controlled by the mechanisms of exemplary power. The public display of punishment, dependent upon its audience, was immediately challenged and subverted by the discourse of martyrdom. The execution was followed shortly by the publication of *Eikon Basilike*, the "King's Book," which interpreted Charles's refusal to submit to the court not as obstinacy but as constancy, and his death not as just punishment for treason but as martyrdom. The cult of royal martyrdom that the *Eikon Basilike* initiated helped to sustain discontent through the Interregnum and flourished after the Restoration; paradoxically, the royal martyr would not die.

In 1649 in his prose *Eikonoklastes*, John Milton set out to break down the image of the martyr-king, to replace false spectacle with true martyrdom as witness to God alone. And, in 1671, he again takes strenuous countermeasures, rewriting in the private, unemotional Son of God in *Paradise Regained* a true martyr who cannot be associated with the Stuart kings. *Paradise Regained* continues on Milton's prose polemic against the idolatrous spectacles of kingship by radically rewriting both recent English history and the centuries-old literary and cultural tradition of Christ as royal martyr.



## I

DESPITE their victory over Charles in the field, the revolutionaries struggled in the trial and execution to win the ideological battle. On January 6, 1649, the Commons accused Charles of tyranny, treason, and murder, charging that he had "a wicked designe totally to subvert the antient and fundamentall lawes and liberties of this nation. And in theire place to introduce an arbitrary and tiranicall government . . . and hath prosecuted it with fire and sword, levied and maintayned a cruell warre in the land against the Parliament and kingdome."[2] The public trial of Charles I showed a transitional stage of power between what Michel Foucault has delineated as the arbitrary torture perpetrated by the ancien régime in France—a means of inducing horror and terror in the viewer—and representative punishment that links the ideas of crime and penalty in the minds of the viewers.[3]

The trial and execution were part of the dramaturgy of state, designed to convince its audience that the text of Charles's life must be read as treason, his death as "exemplary and condigne punishment." The high court appealed to the rhetoric of justice and divine providence to supplement or, more accurately, occlude the force underlying the trial. John Cook, lawyer for the prosecution, described the proceedings as "the most Comprehensive, Impartial and Glorious piece of Justice that ever was acted and Executed upon the Theatre of *England*."[4] The Court of High Commission had not only a juridical but a moral and theological function. Shifting among various Old Testament models by which their actions could be interpreted and justified, the court fastened on the notion of blood-guilt. According to Cook, they acted for a higher court in trying and judging Charles, "whom God in his wrath gave to be a King to this Nation, and will, I trust, in great love, for his notorious Prevarications and Blood-guiltiness take him away from us." In a drama that was both allegorical and didactic, Charles stood "to give an account of his stewardship and to receive the good of justice, for all the evil of his injustice and cruelty."[5]

By staging the trial as a public display, the regicides strove to justify but also exposed to open challenge the legitimacy of their cause. And Charles refused to play his given role. The king acted out the part not of a penitent sinner, which would have confirmed their case, but of a constant sufferer for liberty and truth. Refusing to recognize the authority of the court, he continually exposed the force that the display of justice attempted to cover: "It is not my case alone, it is the Freedom and the Liberty of the people of England; and do you pretend what you will, I stand more for their Liberties. For if power without law may make lawes, may alter the fundamental laws of the kingdom, I do not know what subject he is in England, that can be sure of his life or any thing that he calls his own."[6] Charles rewrote the script, recasting the regicides' justice as a power that unlawfully threatened king and subject alike. As a king betrayed and tried by his own subjects, not allowed to speak in a court claiming justice, Charles soon found a more effective paradigm by which he could sustain and explain his case—that of martyrdom, and, in particular, the royal martyrdom of Christ.



The scaffold as a theater for punishment, twinned with the public trial, showed the force of law and justice, inscribed in the very body of the condemned. Yet the display of the punished traitor did not produce a single meaning. There is, as Foucault explains, "an ambiguity in this suffering that may signify equally well the truth of the crime or the error of the judges, the goodness or evil of the criminal, the coincidence or the divergence between the judgement of men and that of God."[7] Ironically, the Independents themselves made Charles a martyr by trying and executing him publicly. Charles's speech and demeanor during his trial and execution, fully reported and put into circulation, had unexpected consequences. On the scaffold, as during the trial, Charles refused to play his assigned role. No scaffold confession, acknowledging his own guilt and the justice of the state that punished him, was forthcoming.

On the contrary, Charles asserted his innocence and modeled himself on the royal martyr, Christ. Like Christ, he forgave his enemies: "I have forgiven all the world, and even those in particular that have been the chief causes of my death. . . . I pray God forgive them." Claiming to die as "the Martyr of the people," Charles looked to a crown of martyrdom: "I go from a corruptible to an incorruptible crown, where no disturbance can be, no disturbance in the world." He bravely met the execution that followed: "After a little pause, the King stretching forth his hands, the Executioner at one blow severed his head from his body, and held it up and shewed it to the people, saying, 'Behold the head of a Traitor.'"[8] But already the theater of punishment was crumbling.

FIGURE 1 German print of the execution of Charles I (1649). *By permission of the British Library.*

In ceremonies of public execution the main character was the people, whose presence and belief were required for the performance. But the audience at Charles's execution was unreliable. Philip Henry reports that the soldiers, apparently fearing a negative reaction, immediately dispersed the crowd: "There was according to Order one Troop immediately marching from-wards charing-cross to Westm[inster] & another from-wards Westm[inster] to charing cross purposely to masker the people, & to disperse & scatter them, so that I had much adoe amongst the rest to escape home without hurt."[9] Cromwell's troops did not allow the people to gaze for long upon the grisly scene with the severed head.



A German print of the spectacle of execution (Fig. 1) shows how much the crowd dominated the scene. On the scaffold, the executioner holds the severed head of Charles aloft, while blood sprays out voluminously from the decapitated body. The soldiers who would soon disperse the crowd thickly surround the stage. The foreground of the print, however, belongs to audience reaction. Most of the spectators turn their backs, engrossed in the display. But on the left, one man appears to weep and a woman shields her eyes, and on the right, another woman receives assistance after fainting. Numerous onlookers in and even atop Whitehall give the impression of a massive crowd, upon which the display depended.

Yet the audience did not cooperate in the official spectacle but sought another meaning, another kind of tragedy. A royalist newspaper, *Mercurius Elencticus*, reports that the people rushed to buy relics of the dead king. For the people Charles was a martyr, for the soldiers a means of making money: "When they had murdered him, such as desired to dip their handkerchiefes or other things in his blood, were admitted for moneys. Others bought peeces of board which were dy'd with his blood, for which the soldiers took of some a shilling, of others half a crowne, more or lesse according to the quality of the persons that sought it. But none without ready money." The soldiers continued to profit: "And after his body was coffin'd, as many as desired to see it were permitted at a certaine rate, by which meanes the soldiers got store of moneys, insomuch that one was heard to say 'I would we had two or three more such Majesties to behead, if we could but make such use of them.' "[10] The soldier's wish would be granted, although not in the form he might have imagined. Charles would indeed reappear in the ensuing cult of royal martyrdom that left the regicides and Cromwellian government with many Charleses to confront, many new majesties to behead.

## II

THE PUBLICATION of *Eikon Basilike* immediately after Charles's execution marked a new stage in the struggle between the monarch and his foes.

"Prayers and tears" would ultimately be more effective than the weapons of warfare that had failed to make good the king's cause, the discourse of martyrdom more effective than the spectacle of treason. After the Restoration, the probable coauthor (or true author) of the *Eikon Basilike*, John Gauden, exulted in martial metaphor over its publication: "When it came out, just upon the King's death; Good God! What shame, rage and despite filled hys Murtherers! What comfort hys friends! How many enemyes did it convert! How many hearts did it mollify, and melt! . . . What preparations it made in all men's minds for this happy restauration. . . . In a word, it was an army, and did vanquish more than any sword could."[11]

Although much of the *Eikon Basilike* gives a detailed defense of Charles's political actions and decisions, most compelling were its rhetoric of piety and claim to a Christ-like martyrdom that skillfully adapted the precedent of John Foxe's "Book of Martyrs."[12] The *Eikon Basilike* impresses Charles's story with the distinctive contours of Foxe's martyrology as the king endures affliction, remains true to his conscience, and suffers the rage and malice of his enemies. But the "King's Book" also conflates Charles's sufferings with Christ's, merging the Foxean portrait of the martyr with the rich and resonant biblical and literary tradition of royal martyrdom. In so doing, the *Eikon Basilike* developed a powerful discourse by which to idealize Charles and stigmatize his enemies.

Like the "Book of Martyrs," *Eikon Basilike* is self-consciously concerned with defining and portraying true martyrdom. Charles explicitly claims this status: "They knew my chiefest arms left me were those only which the ancient Christians were wont to use against their persecutors—prayers and tears. These may serve a good man's turn, if not to conquer as a soldier, yet to suffer as a martyr" (47). And he denies martyrdom to his political opponents: "Some parasitic preachers have dared to call those 'martyrs' who died fighting against me, the laws, their oaths, and the religion established. But sober Christians know that glorious title can with truth be applied only to those who sincerely preferred God's truth and their duty in all these particulars before their lives and all that was dear to them in this world" (118–19). Charles claims the martyrs' constancy, commenting, "Here I am sure to be conqueror if God will give me such a measure of constancy as to fear him more than man and to love the inward peace of my conscience before any outward tranquillity" (38), for "what they [my enemies] call obstinacy, I know God accounts honest constancy" (138). Charles also prays: "*Give me that measure of patience and constancy which my condition now requires*" (139). Such frequent references to conscience, patience, and constancy create a compelling portrait of Charles, the martyr-king.

While the "King's Book" portrays Charles as suffering and dying for the church as well as for the more strictly political cause of monarchy, the issues are inseparable because this martyr's truth is even more bound to an internal political power struggle than in Foxe's massive tome. While it would be naive to deny the political implications in Foxe's virulently anti-Catholic accounts of martyrdom, his Marian martyrs at least debate over theological issues, albeit with political import—transubstantiation, purgatory and the penitential system (confession, indulgences, meritorious works), marriage of the clergy, and papal supremacy. *Eikon Basilike* appropriates and further politicizes the discourse of martyrdom, employing its rhetoric to interpret such specific events and points of dispute in the English civil war as "His Majesty's Calling This Last Parliament," "The Listing and Raising Armies against the King," "Their Seizing the King's Magazines, Forts, Navy, and Militia," and "The Various Events of the War: Victories and Defeats" (vii–viii).



But despite the increased attention to details of contemporary political events, Gauden (with Charles) is able to draw much more fully than Foxe on the powerful biblical and literary tradition of Christ as royal martyr. Foxe's own relationship to monarchy was complex, if not problematic.[13] Foxe wrote to support Elizabeth and the established Church, to advise the queen in her destined role as true sovereign; yet the martyrdoms he most vividly and elaborately recounts are those of middle- and lower-class subjects under another monarch—bloody Queen Mary. Although Foxe briefly recounts Christ's passion and crucifixion, he makes no real use of the resonant biblical and literary tradition of Christ as royal martyr. *Eikon Basilike* thus both draws on and dramatically revises the Foxean tradition in its compelling portrait of the martyr-king.

As its title indicates, *Eikon Basilike* conveys its message through image as well as word, including a literal image or emblematic portrait of the martyr-king in the frontispiece engraved by William Marshall (Fig. 2). Here the *Eikon* diverges from Foxe, whose volumes were illustrated by grisly and horrific drawings of executions; the king is, rather, depicted in an ennobling, if tragic, Christ-like pose. The frontispiece depicts the kneeling king, his gaze directed at the heavenly crown of glory that he earns, like his Saviour, through a crown of thorns. His jeweled earthly crown lies spurned at his feet. The emblematic picture stresses, above all, the constancy of the martyr-king. In the background are pictured a rock unmoved by stormy seas ("And as th' unmoved Rock out-brave's / The boist'rous Windes and raging waves / So triumph I") and a palm tree which grows despite being held down by weights ("Though clogged with weights of miseries / Palm-like Depress'd, I higher rise"). The frontispiece evokes the passion of Christ in Gethsemane, the ideal of passive suffering and constancy.[14] The picture recalls but does not represent actual physical suffering or punishment; such images, as we shall see, were reserved for Charles's foes, while Charles remains beatifically Christ-like in the iconography of the execution.

Associations with Christ's sufferings, passion, and death resonate throughout the "King's Book," elevating Charles's cause and stigmatizing his political enemies as traitors. "His Majesty's Retirement from Westminster" and his refusal to comply with Parliamentary demands are presented as a choice of kingly martyrdom: "I will rather choose to wear a crown of thorns with my Saviour than to exchange that of gold, which is due to me, for one of lead" (28). Foregrounding his divine type, Charles implicitly compares "Raising Armies against the King" with the crucifixion of a forgiving Christ: "*When Thy wrath is appeased by my death, O remember Thy great mercies toward them and forgive them, O my Father, for they know not what they do*" (46). The "Troubles in Ireland" (in which the king stood ac-

FIGURE 2 Charles I at prayer, from *Eikon Basilike* (1649). *By permission of Rare Books and Special Collections, the Pennsylvania State University Libraries.*

cused of fomenting a Catholic uprising) are depicted in terms of Christ's suffering on the cross: "Therefore with exquisite malice they have mixed the gall and vinegar of falsity and contempt with the cup of my affliction" (63). Similarly, the "Scots Delivering the King to the English" is compared to Judas's selling of Christ: "If I am sold by them, I am only sorry they should do it and that my price should be so much above my Saviour's" (137).

Finally, in the "Meditations upon Death" which conclude *Eikon Basilike*, Charles moves from commenting on and justifying specific actions to constructing more fully the myth of the royal martyr by which his life and death may be interpreted. Charles refers to "those greater formalities whereby my enemies, (being more solemnly cruel) will, it may be, seek to add (as those who crucified Christ) the mockery of justice to the cruelty of malice" (174). Echoing Christ's words in the garden of Gethsemane, Charles professes willingness to accept the bitter cup: "*Thou givest me leave as a man to pray that this cup may pass from me; but Thou hast taught me as a Christian by the example of Christ to add, not my will, but Thine be done*" (181). He claims conformity with Christ's martyrdom: "If I must suffer a violent death with my Saviour, it is but mortality crowned with martyrdom" (179). And Charles is explicit in acknowledging that his martyrdom will be a paradoxical victory: "My next comfort is that He gives me not only the honor to imitate His example in suffering for righteousness' sake, (though obscured by the foulest charges of tyranny and injustice), but also that charity which is the noblest revenge upon and victory over, my destroyers" (176). Like Foxe's martyrs whose constancy in burning at the stake astonished and amazed onlookers, and like Christ on the cross, to whom the Roman centurion paid tribute, Charles experienced death but no defeat. The regicides' apparent failure to understand the power of martyrdom was a crucial and ultimately irreparable mistake.



## III

THE "King's Book" brilliantly subverted the exemplary power of the state, recasting the public trial and execution of Charles as a drama of suffering and martyrdom. Gauden's colleagues responded in kind. The book initiated an outpouring of elegies and hyperbolic laments on Charles the royal martyr.[15] Focusing on his final days and his death, the martyrologies greatly elaborated the parallels with Christ's passion and crucifixion, now paying little attention to details of the political struggle. Diverging from Foxe and elaborating on the *Eikon Basilike*, the martyrologies constructed a full picture of Charles as a uniquely royal martyr. For the first time, Charles was given a sympathetic—even weeping—audience. *An Elegie upon the Death of Our Dread Soveraign* (1649) is typical:

Com, com, let's Mourn; all eies, that see this *Daie*,
Melt into Showrs, and Weep your selvs awaie:
O that each Private head could yield a Flood
Of Tears, whil'st *Britain's Head* stream's out His Blood.[16]

Flouting state censorship, the martyrologies poignantly linked Charles with Christ in his passion and death, blackening the regicides with the powerfully resonant figure of the crucifixion.



The martyrologies recast the alleged justice of Charles's public trial and execution as a false, theatrical reenactment of Christ's trial and crucifixion. *A Deepe Groane Fetch'd* (1649) elaborates the tragic play:

Such was their Bedlame Rabble, and the Cry
Of *Justice* now, 'mongst them was *Crucifie:*
*Pilates* Consent is *Bradshawes* Sentence here;
The *Judgement hall's* remov'd to *Westminster.*
Hayle to the Reeden Scepture the Head, and knee
Act o're againe that Cursed Pageantrie.[17]

But royalist tracts used the metaphor of theater both to undercut the falsity of the "Cursed Pageantrie" at Westminster and Whitehall and simultaneously to construct Charles as a royal martyr, a fissure that Milton and others would fully exploit.

The main focus of the elegies was thus on the royal martyr, the royal actor himself. The trial might be a mockery, but so was the trial of Christ, to whom Charles bears an unparalleled resemblance. *An Elegie Upon the Death of Our Dread Soveraign* (1649) explains: "This *Scene* was like the *Passion-Tragedie,* / His *Saviour's Person* none could Act, but Hee." Focusing thus on the final days and hours of the king's life, elegies and sermons multiplied links between the sufferings of Charles and Christ, much to the detriment of the king's accusers. *A Hand-Kirchife for Loyall Mourners* (1649) asserts:

It is a heavy thing to think on, that he should suffer by his own Judasses. But a joyfull and glorious thing it is to think on, that he suffered so like his own Jesus, so like him in the manner, and circumstances of his sufferings being betrayed by his owne servants, arraigned before Jewes and *Pilate,* at the best, reviled, reproached, and they say spit upon by an unworthy varlet, scorned and contemned & condemned unto death: so like him in the temper of his sufferings, with so much meeknesse and fortitude, undauntedness of spirit, and submission to the will of God.[18]

A number of tracts and sermons insist that the parallels between Charles and Christ are both striking and unique. *The Scotch Souldiers Lamentation* (1649) concludes: "There have beene many Martyrs, but no Martyr-Kings that I know of but my blessed Saviour Christ Jesus, and my late gracious Soveraigne Lord King Charles."[19] The royalists used the theatrical metaphor both to undercut the Puritan show and to idealize Charles as martyr-king.

The cult of the royal martyr circulated by image as by printed word; following the *Eikon Basilike*, Charles I was represented in a number of Christ-like poses. In 1649, *The Subjects Sorrow* (Fig. 3) showed Charles fully clothed (and not decapitated), lying atop a monument but curiously animated in that his hand reaches up toward the cross.[20] The Christic overtones that remain allusive and implicit in *Eikon Basilike* are overt and obvious here in the image of the cross and the appended verse, "for thine's like to thy Saviours suffering." The suffering is lamented, likened to Christ's, and yet not visually represented; the beatific image is not marred.



*The Subjects Sorrow* spells out the meaning of the iconography in "The Frontispiece Opened":

> Loe where K. Charls a Monarch Martyr lies,
> His Kingdomes and the Churches Sacrifice:
> His Crowne and Scepter glorious vanitie
> He waves and hastens to Mount Calvarie
> Where taking up his Saviour Christ his Crosse,
> Angels him Crowne; good Subjects waile His losse.

Visual representations of the martyr-king generally avoided the severed head, replacing the spectacle of punished treason with the iconography of Christic passion.

The (now) best-known rendition of Charles I as tragic actor is, however, not royalist but that of Andrew Marvell's *An Horation Ode*. The *Ode*, ostensibly in praise of Cromwell, first gives the stage or "tragick scaffold" to Charles I:

> *He* nothing common did or mean
> Upon that memorable Scene:
>   But with his keener Eye
>   The Axes edge did try:
> Nor call'd the *Gods* with vulgar spight
> To vindicate his helpless Right,
>   But bow'd his comely Head,
>   Down as upon a Bed.[21]

Critics have long noted and debated the significance of the strikingly dual focus of the *Ode*: Charles I and Cromwell as competing actors, in competing spectacles.[22] Although he does not make Charles a Christic figure, Marvell does accord him all the tragic dignity of the martyrologies. In-

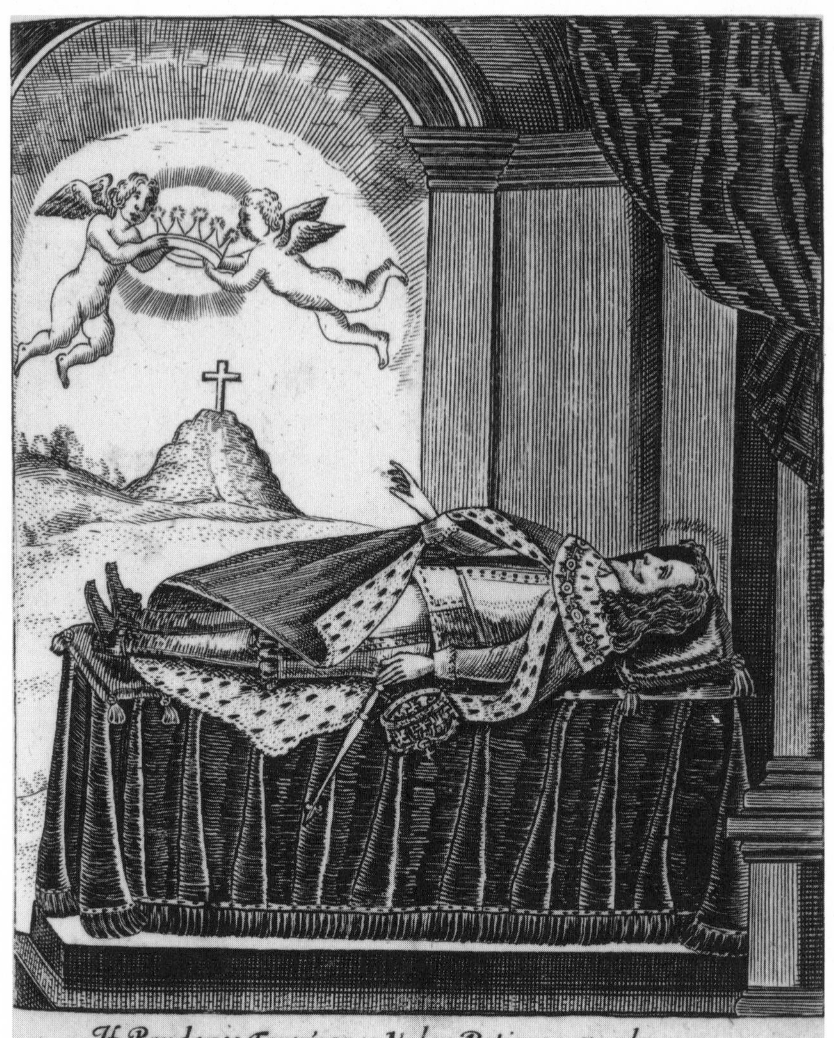


FIGURE 3 Charles I on coffin, from *The Subjects Sorrow* (1649). *By permission of the British Library.*

deed, he extends the guilt, putting the king onstage, "while round the armed Bands / Did clap their bloody hands."

Marvell does not exclude the horrors of the execution avoided by both royalist and republican; indeed, as Thomas Corns has argued, he adds surreal, nightmarish details.[23] While both sides avoided gazing on the severed head, usually back in place in royalist iconography and put just out of view in republican defenses, Marvell both presents the head and makes it bloody:

> So when they did design
> The *Capitols* first Line,
> A bleeding Head where they begun,
> Did fright the Architects to run;
> And yet in that the *State*
> Foresaw its happy Fate.

Such tensions would seem to undercut Cromwell, but the poem indeed reenacts what it describes: Cromwell's power is even greater for forcing allegiance through such a victory over such a foe.

Annabel Patterson has written that Marvell's *Ode* takes its place between *Eikon Basilike* and *Eikonoklastes*, mediating pathos and ethos.[24] The *Ode* also occupies a middle ground, however polemical, in its attitude toward spectacle. We have seen that *Eikon Basilike* fully exploits the figure of tragic martyr-king. Marvell, in turn, stages both king *and* Cromwell as actors in competing spectacles (we will return to Cromwell as Roman conqueror in chapter 4). But in his response to the "King's Book," Milton much more drastically rejects the theatrical show, both the deifying people and their idol-king.

## IV

In publishing the text of Charles's trial and execution and allowing the *Eikon Basilike* and the martyrologies to escape censorship, the Independents had seriously miscalculated the effects of the public execution. Too late, the new government commissioned John Milton, who had recently been appointed to the post of Latin secretary, to answer the "King's Book." Milton had previously written, uninvited, a defense of the regicide in *The Tenure of Kings and Magistrates* and was thus perhaps a logical choice. Milton's *Eikonoklastes*, although primarily a point-by-point rebuttal of the *Eikon Basilike*, also recognizes the cult of royal martyrdom that the "King's Book" had fostered. Milton rebukes the preachers who "howle in thir Pulpits" after the dead Charles, and he tries (futilely, in the event) to repel the rhetoric of martyrdom with a combination of scorn and reason.

Milton attacks the *Eikon Basilike*, first of all, by reversing and blackening the charges of stagecraft: Charles's alleged martyrdom is false theatricality, dependent on a deluded and idolatrous audience.[25] The frontispiece of the *Eikon Basilike*, with the kneeling Charles, aims, according to Milton, to "Martyr him and Saint him to befool the people" (*CPW* 3:343). The "conceited portraiture" of Charles is sleight-of-hand stagework, "drawn out to the full measure of a Masking Scene, and sett there to catch fools and silly gazers" (342). Such "quaint Emblems and devices begg'd from the Old Pageantry of some Twelf nights entertainment at *Whitehall* will doe but ill to make a Saint or Martyr" (343). The "King's Book" is to be rejected as false and theatrical: "Stage-work will not doe it; much less *the justness of thir Cause*" (530).

And yet the people are easy prey. Milton heaps scorn not only on the royal actor but on his gullible, doting, idolatrous audience: "The People, exorbitant and excessive in all thir motions, are prone ofttimes not to a religious onely, but to a civil kinde of Idolatry in idolizing thir Kings" (343). The "King's Book" shows "what a miserable, credulous, deluded thing that creature is, which is call'd the Vulgar" (426). Charles will never "stirr the constancie and solid firmness of any wise Man" but instead will only "catch the worthles approbation of an inconstant, irrational, and Image-doting rabble" (601). The people, like a "credulous and hapless herd, begott'n to servility, and inchanted with these popular institutes of Tyranny" are themselves witness to "thir own voluntary and beloved baseness" (601).

Charles's claim to martyrdom, then, is false and theatrical; the people's responses to such a claim, idolatrous and deluded. Milton scornfully dismisses Charles's claim to a Christ-like crown of thorns, since Charles, unlike Christ, suffers for his own faults: "Many would be all one with our Saviour, whom our Saviour will not know. They who govern ill those Kingdoms which they had a right to, have to our Saviours Crown of Thornes no right at all. Thornes they may find anow, of thir own gathering, and thir own twisting . . . but to weare them as our Saviour wore them is not giv'n to them that suffer by thir own demerits" (417–18). According to Milton, Charles's self-promotion undermines his own cause since "martyrs bear witness to the truth, not to themselves": "If I beare witness of my self, saith *Christ*, my witness is not true. He who writes himself *Martyr* by his own inscription, is like an ill Painter, who, by writing on the shapeless Picture which he hath drawn, is fain to tell passengers what shape it is; which els no man could imagin" (575). Suffering or dying with constancy, Milton objects, does not make a martyr: "Lastly, if to die for *the testimony of his own conscience*, be anough to make him Martyr, what Heretic dying for direct blasphemie, as som have don constantly, may not boast a Martyrdom?" (576).

In discounting Charles's suffering and emphasizing the truth for which genuine martyrs suffer, Milton implicitly revives the etymology of martyrdom, "witness." If Milton primarily focuses in *Eikonoklastes* on denying Charles I the name of martyr, he also constructs his own text as a counter-example—a true martyr or witness to the truth before God and man. *Eikonoklastes* comes to counter the king's false claims to the truth, impelled by the king's "making new appeale to Truth and the World" and leaving "this Book," *Eikon Basilike*, "as the best advocat and interpreter of his own actions," so that "his Friends by publishing, dispersing, commending, and almost adoring it, seem to place therein the chiefe strength and nerves of thir cause" (340). Milton will oppose the *Eikon Basilike* by "remembring them the truth of what they themselves know to be heer misaffirm'd" (338). Milton insists that this truth needs no reinforcement, but is simply sent out "in the native confidence of her single self, to earn, how she can, her entertainment in the world, and to finde out her own readers; few perhaps, but those few, such of value and substantial worth, as truth and wisdom, not respecting numbers and bigg names, have bin ever wont in all ages to be contented with" (339–40).



Yet Milton's truth, like the king's, is embedded in and shaped by seventeenth-century politics, part of political debate and ideological struggle. When, as confuter of Charles I, Milton claims to be part of the "sole remainder" or remnant selected by God "to stand upright and stedfast in his cause; dignify'd with the defence of truth and public libertie" (348), he politicizes not only martyrdom but the truth to which martyrs bear witness. Later in the work, he more radically conflates truth with justice and claims both were operative in executing the king: "Either Truth and Justice are all one, for Truth is but Justice in our knowledge, and Justice is but Truth in our practice . . . or els, if there be any odds, that Justice, though not stronger then truth, yet by her office is to put forth and exhibit more strength in the affaires of mankind" (583–84). Writing thus, Milton hopes to "set free the minds of English men from longing to returne poorly under the Captivity of Kings, from which the strength and supreme Sword of Justice hath deliverd them" (585). Like the royalists, Milton strives to appropriate and deploy justice and truth for his political cause: once again, it is clear that such truth is a thing of this world, produced and defined in ideological struggle.

Central to *Eikonoklastes*, then, is Milton's rebuttal of Charles's claim to cap the Foxean tradition of martyrdom. To Charles's false, theatrical martyrdom, Milton opposes his own witness to the truth, a revised and reconstituted kind of martyrdom. Ironically, *Eikonoklastes* itself suffered the fate of a martyr—being burned by the public hangman on the continent in the 1650s and in England after the Restoration. But Milton himself was left alive, to contemplate new modes of witness, of standing upright for the truth.

## V

In England, Charles I was apparently viewed by many as a martyr throughout the Interregnum; there is evidence that January 30 was covertly observed as an anniversary fast even before the Restoration. Letters and diaries refer to Charles as martyr; there was concern with his relics, as, for instance, when in 1652 Henry Oxinden sends Elias Ashmole "King C. his haire."[26] But the cult of the royal martyr especially flourished with the restoration of Charles's son to the throne of England. After 1660 Anglican clergy and others republished and embellished literally dozens of *lachrymae ecclesiasticae* over the death of Charles I; the martyrology cult played a crucial role in the Anglican view of the restoration as divine intervention on behalf of God's rightful ecclesiastical and political order. Despite the promise of freedom for tender consciences made by Charles II at Breda, the Anglican clergy succeeded in their support for measures establishing the church and repressing dissent. To conjure with the myth of Charles I as Christic martyr in the 1660s effectively blackened and stigmatized religious dissent as political subversion.



*The Martyrdom of King Charls I. Or His Conformity with Christ in his Suffering*, a sermon preached at Breda before Charles II by the Bishop of Down, is a clear and representative example of both the power of the traditional martyrology themes—Charles I rejected, afflicted, suffering, crucified—and their political application. After a lengthy comparison of Charles I and Christ, the bishop concludes: "Thus you see, that, as the Princes of the world Crucified the Lord of Glory, so others worse than they have Crucified our glorious Lord. . . . [Some of the Jews] repented, and became very zealous to advance the Kingdome of Christ; so let us be zealous to advance the Kingdome of our glorious Martyr, in the person of his Son."[27] Remorse and sorrow for the martyred father is translated into loyalty and support for the son.

Other political applications follow, as the bishop then goes on to assert sacral kingship and, concomitantly, the true established church. The "doctrine of opposing, deposing, and killing of Kings," he insists, was broached in the Court of Rome and "licked up" by the Puritans. The bishop points to the Anglican Church, setting the pattern for the arguments to come against toleration or comprehension:

> That [Anglican] religion onely, among all Christian religions, doth promise safety and security to kings, submitting them neither to Pope, Parlia-

ment, Presbytery, nor People, but into God only, by whom and for whom they reign. In the profession and maintenance of that Religion, which your glorious Father seal'd with his blood, God will yet establish your throne, and make you to possess the Gates of your enemies.[28]

The martyrdom of Charles I becomes a powerful argument for the establishment of the Anglican church and against toleration of religious nonconformity.





The denigration and punishment of the regicides and other enemies of Charles I also served to enhance the cult of the royal martyr. We shall see in chapter 2 how the executions and exhumings of the regicides were deployed as counterspectacles to the execution of Charles I. Accounts of the trial and execution of Charles mythologized the king through print and iconography. *The Great Memorial* (1660) depicts a kingly and very much living, if somber Charles (Fig. 4).[29] In the background is the stage, thronged by spectators, where a masked executioner waits with raised axe. The accompanying verse explicitly links Charles with Christ: "And where's the Slaughter-house Whitehall must be, / Lately his Palace, now his Calvarie." Again, Charles's suffering is evoked but not represented, not allowed to endanger the image of Christ. Indeed, in another contemporary print, Charles holds up his hands as if to show the Christ-like wounds; in royalist iconography, the Stuart king is, apparently, not beheaded but crucified.

But the event that fixed in the public mind the image of the royal martyr was the establishment of an annual fast day to commemorate the anniversary of Charles's death. In December 1660, a royal proclamation, following a Parliamentary act, set aside January 30 as "an anniversary day of fasting and humiliation, to implore the mercy of God, that neither the guilt of that sacred and innocent blood, nor those other sins by which God was provoked to deliver up both them and their king into the hands of cruel and unreasonable men, might at any time after be visited upon them or their posterity."[30] Lavish praise of Charles I was twinned with the unparalleled act of exhuming the bodies of his enemies—Oliver Cromwell, Henry Ireton, and John Bradshaw. The fast day sermons extolled the royal martyr, exulted over divine vengeance on his enemies, and pointed to the Anglican Church as the true protector of sacral kingship.

Like Foxe's "Book of Martyrs" dedicated to Elizabeth, the sermons of the Anglican clergy and the martyrology tracts that were republished and circulated in the early 1660s pointed to Charles II as monarch restoring the true church; and, also like Foxe, they instructed and guided Charles in the manner of the church's establishment. The cult of the royal martyr exonerated the Anglican clergy and blackened all those who had any role in the regicide—including the Presbyterians and Independents. Hence, the cult

FIGURE 4 Charles I with execution in background, from *The Great Memorial* (1660). *By permission of the British Library.*

FIGURE 5 Charles II on the throne, from *The Manner of the Solemnity of the Coronation* (1661). *By permission of the British Library.*

also had a role in shaping the increasingly intolerant ecclesiastical policy of the 1660s. The fast day sermons were a powerful forum to articulate political and ecclesiastical policy, to reach the minds—and hearts—of the people.





In the panegyric greeting the arrival and coronation of Charles II, the martyrdom of Charles I was further used in expressions of regret that enhanced and legitimated the new monarchy. The son was linked with his martyred father through a new motif of resurrection imagery, as in Arthur Brett's *The Restauration* (1660): "His Son should with more Glory rise, / Because he on a Scaffold dies."[31] Charles I as crucified Christ gave way to Charles II as the resurrected Christ. In Abraham Cowley's *Ode, Upon His Majesties Restoration and Return* (1660), the martyr's blood is the seed that is reborn through the son:

> The *Martyr's blood* was said of old to be
> The *seed* from whence the *Church* did grow.
> The *Royal Blood* which dying *Charles* did sow
> Becomes no lesse the *seed* of *Royalty*.
> 'Twas in *dishonour sown*,
> We find it now in *glory grown*,
> The *grave* could but the *dross* of it devour;
> 'Twas *sown* in *weakness*, and 'tis *rais'd* in *power*.[32]

In descriptions of the coronation, Charles's glory is linked with the glory of his father's martyrdom. An illustration of Charles II on the throne in *The Manner of the Solemnity of the Coronation* (Fig. 5) construes the lavish material glory, rich robes, draped throne, crown, and scepter as the analogue to the glory of his martyred father. Charles II is "Heire of the royall Martyr," who is recalled in Christ-like terms:

> Since the rude Souldier pierc'd our Saviours side:
> Who such a Father had'st, art such a Son;
> Redeem thy people and assume thy own.
> Ascend thy Ancestors Imperial seat,
> Of *Charles* the Good, thou second *Charles* the Great,
> That adds the worth, this lustre to the Crown,
> Whose solid Glories weighd Usurpers down.[33]

Now the graphic image of the crucifixion, of the sword piercing Christ's side, is displaced by the material splendor that evinces the solid glories of the Stuart martyr and his son.

Even more striking—and surprising—in the Restoration panegyric is that Charles II himself is depicted as a martyr who has suffered for the truth. A poem in *Britannia Rediviva* puts the motif most succinctly: "Heir to thy Fathers Sufferings, and his Crown! / He Dy'd a Martyr, thou hast Lived one."[34] Cowley's *Ode, Upon His Majesties Restoration* treats Charles II as martyr with reference to his past afflictions: "Thy *Royall Father's* came at last: / Thy *Martyrdom's* already past."[35] When Charles II entered into London on May 28, 1660, Sir Harbottle Grimston, Speaker to the House of Commons, praised his patience in affliction: "We doubt not but Your Name is Registered in the Records of Heaven, to have a place in the highest from amongst those glorious Martyrs, of whom it is reported that through faith in Christ, and patience in their suffering, they converted their very Tormentors, and conquered those barbarous bloody Tyrants, under whom they then suffered."[36] Striking echoes of the martyrdom of the father recur in the stress on son's patience in suffering, the turn from an earthly to a heavenly perspective, and the characterization of political enemies as tormentors and tyrants. But the Christ analogy is significantly muted here. Unlike his father, Charles II is not uniquely compared with the crucified Christ, but takes his place in the great company of martyrs.



More frequent than this overt treatment of Charles II as martyr is a stress on his patience in suffering, not explicitly identified with martyrdom, and yet, as we have seen, a distinctive quality of Foxean martyrs. As with the father, the patience of the son is lavishly praised: "Much-suffering Monarch, the first English born / That has the Crown of these three Nations worn, / How has Your patience, with the barbarous rage / Of Your own soyl, contended half an Age."[37] Charles II, like his father, achieves victory through patient suffering, as in Alexander Brome's *A Congratulatory Poem* (1660):

> you that did endure
> What e're the *wit* or *Malice* of your foes
> Could lay on you or yours, yet stoutly chose
> To suffer on, rather than to *Retort*
> Their injuries, and grew *Victorious* for't;
> And by your patient suffering did subdue
> The *Traytors* fury, and the *Traytors* too.[38]

*A Poem To his most Excellent Majesty* (1660) puts the matter succinctly, praising, "Your Patience, which You may singly own, / Since none (but You) suffer'd into a Throne."[39]

Praise of Charles II as patient sufferer, even martyr, does not seem to have outlasted the panegyric of the early 1660s, but that we find it there at all reflects the ongoing power of Christ-like martyrdom as a means of legitimating and idealizing the Stuart monarchy. The martyrdom of Charles I remained a powerful symbol against political disorder and even against ecclesiastical tolerance. January 30 continued to be observed as a day of fast and humiliation until 1859. John Evelyn dutifully records his attendance each year. In 1685, one Francis Turner comments on its continuing emotional and political power: "Not a few of those that were carry'd away with the Dissimulation of the men of malice among us, have been converted by the blessing of God, and the preaching every Thirtieth of January more than three thousand sermons."[40] Charles I, the martyr-king, remained alive and well in England.



## VI

IN THE vituperation of the Good Old Cause and of its supporters after 1660, Milton's *Eikonoklastes* found an unenviable place. *The Character of the Rump*, published in London in March 1660, attacks Milton as "an old Heretick both in Religion and Manners" and asserts (with hyperbole) that "the Sun-beams of his scandalous papers against the late Kings book, is the Parent that begot his late new Commonwealth" (*LR* 4:305). In April, Roger L'Estrange, soon to be chief censor for the new government, suspects a seditious pamphlet to be "a Blot of the same *Pen* that wrote *Iconoclastes.* It runs foule;—tends to Tumult;—and, not content, Barely to Applaud the Murther of the King, the execrable Author of it vomits upon his Ashes; with a Pedantique, and Envenom'd scorn, pursuing still his sacred Memory."[41] Although the tract is probably not Milton's, L'Estrange's reasons for thinking so are significant, revealing the notoriety of the author of *Eikonoklastes.*

On August 13, 1660, a Royal Proclamation was issued against Milton's *First Defense* and *Eikonoklastes*, "in both which are contained sundry Treasonable Passages against Us and Our Government, and most Impious endeavours to justifie the horrid and unmatchable Murther of Our late Dear Father, of Glorious Memory." The Proclamation, jointly against leveller John Goodwin, goes on to state that since "the said *John Milton*, and *John Goodwin*, are both fled, or so obscure themselves, that no endeavors used for their apprehension can take effect," the books themselves are to be apprehended "to the end that Our good Subjects may not be corrupted in their Judgments, with such wicked and Traitrous principles." All persons are commanded to turn over the books to the mayor, bailiffs, or magistrates, who are also given authority to seize the books, turning in the names of offenders to the Privy Council. The books are then "to be delivered to the respective Sheriffs of those Counties . . . to be publickly burnt by the hand of the Common Hangman" (*LR* 4:328–30). On August 27, *The Publick Intelligencer* had this entry: "According to a former Proclamation, several Copies of these infamous Books made by *John Goodwin* and *John Milton* in Justification of the horrid Murder of our late glorious Sovereign King

*Charles* I. were solemnly burnt at the Sessions House in the *Old-Bailey* by the Hand of the Common Hangman" (*LR* 3:334)

Milton was thus intimately connected in the public mind with *Eikon Basilike.* In 1662, Clarendon mentions Milton in a letter that indicates that John Gauden was the true author of *Eikon Basilike:* "Truly when it ceases to be a secrett I know nobody will be glad of it but Mr. Milton" (*LR* 4:369). In a lavish edition of *The Workes of King Charles the Martyr* in 1662, Richard Perrinchief singles out Milton among the "mercenary Souls" hired to attack the *Eikon Basilike:*



> Especially one base Scribe, naturally fitted to compose Satyres and invent Reproaches, who made himself notorious by some licentious and infamous Pamphlets [on divorce], and so approved himself as fit for their service. This Man they encouraged (by translating him from a needy Pedagogue to the office of a Secretary) to write that Scandalous book *Eikonoklastes* (an Invective against the *King's* Meditations) and to answer the learned *Salmasius* his Defence of *Charles the First.* But all was in vain.[42]

Milton's close association with the regicide was noted and unpopular.

After 1660, Milton clearly could no longer speak out directly on the issue of the royal martyr. Yet although Milton's "left hand" no longer produced polemical prose, in the more allusive medium of poetry he continued his fight against kingship. *Paradise Regained*, seemingly so remote from contemporary political issues, is centrally concerned with depicting a Christ who cannot be associated with the Stuart monarchy.[43] Milton's Son of God recalls and rejects the *Eikon Basilike* and the martyrdom of Charles I, including the complex and various uses of royal martyrdom in the 1660s. If in *Eikonoklastes* Milton primarily sought to rewrite the figure of Charles I so as to deny him martyrdom with Christ, in *Paradise Regained* he strives, even more radically, to rewrite the meaning of martyrdom. Milton constructs a Son of God who embodies many of the characteristics of Foxe's martyrs—constancy in affliction, plain-speaking of the truth, self-composure. Yet the Son is no martyr in the traditional sense of suffering; he is a victor who does not die to achieve his conquest. *Paradise Regained* counters the royalist appropriation of the discourse of martyrdom by radically rewriting both recent English political history and the centuries-old literary and cultural tradition of the royal martyr.

The longstanding problems of the poem are significant in regard to this revisionary project. The Son of God in *Paradise Regained* has been termed a "celibate detective," "heartless, prissy, or downright cold," and an "inhuman snob."[44] The Son refuses to act or even to show any emotion. Faced with its spare style, austere setting, and paucity of action, readers have found the poem, as well as its hero, baffling and cold.[45] Even the most basic questions remain unsettled. Why this subject? Why not the crucifixion? Is there development? Does the Son learn anything? Is there a miracle atop the temple tower? Why does Satan fall astonished? Such cruxes are not resolved by analyzing the poem as brief epic; indeed, Milton's use of that genre is equally puzzling. Why no heroic action, figurative richness, poetic allusiveness, divine intervention?[46]



Viewing *Paradise Regained* as participating in the political discourse of martyrdom provides a new interpretive paradigm for a number of these issues. Here epic action, narrative, and plot are circumscribed by the single action of the martyr who must speak the truth, repeatedly, constantly. The hero's actions consist precisely in his witness to the truth—speaking out, enduring fraud and force, standing upright to the end. Divine intervention becomes the inward consolation by which martyrs are fortified. Epic allusiveness and figurative richness become Satanic snares, pitfalls to the plain and simple truth. While the royalist tracts and sermons on Charles I focus on the passion and crucifixion of Christ, for Milton the temptation not only prepares for but essentially replaces the passion and crucifixion. Paradise is regained not by theatrical suffering but by an intellectual debate in the wilderness; the genre is not tragedy but brief epic, the protagonist not the crucified, kingly Christ, but the constant, unmoved Son of God.

Unlike the martyr-kings, father and son, *Paradise Regained* offers no physical suffering and death, no pathos, no public spectacle, no weeping audience. The poem is deliberately antitheatrical or, rather, it links theatricality with Satan, who has a full complement of props, costumes, scenery, and dramatic ploys. While Satan seems to do all the acting, he also continually presses the Son to say or do something dramatically interesting.[47] The character of the Son—private, terse, unemotional—is the opposite of the kings who act out a well-calculated pageant before a gullible audience. The royalists may have the theater, but Milton has the truth.

The contemporary political discourse that linked both Stuart kings with Christ thus clarifies Milton's choice and treatment of his subject in *Paradise Regained.* There is, to begin with, the simple, essential, but continually overlooked point that the hero of *Paradise Regained* is never called Christ. He is the "Son of God" (thirty-six times), the "Son" (fifteen times), "our Saviour" (eighteen times), "Jesus" (five times), "Messiah" (seven times), but never Christ, the one in whom the kingly line of David had been fulfilled. Critics, however, invariably call this character Christ, thus coloring the character and poem with the sacramental associations of earthly kingship that Milton consciously avoided.

The Christ of the synoptic gospels is dramatically attractive as he suffers for others and forgives and prays for his enemies. The passion of Christ is central in the gospels, and it was the language of the passion narratives that Charles I had so powerfully appropriated. Christ's passion takes place in the capital, Jerusalem; his agony in the garden, trial, condemnation, and carrying of the cross are all publicly accessible events. The Christ of the gospels does not eschew the notion of kingship, although he also states, paradoxically, that "my kingdom is not of this world" (John 18.36). Charged before Pilate with claiming to be the king of the Jews, Christ simply replies, "Thou sayest it" (Matthew 27.11; Mark 15.2; Luke 23.3).[48] The passion of the gospel Christ is compelling because of the pathos he evokes—as a figure tragically misunderstood and unjustly put to death. What Milton leaves out of a poem on the regaining of paradise is, from this perspective, astonishing. In rejecting the passion narratives as models for telling how Christ regains paradise, Milton represses the main emphases of the gospels—Christ misunderstood, suffering for others, and redeeming humanity through his death and resurrection. The witness of Milton's Son of God counters and challenges the pathos and dramatic appeal not only of the theatrical martyr-kings, but of the Christ whom they imitate.



Suffering and death, the traditional marks of martyrdom, are evoked in *Paradise Regained*, but then only to be pushed beyond the margins of the narrative. God the Father explains the Son's future mission

> To conquer Sin and Death the two grand foes,
> By Humiliation and strong Sufferance:
> His weakness shall o'ercome Satanic strength
> And all the world, and mass of sinful flesh.
>
> (I.159–62)

The Son knows from the beginning that his claim to the promised kingdom will ultimately consist in a traditional martyr's witness: "my way must lie / Through many a hard assay even to the death, / Ere I the promis'd Kingdom can attain" (I.263–65). Satan, too, discerns in the stars the Son's future suffering and death: "Sorrows, and labors, opposition, hate, / Attends thee, scorns, reproaches, injuries, / Violence and stripes, and lastly cruel death" (IV.386–88). Rejecting an earthly kingship, the Son defends his God-appointed mission thus:

> What if he hath decreed that I shall first
> Be tried in humble state, and things adverse,
> By tribulations, injuries, insults,
> Contempts, and scorns, and snares, and violence,
> Suffering, abstaining, quietly expecting
> Without distrust or doubt, that he may know
> What I can suffer, how obey? who best
> Can suffer, best can do; best reign, who first
> Well hath obey'd.
>
> (III.188–96)

While the Son's rejoinder to Satan here seems to refer to future martyrdom, his speech (which significantly omits any mention of the crucifixion) also strikingly describes the action of *Paradise Regained* itself.

In a very material sense, then, the wilderness temptation—during which the Son is tried by "injuries, insults, / Contempts, and scorns, and snares, and violence" and responds by "Suffering, abstaining, quietly expecting / Without distrust or doubt"—functions in Milton's poem as a replacement for traditional martyrdom. The Son's suffering here consists in endurance as he abstains from earthly political power. Martyrdom thus delineated can encompass all the faithful in Restoration England (including those who do not suffer the ultimate witness of death). In Milton's hands, the martyrdom of the Son of God becomes an inclusive condition, no longer unique and no longer linked with his kingship—or that of the Stuart monarchs. Indeed, martyrdom significantly passed in the 1660s and 1670s from the monarchy to other sufferers in the wilderness, the Baptists, Congregationalists, Anabaptists, and especially the Quakers persecuted under the harsh Clarendon Code. Milton's model of martyrdom provides crucial hope and encouragement to his fellow dissenters.



Although the Son does not suffer death in *Paradise Regained*, he nonetheless shows throughout his temptations the constancy that centrally defines Foxean martyrs. This, however, has been perhaps his most frustrating and puzzling trait for readers. In response to Satanic temptations, the Son replies "sternly," (I.406), "with unalter'd brow" (I.493), "temperately" (II.378), "patiently" (II.432), "calmly" (III.43), "fervently" (III.121), "unmov'd" (III.386; IV, 109), "with disdain" (IV.170), and "sagely" (IV.285). During the Satanic storm he is "patient" (IV.420), "unshaken" (IV.421), and "unappall'd" (IV.425). Satan names the trait that constitutes the Son's central defense when he rejects Belial's suggestion of a temptation involving women: "with manlier objects we must try / His constancy" (II.225–26). The simile that opens Book IV of *Paradise Regained* recalls the frontispiece to *Eikon Basilike* as well as the claims, made by both Charles I and Charles II, of constancy in faith through storms of popular rage:

> [As] surging waves against a solid rock,
> Though all to shivers dash't, th'assault renew,
> Vain batt'ry, and in froth or bubbles end;
> So Satan.
>
> (IV.18–21)[49]

Likewise, Satan later complains that he has found the Son "Proof against all temptation as a rock / Of Adamant, and as a Center, firm" (IV.533–34). This constancy reaches its apex (literally and dramatically) in *Paradise Regained* in the temptation of the Tower, when the Son stuns Satan by the untheatrical action of standing still: "To whom thus Jesus. Also it is written, / Tempt not the Lord thy God; he said and stood. / But Satan smitten with amazement fell" (IV.560–62).

And yet, as Milton himself had argued in *Eikonoklastes*, such constancy is in itself insufficient. Milton wants to show that the Son of God is constant in witness to the truth. The Son declares early in *Paradise Regained* that even as a child he felt himself "born to promote all truth, / All righteous things" (I.205–6). Military might allures him to subdue tyrannic power and to these specific ends: "Till truth were freed, and equity restor'd" (I.220). By contrast, Satan is repeatedly defined in terms of falsehood. The Son reproaches Satan as "compos'd of lies / From the beginning, and in lies wilt end" (I.407–8). Later, he charges Satan: "For lying is thy sustenance, thy food. / Yet thou pretend'st to truth" (I.429–30). Even Satan praises (though guilefully) the Son's truthfulness:



> Hard are the ways of truth, and rough to walk,
> Smooth on the tongue discourst, pleasing to th' ear,
> And tunable as Silvan Pipe or Song;
> What wonder then if I delight to hear
> Her dictates from thy mouth?
>
> (I.478–82)

This praise is blandishment, offered in response to the Son's characterization of himself in terms of truth:

> God hath now sent his living Oracle
> Into the World to teach his final will,
> And sends his Spirit of Truth henceforth to dwell
> In pious Hearts, an inward Oracle
> To all truth requisite for men to know.
>
> (I.460–64)

Truth, as embodied in the Son, becomes inward, not visible, not subject to display. Such a definition is politically charged, formed in a nexus of political struggle. Thus *Paradise Regained* dissociates truth from kingship: unlike Charles II, who suffers into a throne, the Son rejects an earthly throne and redefines kingship as guidance in the truth:

> But to guide Nations in the way of truth
> By saving Doctrine, and from error lead
> To know, and knowing worship God aright,
> Is yet more Kingly.
>
> (II.473–76)

Once the Son has definitively denied any association with earthly political power, the narrator concludes: "So spake *Israel's* true King, and to the Fiend / Made answer meet, that made void all his wiles. / So fares it when with truth falsehood contends" (III.441–43).

Finally, then, as opposed to the false witness of earthly king, the Son's true witness is private. While Charles I courts publicity as a martyr, penning his meditations and seeking through theatrics to stir up the people, and Charles II enters London in a lavish and magnificent triumphal progress, Milton's Son of God is alone in the wilderness. Milton moves the public role of Christ—not only his suffering and death, but his entire ministry—beyond even the reader's view. Although the poem opens with the public baptism of the Son, the action then relocates to a private sphere. Most unlike the Stuart monarchs, Milton's Son of God is found "tracing the Desert wild, / Sole, but with holiest Meditations fed" (II.109–10).





Satan mocks the Son's circumstances:

> Thou art unknown, unfriended, low of birth,
> A Carpenter thy Father known, thyself
> Bred up in poverty and straits at home;
> Lost in a Desert here and hunger-bit.
> (II.413–16)

He tempts the Son to seek fame: "These Godlike Virtues wherefore dost thou hide? / Affecting private life, or more obscure / In savage Wilderness" (III.21–23). But the Son harshly rejects public acclaim, the "people's praise," in language that strikingly recalls Milton's earlier polemic against the "herd" in *Eikonoklastes:* "And what the people but a herd confus'd, / A miscellaneous rabble, who extol / Things vulgar, and well weigh'd, scarce worth the praise?" (III.49–51). The link with Milton's *Eikonoklastes* clarifies the otherwise puzzling severity of these lines. Milton's Son of God, unlike the Stuart monarchs, rejects popular fame because he witnesses not to himself but to God: "Shall I seek glory then, as vain men seek / Oft not deserv'd? I seek not mine, but his / Who sent me, and thereby witness whence I am" (III.105–7).

The human bystanders in *Paradise Regained* neither see nor hear about the Son's temptation in the wilderness. Andrew and Simon are disappointed and baffled by the Son's disappearance; nonetheless they summon up their faith:

> But let us wait; thus far he hath perform'd,
> Sent his Anointed, and to us reveal'd him,
> By his great Prophet, pointed at and shown,
> In public.
> (II.49–52)

Mary has not even seen the baptism, but only hears that her son, "Private, unactive, calm, contemplative" (II.81), has now been "acknowledg'd . . . / By *John* the Baptist, and in public shown, / Son own'd from Heaven by his Father's voice" (II.83–85). Apprehensive about her son—"But where delays he now? some great intent / Conceals him" (II.95–96)—Mary too keeps faith: "But I to wait with patience am inur'd'" (II.102). The poem hence provides a model for the faithful few in Milton's Restoration audience, as the poet conceived them and his hero alike. The Son's true witness never finds a human audience in the poem. After he has withstood Satanic temptation, the Son simply goes home: "hee unobserv'd / Home to his Mother's house private return'd" (IV.638–39).



Yet the Son is not wholly unobserved for he has, in the first place, a divine audience. God the Father explains that he is sending the Son

> That all the Angels and Ethereal Powers,
> They now, and men hereafter, may discern
> From what consummate virtue I have chose
> This perfect Man, by merit call'd my Son,
> To earn Salvation for the Sons of men.
> (I.163–67)

Satan too, of course, closely tracks the Son's witness and is ultimately stunned and defeated by it. In a sense, having given up the theatrical, Milton takes it back again: the Son's constancy and witness effect the same result as the dramatic display—overwhelming and amazing Satan.

Finally, the Son is not unobserved because Milton himself is publishing by textualizing the epic Christ's "private" witness in the wilderness. The narrator will

> tell of deeds
> Above Heroic, though in secret done,
> And unrecorded left through many an Age,
> Worthy t' have not remain'd so long unsung.
> (I.14–17)

In order to lodge his insistence that the true Son of God has no real earthly audience, Milton must speak to some earthly audience. This audience might be those few of "value and substantial worth" with whom, in *Eikonoklastes*, Truth is contented. For Milton, the very inaccessibility of *Paradise Regained* throughout its reception history, its lack of drama and popular appeal, would paradoxically confirm the truth of his discourse. The monarchy may have the public theater, but Milton's is the truly heroic witness.

# *Samson Agonistes* and the Regicides

> 17 [October 1660] This day were executed those murderous Traytors at Charing-Crosse, in sight of the place where they put to death their natural Prince, & in the Presence of the King his sonn, whom they also sought to kill: take[n] in the trap they laied for others: The Traytors executed were *Scot*, *Scroope*, *Cook*, *Jones.* I saw not their execution, but met their quarters mangld & cutt & reaking as they were brought from the Gallows in baskets on the hurdle: o miraculous providence of God.
>
> John Evelyn, *Diary* 3:259

When Charles II was restored to the throne of England, amid tumultuous and decidedly unpuritanical celebration, he was inclined to be lenient to most of his old enemies. In the generous but shrewd Declaration of Breda, Charles had offered a free and general pardon to all persons connected with the Interregnum regime, with the exception of those persons whom Parliament would exempt. The Convention Parliament proved to be more vengeful than the king himself, and in mid-October 1660 it tried and condemned for high treason twenty-eight of those men who had signed the death warrant or sat as judges at the trial of Charles I. Almost immediately, ten of these were executed as traitors in a spectacular and grisly display of monarchical power, backed by appeal to divine providence. These executions were followed in January by the disinterment and desecration of the bodies of Oliver Cromwell, Henry Ireton (Cromwell's son-in-law), and John Bradshaw (who presided over the trial of Charles I). The restored power of the king was inscribed in the disemboweled and dismembered bodies of the "murderous Traytors," who were exposed alive and dead to the public view.[1]

The executions and the exhumings continued the contestatory discourses of martyrdom and treason introduced at the execution of Charles I. But there was now more recognition of the potential for different and subversive interpretations of the spectacle and more attempt to control such reinterpretation, in part by carrying out the exhuming on the day of the anniversary fast for the martyr-king, Charles I. Royalist and republican martyrologies competed to control the site of punishment, each self-fashioned as iconoclastic and seeing idolatry in the other. The spectacle of punishment remained an emotionally powerful tool, subject to challenge, subversion, and reappropriation.



As it meditates on the spectacles of punishment in Restoration England, Milton's *Samson Agonistes* exposes the twin and interchangeable threats of iconoclasm and idolatry. The odd ambivalence of the work, often explained away in the interest of theological orthodoxy, reflects the ambivalences of these political spectacles of punishment. But the tragedy finally moves to question not only true and false appropriations but the nature and efficacy of the spectacle itself. In *Samson Agonistes* the people are self-enslaved, and Samson's act of violence cannot set them free.

## I

The trials and executions of the regicides, like the trial of Charles I, were public displays of state justice. Those men who had signed the death warrant of Charles I, or, in a few cases, had simply participated prominently in his execution, were tried for treason, for encompassing the death of the king. The executions of the regicides were, first of all, a visual display of power, the spectacle of the law inscribing itself on the body of the condemned. Since the men were disemboweled and quartered as well as hanged, the display was more visually grotesque and physically horrifying than was the beheading of the monarch. On October 17, 1660, Peter Mundy witnessed the executions of Mr. Clement, Mr. Scot, Colonel Scroope, and Colonel Jones:

> They hang near half quarter of an houre while the hangman strips them starcke naked and cutts them downe, and then presently, while they are hott, (I say not alive), cutts of[f] their privities, casts them first into the fire, the[n] opens them [and] disembowells them, casting their entraills into the fire allsoe, lastly holding up their hearts in hand one after another, cries to the people—"See the heart of a traitor." It is don alike to all. (*Travels*, 125–26)

Alive or dead, the dismembered bodies were exhibited for public view. On the sixteenth Mundy had watched the execution of Hugh Peters, commenting dispassionately: "Their quarters brought backe openly, part in a great (porters) baskett and part on the slead, forequarters and hind quarters throwne together like butchers meat brought from the shambles, the leggs over the baskets for their bigness, fullnesse and fattnesse judged to bee Mr. Peters" (125). The body parts constituted an ongoing display of punished treason, as Mundy records: "The quarters of these that were executed wer[e] set over the gates of the Citty, stuck on and fastned unto long poles set upright, to be discerned afarre ofte. . . . Never the like was seene before at any tyme in the Citty of London" (126–27).





Mundy emphasizes the horror-producing spectacle. But this exemplary power was supplemented by a less spectacular and more pervasive form of power, as official accounts appeared to ensure that the spectators would properly interpret the drama they had watched. These accounts appealed to the rhetoric of divine providence and justice to supplement the law and monarchical power. The weekly newspaper, *Mercurius Publicus*, reports that Thomas Scot,

> who last year publickly boasted that he was one of those that adjudg'd his late MAJESTY to death, and desired *he might have that written upon his Tomb* in some sort now has his desire; only he hath no Tomb, for after (according to Law) he was half-hang'd, cut down, his Members cut off and burnt in his sight, his quarters were convey'd back upon the Hurdle that brought him to be dispos'd so far asunder, that they'll scarce ever meet together in one Tomb.[2]

The bitter irony underscores, in this account, the heinousness of the crime.

Royalist accounts emphasize the behavior of the criminal on the scaffold, the continuing impenitence or confession which, in either case, justified the punishment. *A True and Perfect Relation of the Grand Traytors Execution* (1660) comments on the execution of Harrison that "many of his acquaintance did seem to triumph to see him die so Confidently; whiles numbers of true Christians did grieve in earnest to see him die so impenitently"; and, on John Carew's continuing defiance: "It is a sad thing for a dying man to add more Coles to that Fire which by the Laws of Nature and Christianity he is bound to extinguish."[3]

Scaffold confessions also served to supplement and confirm the exemplary punishment. *Mercurius Publicus* reports that John Cook "express'd exceeding much Penitence; and (which best became him) heartily pray'd for his MAJESTY that now is" (670); Gregory Clement at his death "express'd a great deal of sorrow and penitence, confessing, That he most justly suffered both from God and man, and that his Judges had done nothing but according to Law, begging the Prayers of all spectators" (672).

Royalist accounts were also attentive to the response of the spectators, the true target of the display. On October 18, 1660, Secretary Nicholas writes that "the people are so satisfied that they even shout with joy on the death of the more hardened of the traitors" (*CSPD* 1:316). *Mercurius Publicus* reports that the death of the unpopular regicide Hugh Peters was "the delight of the people, which they exprest by several shouts and acclamations, when they saw him go up the ladder, and also when the Halter was putting about his Neck, but also when his head was cut off, and held aloft upon the end of a spear, there was such a shout as if the people of *England* had acquired a Victory" (670–71).



These accounts produced and controlled treason, finally, by demonizing the regicides through vivid reminders of the execution of the martyr-king. *Mercurius Publicus* notes the irony that Harrison is hung "with his face towards the *Banqueting-house* at *White-hall* (where that precious innocent bloud of our late Sovereign Lord King *Charles the First* was spilt) by this *Harrison*, and the rest of those bloudy Regicides" (660). The broadsheet *A True and Perfect Relation* associates the regicides with the hated Jesuits: "Thus we plainly may perceive how the Kings of Christendome are daily crucifyed (as Christ their Lord was) between two Thieves the *Jesuits* and the *Sectaries*, who have designed all those Princes to destruction, whom in their own Trayterous and Irreligious Hearts they have condemned for Tyranny." *A Looking-Glass for Traytors* relates the indictment which charges that the regicides, "not having the fear of God before their eyes, but being led by the instigation of the Divel, had maliciously, traiterously, and advisedly imagined, consulted, contrived, and compassed the death of his late Majesty Charles the first of ever blessed memory."[4]

The blackening of the regicides was furthered by the circulation of prints and drawings of their execution, images that differ strikingly from the representations of the king's execution. The iconography of the regicides' execution dwells, as do the printed texts, on the grisly horrors of hanging, drawing, quartering, and beheading. Whereas the king is depicted fully clothed, in one piece, and lifelike even when lying on his coffin, the regicides are represented in various stages of hanging, decapitation, and dismemberment. *A True and Perfect Relation* thus supplements written text with visual display, juxtaposing the execution of Charles I with the execution of his murderers (Fig. 6).

In the illustration on the left, the execution of Charles I is represented as a solemn ceremony; soldiers stand close to the scaffold in parallel formation with their muskets drawn, and the king beckons to Bishop Juxon, perhaps to give him the famous injunction, "Remember." In contrast, the illustration of the execution of the regicides shows them dead or dying in a vivid, grisly display. A hangman holds a decollated head above the knife that has just cut it off; a caption reads, "A Traytors head." Another regi-

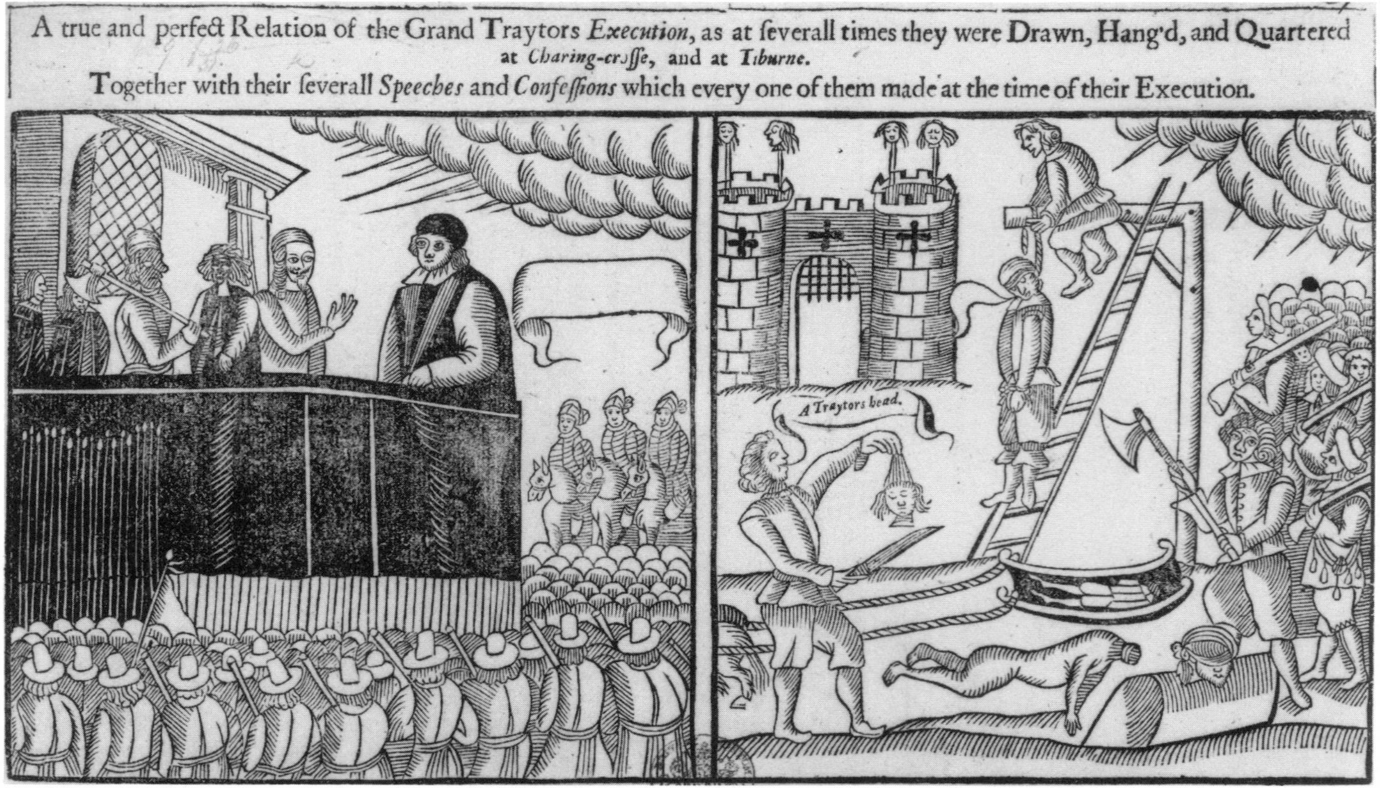

A true and perfect Relation of the Grand Traytors *Execution*, as at severall times they were Drawn, Hang'd, and Quartered at *Charing-crosse*, and at *Tiburne*.

Together with their severall *Speeches* and *Confessions* which every one of them made at the time of their Execution.



FIGURE 6 Executions of Charles I and of the regicides, from *A True and Perfect Relation of the Grand Traytors Execution* (1660). *By permission of the British Library.*

cide, tied at the hands, dangles from the scaffold with head askew and eyes closed, ready (or almost ready) to be cut down, castrated, and dismembered. On the ground is a naked body and severed head, and a sledge upon which appears to be the bottom half of another corpse. The people stand not in regular formation but in disarray. This spectacle is not a solemn tragedy but a brutal horror, designed to bring upon the regicides all the ignominy of the felon, to repulse and deter.



But, as with the execution of Charles I, the spectacle of public punishment, once put into circulation, could not be fully controlled and had unexpected and contrary effects. Hence sympathizers with the regicides interpreted their executions as a spectacle of martyrdom, a display of divine witness not to monarchical power but to the Good Old Cause. *The Speeches and Prayers of Major General Harrison [et al]*, published in 1660 and circulated widely enough so that the printers were later prosecuted and fined, presents (alleged) speeches and letters of the regicides that construe their sufferings as martyrdom.[5] *The Speeches and Prayers* constructs what might be called a poetics of martyrdom: the regicides in this account reappropriate for the Good Old Cause the rhetoric of martyrdom shaped by Foxe and so effectively deployed after the execution of Charles I. Unlike these earlier martyrologies, however, it should be noted that there were no accompanying illustrations; this account avoids the actual display of punishment with its degrading criminality, opposing and rewriting that image by word alone.

*The Speeches and Prayers* thus directly counters the strategies of display, rewriting treason and justice as suffering and witness to the Good Old Cause. From the scaffold, Thomas Scot recognizes the ambiguous and exemplary nature of the spectacle: "O blessed Lord, thou hast called him forth as a publick Spectacle to some, in a condition of Shame and Reproach; to others, of Comfort; and to thy Blessed Self, as one that is a Witness for Thee, that hath served Thee with all faithfulness in his trust and publick capacity and imployment" (62). The Good Old Cause is seen as inscribed in the bodies and blood of its martyrs, as Major-General Harrison attests: "As he was going to suffer, one in a Derision called to him and said, Where is your *Good Old Cause?* He with a cheerful smile clapt his hand on his Brest, and said, *Here it is, and I am going to seal it with my bloud*" (6–7).

In this account, the regicides, like Foxe's martyrs, exhibit not only constancy and courage, but cheerfulness, even merriment in the face of death. At the sight of the gallows, Harrison is "transported with joy" (7); he asserts, "if I had ten thousand lives, I could freely and cheerfully lay them down all to witnesse to this matter" (8). Carew's cheerfulness is much noted: "It was also observed that the cheerfulness of his countenance all the way as he went to the Gibbet remained, to the encouragement of the Faithfull, and admiration of enemies, uttering by the way many chearfull expressions setting forth his joy in the Lord" (15). The "courage and chearfulness" of Jones and Scroope "caused great Admiration and Compassion in the Spectators, as they passed along the Streets, to *Charing-Crosse*, the place of their Execution" (70). A second martyrology on the later executions of Okey, Barkstead, and Corbet depicts similar cheerfulness: Colonel Barkstead, seeing his wife waving a handkerchief at him, "took off his hat and several times shaking it over his head, cried out with an astonishing chearfulness, To heaven, to heaven, to heaven, my love, and leave you in the storm!"[6]





This cheerfulness is witness to divine consolations, again as is typical of Foxe's martyrs. Carew receives divine consolations after his arrest and at his execution: "Indeed, the rage of the people all the way was such, that had he not been indued with strength from on High, he could not have undergone the wicked and Barbarous Deportment and Carriage of the Giddy multitude which he was subjected to" (11). After praying on the scaffold, Carew exclaims: "Oh blessed be God! Oh! how many are the Refreshments I have had from the presence of my God and Father, sweet, and secret Communion betwixt him and my soul today" (23–24). Thomas Scot states on the scaffold: "This very day, thy poor Servant that now stands to suffer, had joy and much Consolation from God, and from his Cause, more than ever he had before" (63). In the later executions, when a bystander takes the comforting spirits to be literal—"O Barkstead! you have got the comforter! (meaning a little strong-water bottle that he had in his hand)"—Barkstead replies, "Blessed be God, he had a better comforter than that, or else he should not be able to stand there so chearfully as he did."[7]

As described in *The Speeches and Prayers*, the regicides rewrite the text of their punished bodies to deny the charges of treason. They block and subvert the scaffold confession that would reaffirm the justice of their punishment, reiterating, like Foxe's martyrs (and like Charles I) that their consciences are clear. Harrison, for instance, avers that "though I am wrongfully charged with murder and bloudshed, yet I must tell you I have kept a good Conscience both towards God, and towards Man" (7). Similarly, Cook asserts: "I bless the Lord I have nothing lying upon my conscience, but I can unbosome my self to every one, and to the throne of free grace, in the simplicity of my spirit, I have endeavoured to doe nothing but with a good conscience" (34). The regicides thus redeploy exactly that discourse which had rescued and continued to legitimate sacral kingship.

Like Foxe's martyrs (and like Charles I), the regicides further subvert the spectacle of punishment by reiterating their hope for a crown of martyrdom. Carew thus comforts his grieving relatives: "O my friends, if you did know and feel what joy I have, and what a Glorious Crown I shall receive from the hand of Christ (for this work) you would not Mourn, but Rejoyce, that I am counted worthy to be a witness to this Cause" (12). Brought to the gibbet, Carew consoles his nearby friends: "Before he went up the ladder (his hands being bound) he exhorted severall friends standing by to be faithful unto death; and not to be ashamed of the Cause for which they suffered, and they should receive a Crown of life" (15–16). Axtell encourages his fellow prisoner Hacker: "Come brother be not so sad, by this time tomorrow we shall be with our Father in Glory, and what hurt will they do us to bring us through the Crosse to the Crown" (83).



But this crown is a heavenly crown and cannot cohere with the Stuart monarchy. The regicides thus make the discourse of martyrdom antimonarchical once again: the martyr's crown is contrasted with, and as it were precludes, the kingly crown. Cook asserts: "Little doe my Enemies think what a Friendly part they do me, to hasten me to my Fathers Kingdom, to my Crown and Glory; I had rather go to my Dear Jesus with my Chain and Crosse, then to sit down with an Earthly King on his Throne and wear a Crown of Gold" (27).

The regicides are conscious—like Foxe's martyrs and like Charles I—that they bear the martyr's witness. Cook looks to Hebrews for the book of martyrs: "*Heb.* 12. has an ineffable sweetnesse in it, *Ch* 11 is the little book of Martyrs. . . . Christ and the saints behold you and yee are witnesses for Christ as they were" (44). They dwell as well on the witness of God. Hence, Harrison encourages his brethren: "Therefore be cheerful in the Lord your God, hold fast that which you have and be not afraid of suffering. . . . Be not discouraged by reason of the cloud that now is upon you; for the Son will shine, and God will give a testimony unto what he hath been a doing, in a short time" (10).

But finally the discourse of martyrdom reinterprets not only the actions of the regicides, but the actions of their enemies. Reversing the charge of treason, the regicides posit a higher court by which England will be judged. Cook is a typical and eloquent spokesman:

> My rejoycing is in a good God, a good Cause, a good Conscience, I have the Justice of Heaven on my side, and Gods loving kindnesse which is better then life, if we find injustice and cruelty here, mens Law at *Westminster* will be adjudged Treason in Heaven. . . . At the revelation of the righteous judgement of God, it will appeare before men and Angels, that we are not Traytors, nor Murtherers, nor Phanatiques, but true Christians, and good Commonwealths men. (48–49)

The regicides contrast the judgments of God and man: man has judged them, but God will justify them. The reversing of treason and martyrdom continues, and the execution of the king, more than a decade earlier, continues to be the central contested site.

Having embraced martyrdom, Cook asserts that their blood will in fact be an ongoing spectacle which will bring destruction upon their enemies: "Farewell my Dear Lamb, I am now going to the soules under the Altar, That cry how long O Lord holy and true; dost thou not Judge and Avenge our bloud on them that dwell on the Earth, and when I am gone, my bloud will cry and do them more hurt then if I had lived" (29). Carew comforts his grieving friends: "The Lord will bring my bloud (saith he) to cry with the rest of the Martyrs, *How long, O Lord, Holy and True, &c.*" (14). Their blood "shall come down shortly upon *Babylon*, although they think to heale her, yet they shall give her a greater blow than ever we could have given her in our persons" (15). The regicides' call for apocalyptic judgment, as we shall see in chapter 5, did not go unheeded (at least on earth).



The effects of the display were shown on the true target of the punishment, the spectators at the scaffold. As with the display of Charles's execution, the public punishment had some contrary and undesired effects. The fortitude shown by the regicides apparently astonished the onlookers. In recounting the executions of Axtell and Hacker, *The Speeches and Prayers* recounts a conversion of the spectators: two uncivil onlookers who "cryed out very earnestly, hang them, hang them Rogues, Traytors, Murtherers, Hang-man, draw away the cart," after hearing Axtell's speech and prayer, were "so affected, that they could not refrain from pouring out many Tears upon the place, and went aside to a place a little more retired to weep" (96). Even an unsympathetic contemporary observer, Burnet, writes that although the first trials and executions were attended by "vast crowds, and all people seemed pleased with the sight," the effect then changed dramatically: "the odiousness of the crime grew at last to be so much flattened by the frequent executions, and most of those who suffered dying with such firmness and shew of piety, justifying all they had done . . . that the king was advised not to proceed farther, at least not to have the scene so near the Court as Charing-cross" (*History*, 105–6). Indeed, many of the accused regicides were not executed, but languished and died in prison.

That this discourse of martyrdom had some circulation is shown by agitated royalist responses. *A True and Perfect Relation* ends with a warning to the readers: "I hope neither Peers nor people for the time to come will be so fond to believe [the dying regicides], or so wicked to follow them." *Mercurius Publicus* calls the readers' attention to its "most perfect account of the Arraignment, Tryal, and Judgment of 28 grand traytors, the pretended Judges of his late sacred Majesty" which will be "speedily Printed and Published by Authority . . . to prevent the Readers abuse by Imperfect Notes Irregularly and daily put upon them" (667). One London minister tries to undo the effects of the "newsmongers" and "licentious pamphlets" by denying that Harrison and the other regicides could be martyrs: "The best of them could not dye like religious Martyrs. The cause would by no means permit it; because it was for Martyring a most glorious Martyr, for which they suffered."[8] The ceremony of punishment throughout was designed to point to and reaffirm Charles I as royal martyr. But the royalists, like the revolutionaries earlier, found the spectacle of treason a contested site and in their very denials affirmed the power of the discourse of martyrdom now appropriated by their enemies.



## II

IN DECEMBER 1660, Parliament moved from punishment of the surviving regicides to punishment of the dead. A Captain Silas Titus concluded the debate on the Bill of Attainder by arguing that

> execution did not leave Traitors at their graves, but followed them beyond it: and that since the Heads and Limbs of some were already put upon the Gates, he hoped the House would order the Carcasses of those Devils, who were buried in Westminster, Cromwell, Bradshaw, Ireton, and Pride be taken out of their graves, dragged to Tyburn, there to hang for some time, and afterwards to be buried under the gallows.[9]

The exhuming of Cromwell and his associates was a symbolic undoing of the trial and public execution of the king. The bodies were to be disinterred on January 30, the anniversary of Charles's death. It was also an extension and completion of the punishment of the living regicides—and it took back again, for the royalist cause, the rhetoric of martyrdom. As we have seen, January 30 was set aside as an anniversary day of fasting and humiliation.[10] The unprecedented act of exhuming confirmed Charles I as martyr, answering the call of his sacred blood.

This grisly display of the corpses, dragged to Tyburn reeking and decomposing and there publicly degraded, was depicted as an act of justice upon traitors; the exhuming graphically countered the trial and execution of the king. According to *The Last Farewel of Three Bould Traytors* (1661), "Bloody *Cromwel*, Bloody *Bradshaw* and Tyrant *Ireton* . . . [were] drawn to Tyborn upon two Sledges, *January* 30, 1661. the same day of the moneth as they Murdered our Sovereign Lord King *Charles* the first, of ever blessed Memory."[11] At Tyburn, according to *Mercurius Publicus* (24–31 January), the corpses were "pull'd out of their Coffins, and hang'd at the several angles of that Triple tree, where they hung til the Sun was set; after which, they were taken down, their Heads cut off, and their loathsome Trunks thrown into a deep hole under the Gallows" (64). The dead men were dehumanized, made into something monstrous and animalistic. An eyewitness, Spanish merchant Samuel Sainthill, described how Ireton, "having been buried long hung like a dried rat, yet corrupted about the fundament"; Bradshaw in his winding sheet was better preserved, "the fingers of his right hand and his nose perished, the rest very perfect, insomuch that I knew his face, when the hangman after cutting off the head held it up." Sainthill claimed to have held Bradshaw's toes in his hand, "which the prentices had cut off."[12]



The exhuming once again evinced justice for the cause of monarchy. After the corpses were hanged at Tyburn, the heads were displayed at Westminster, scene of their crime of treason, as Peter Mundy observes: "Their heads were set on a pinnacle at the west end of Westminster Hall, right over the High Court of Justice where the old King was sentenced to dye" (*Travels*, 131). *A New Meeting of Ghosts at Tyburn*, a satiric tract published after the exhuming, depicts Cromwell himself as acknowledging the symbolic reversal: "Now alas, we find the dire effects of our blood and Villany, crying out loud for Justice against us at a High Court of Justice indeed."[13] Secretary Nicholas writes that the corpses "being dragged on sledges to Tyburn, remained hung on the gibbet, in the view of thousands, attracted by so marvellous an act of justice" (*CSPD* 1:506).

Like the execution of the regicides, the exhuming was widely viewed. Thomas Rugg writes of the public enthusiasm for viewing and degrading Cromwell's corpse: "Oliver Cromwels vault beeing broke open, the people crowed very much to see him, who gave sixpence a peece for to see him" (*Diurnal*, 143). *Mercurius Publicus* (24–31 January) reports that as the "odious carcasses" of Cromwell, Ireton, and Bradshaw were drawn upon sledges, "the universal out-cry and curses of the people went along with them" (64). And the Venetian ambassador comments that the disinterment and hanging "was carried out before a great crowd amid the universal approval of the city and of all the people" (*CSPV* 32:246). This audience, unlike the spectators at the execution of the regicides, was not moved to sympathize with the grotesque and dishonored corpses; nor could the corpses resist and subvert the display of treason.

And again the spectacle of punishment was circulated in woodcuts and drawings as well as printed texts. As with the regicides, and unlike the iconography of Charles I, these illustrations are graphic and visually horrifying; the corpses, hangings, and decollated heads are depicted, underscoring the horror of both punishment and crime. A Dutch print (Fig. 7) is especially vivid but otherwise not unlike its English counterparts.[14] Two corpses hang ignominiously from the gibbet; the larger of the two, resembling Cromwell, is turned face forward revealing the distorted facial expression of death. The third corpse, head downward, is being pulled off the sledge. The bodies are clothed (rather than in embalming sheets) but hang limply. The large crowd, including one child holding her mother's hand and another on the shoulders of his father, watches with a keen but dispassionate interest.

Significantly, tracts on the exhuming or other derogatory writings after 1660 often visually demonize or dehumanize Cromwell, depicting him as a shrouded ghost, conspiring with the Devil, or being fed by the Devil into hell.[15] *The Last Farewel of Three Bould Traytors* turns the viewer's gaze away from the site of exhuming, which is depicted in a woodcut, to a second print in which Cromwell and a companion, presumably either Bradshaw or Ireton, are fed by the Devil into the gaping mouth of a monsterlike hell (Fig. 8). The spectacle of the grotesque body falls below tragedy into satire, even farce. Another tract is devoted entirely to a scurrilous exposition on Cromwell's "nose."[16] Such debasement follows what Bakhtin has identified as the grotesque body more than the solemn and horrifying Foucauldian spectacles of punishment that we have traced in the execution of Charles I and the regicides. But unlike the examples explored by Bakhtin, here there is no carnivalesque revitalization, no recuperation from the life forces; the display is pure satire.[17]



The grotesque spectacle of disinterred traitors seemed to be the final turn in the contested spectacles of treason and martyrdom. Unlike the execution of Charles and of the other regicides, the men could not speak, could not subvert the display. Cromwell had died peacefully in his bed and was given a lavish state funeral; no one could plausibly argue that old Noll had been a martyr. Instead, Marchamont Nedham and Payne Fisher published a biting parody of *The Speeches and Prayers* in which the corpses luridly confess to tyranny, fraud, dissimulation, and a variety of sins of the body—adultery, lechery, drunkenness, incest.[18]

Yet a few dissenting views are recorded: Pepys sees the order for disinterment as excessive; "[it] do trouble me that a man of so great courage as [Cromwell] was should have that dishonour, though otherwise he might deserve it enough" (*Diary* 1:309). And the Middlesex court records show charges of sedition for such praise of Cromwell as "Oliver was as good a man as King Charles was," "the Lord Protector was as good a man as the King," or "If Oliver were alive, I would fight for him before any man in England for money" (*MCR* 3:316; 326). But in the realm of public discourse, the government seemed to have the last word on treason and martyrdom. Or, so it seemed.

## III

At the time of the Restoration, John Milton was closely associated with the regicides and came perilously close to their same fate. In January 1660, *The Out-Cry of the London Prenctices* mentions Milton among various scur-

FIGURE 7 Dutch print of the exhuming and hanging of Cromwell, Ireton, and Bradshaw, from *T'Radt van Avontveren* (1661). *By permission of the Trustees of the British Museum.*

rilous suggestions for the disposing of the remains of regicide John Lord Hewson (fortunate enough to have died a natural death): "The one good eye he hath left, wee'l take out of his Head, and bestow it upon blind *Milton*, that it may still be worn as an Ornament in a knaves countenance, and when he leaves it, it shall be given to Surgeons Hall for a rarity" (*LR* 4:298). With the return of the king, as we have seen, contemporaries expected Milton to be punished. An attack on Milton in *The Character of the Rump* (1660) asserts wryly that "he is so much an enemy to the usual practices that I believe when he is condemned to travel to *Tyburn* in a cart, he will petition for the favour to be the first man that ever was driven thither in a *Wheel-barrow*" (*LR* 4:305). Gui Patin hears in Paris in 1660 "that Milton's book against the late king of England was burned by the hand of the common hangman; that Milton is a prisoner; that he may well be hanged" (*LR* 4:327). But, as we saw earlier, Milton was not excepted out

Figure 8 The Devil feeding Cromwell into the mouth of hell, from *The Last Farewel of Three Bould Traytors* (1660). *By permission of the Houghton Library, Harvard University.*

of the Act of Oblivion, although he was imprisoned for a time. An early biographer, Jonathan Richardson, reports in his *Life of Milton* that his son found scribbled on a copy of *Eikonoklastes* a poem entitled "Upon John Milton's not suffering for his Traiterous book when the Tryers were Executed 1660." This verse sets out one explanation for the apparent clemency shown Milton—that his present state of poverty and blindness was worse than death:

> That thou Escapd'st that Vengeance which o'ertook,
> *Milton*, thy Regicides, and thy Own Book,
> Was Clemency in *Charles* beyond compare
> And yet thy Doom doth prove more Grevious farr.
> Old, Sickly, Poor, Stark Blind, thou Writ'st for Bread.[19]

For Milton the fate of the regicides after the Restoration was not only a political but a personal tragedy. Yet he could use the vehicle of literature to interpret and rewrite apparent punishment and defeat. Milton's choice and treatment of a tragedy on the biblical figure of Samson has, in relation to the punishment of the regicides, more specific, extensive, and resonant political implications than have previously been recognized.[20]

Critics have disagreed about the political import of *Samson Agonistes*. For Mary Ann Radzinowicz, the drama provides a model of a people chastened, quieted, and self-disciplined in the face of defeat.[21] For Christopher Hill, *Samson Agonistes* is an allegorical call to arms for seventeenth-century Englishmen: "However difficult the political circumstances, be ready to smite the Philistines when God gives the word."[22] Jackie DiSalvo sees Samson as reflecting the military and revolutionary vocation of seventeenth-century Puritans, particularly of the New Model Army in the 1640s; she argues for an earlier dating.[23] For Nicholas Jose, *Samson Agonistes* "is about a spiritual restoration which counters the political restoration, falsifying its values and claims."[24] Irene Samuel and, more recently, Joseph Wittreich, see the work as repudiating English politics through a violent and deeply flawed Samson.[25] David Loewenstein counters this view by linking the violence to Milton's earlier iconoclasm.[26]

The relationship of *Samson Agonistes* to the execution and exhuming of the regicides has not been explored in any sustained way. Striking differences, of course, hinder any simple allegorical reading. Samson admits great guilt and dies through his own strength and violence, albeit in self-sacrifice; nor does Samson show the distinctive characteristics of the Foxean martyrs—patience, constancy, inner consolations, hope in a heavenly afterlife. The Chorus—and a scholarly tradition that wants to make the text a model of private regeneration, not a public political statement—has seen Samson as martyr, a Christ figure.[27] But through much of the drama, Samson's restless thoughts contrast with the inward consolations of the Son in *Paradise Regained* and of the Foxean martyrs.[28] Milton does not rewrite the regicides—or Cromwell—as martyrs in his tragedy. Yet *Samson Agonistes* nonetheless revises the signs of crime and punishment, exposing and undermining Philistine strategies of power in a final violent display. The triumphant Philistines, insulting over the body of their defeated enemy, have in reality been given over to idolatry, delusion, and impending doom. Samson embodies the violence for which the regicides could only call.

*Samson Agonistes* opens with the body of the condemned on visible display. Captived, blinded, exposed to daily view, Samson's body appears to be the public sign of Philistine triumph and power. Samson sees himself through the eyes of his enemies, by whom he has been blinded, imprisoned, and put to perpetual labor. He fears that despite his divine calling, he will die:

> Betray'd, Captiv'd, and both my Eyes put out,
> Made of my Enemies the scorn and gaze;
> To grind in Brazen Fetters under task
> With this Heav'n-gifted strength.
>
> (33–36)

Samson is not so much suffering from physical pain as he is shamed by his constant visibility, branded with infamy, "the scorn and gaze" of his Philistine foes. Hearing footsteps, Samson expects his enemies, who "come to stare / At my affliction, and perhaps to insult, / Thir daily practice to afflict me more" (112–14). The once-proud champion of Israel is now an object of scorn for the victorious Philistines, of shame for the Israelites. Having fallen, "swoll'n with pride" (532), Samson is now punished with shame. He is momentarily grateful for his blindness: "for had I sight, confus'd with shame, / How could I once look up, or heave the head" (196–97). After Manoa reminds him of the far-reaching implications of his downfall, Samson asserts that the scandal he has brought to Israel is "my chief affliction, shame and sorrow" (457). Samson sees his shaming as the end of his usefulness: "Now blind, disheart'n'd, sham'd, dishonor'd, quell'd, / To what can I be useful, wherein serve / My Nation, and the work from Heav'n impos'd" (563–65). He seems to be an unambiguous spectacle of punishment, shame, and defeat.





The display of the punished criminal body is read by a series of visitors as exemplifying Philistine power and the triumph of Dagon, "as their God who hath deliver'd / Thee, *Samson*, bound and blind into thir hands, / Them out of thine, who slew'st them many a slain" (437–39). Yet the public spectacle of punishment is radically ambivalent.[29] The Chorus, which variously interprets the defeated body as sign of mutable fortune or self-abandonment, looks for the providential meaning of the shifting text. Divine providence, they charge, is contrarious in regard to the elect, as it "throwst them lower than thou didst exalt them high" (689):

> Oft leav'st them to the hostile sword
> Of Heathen and profane, thir carcases
> To dogs and fowls a prey, or else captiv'd:
> Or to th'unjust tribunals, under change of times,
> And condemnation of th'ingrateful multitude.
>
> (692–96)

The words of the Chorus are a strikingly direct allusion to the persecution of the republicans after the Restoration, including the exhuming of the bodies of Cromwell, Ireton, and Bradshaw, and the trials and executions of the surviving regicides.[30] But the dramatic context here is critical. The Chorus sees only the hostile force and the defeat of the elect, voicing a poignant complaint about the precarious fate of former leaders. But the Chorus's despair over the apparent signs of defeat and desertion is premature and self-interested, allowing them to ignore their own complicity in Samson's captive state. The drama will counter rather than confirm their view.

The signs of Philistine triumph in the shamed, defeated body of Samson are only apparent, not real. The Philistines believe that they are victorious, but in reality, God has given them over to idolatry and hence to ultimate destruction. Samson is under divine wrath and has been given divine justice, but the people with whom God is incensed are the Philistines. The Philistines think that, with the help of their god, they have completely done in their foe; they mistakenly think that the humiliation of their defeated enemy is sign of victory. But the spectacle of shame and punishment may be in a different drama, a tragedy in which the power on display is God's.

Thoughout *Samson Agonistes* the Israelites define themselves against the idolatrous Philistines. Samson's opening words tell us that "This day a solemn Feast the people hold / To *Dagon* thir Sea-Idol" (12–13). Manoa focuses on the idolatry of the Philistine feast:

> So *Dagon* shall be magnified, and God,
> Besides whom is no God, compar'd with Idols,
> Disglorified, blasphem'd, and had in scorn
> By th' Idolatrous rout amidst thir wine.
> (440–43)

Samson's response to Manoa equates all of the Philistines with their idol, Dagon: "all the contest is now / 'Twixt God and *Dagon*" (461–62).

The Philistines who appear on stage only heighten the idolatry. The Chorus implicitly links Dalila with the sea-god Dagon in its description of her as a "thing of Sea or Land" (710), or, more extensively, as

> a stately Ship
> Of *Tarsus*, bound for th' Isles
> Of *Javan* or *Gadire*
> With all her bravery on, and tackle trim.
> (714–17)[31]

The cult that Dalila imagines for herself extends in its false veneration the idolatrous worship of Dagon, an undue reverence that exemplifies the blindness of the idolatrous nation:

> I shall be nam'd among the famousest
> Of Women, sung at solemn festivals,
> Living and dead recorded, who to save
> Her country from a fierce destroyer, chose
> Above the faith of wedlock bands, my tomb
> With odors visited and annual flowers.
> (982–87)

Harapha, too, is closely linked with Dagon for whom he fights; he swears by "*Baäl-zebub*" (1231). The Officer's summons to Samson foregrounds the idolatry of the feast: "This day to *Dagon* is a solemn Feast, / With Sacrifices, Triumph, Pomp, and Games" (1311–12).

In his initial refusal to obey the summons, Samson likewise emphasizes the idolatry, fearing to "add a greater sin / By prostituting holy things to Idols" (1357–58) and arguing that in his prison labor he serves "Not in thir Idol-Worship, but by labor / Honest and lawful to deserve my food / Of them who have me in thir civil power" (1365–67). When he nonetheless agrees to go, Samson still emphasizes the idolatry:



> Lords are Lordliest in thir wine;
> And the well-feasted Priest then soonest fir'd
> With zeal, if aught Religion seem concern'd:
> No less the people on thir Holy-days
> Impetuous, insolent, unquenchable.
> (1418–22)

Samson's summons to the festival of Dagon seems to be the culmination of his shame and defeat. The Philistine "City rings, / And numbers thither flock" (1449–50). As Nicholas Jose observes, "The Philistine triumph is symbolised by the building, both temple and theatre, where the spectacle takes place."[32] The drama the Philistines are about to stage is allegorical and didactic, with Samson exemplifying the power and victory of Dagon. At first, Samson is unwilling to take on the shame, "to be thir fool or jester" (1338) or to "play before thir god, / The worst of all indignities, yet on me / Join'd with extreme contempt" (1340–42). But based on inner "rousing motions" (1382), he seems to begin to think of the festival as a possibility for reversing the shame: "This day will be remarkable in my life / By some great act, or of my days the last" (1388–89). This internal impulse is validated by the apocalyptic spectacle with which Samson ends his life, overturning and appropriating the display of Philistine power.[33]

The ending of *Samson Agonistes* replaces the spectacle of Philistine triumph with a divine spectacle of punishment. Samson's violent death induces fear and horror in the Messenger who, coming from "the place of horror," recounts the off-stage spectacle:

> O whither shall I run, or which way fly
> The sight of this so horrid spectacle
> Which erst my eyes beheld and yet behold?
> For dire imagination still pursues me.
> (1541–44)

The Messenger describes how Samson was displayed as sign of Philistine power, "brought forth to show the people / Proof of his mighty strength in feats and games" (1601–2). The festival takes place, significantly, in a "spacious Theater" (1605). As the Messenger explains, Samson is "as a public servant brought, / In thir state Livery clad" (1615–16). The spectators respond accordingly: "At sight of him the people with a shout / Rifted the Air clamoring thir god with praise, / Who had made thir dreadful enemy thir thrall" (1620–22).

But, like the regicides, Samson's speech and behavior on the scaffold—or stage—overturns the intended meaning of the display, this time literally:



> Hitherto, Lords, what your commands impos'd
> I have perform'd, as reason was, obeying,
> Not without wonder or delight beheld.
> Now of my own accord such other trial
> I mean to show you of my strength, yet greater;
> As with amaze shall strike all who behold.
> (1640–45)

The spectacle of apocalyptic violence recounted at the end of *Samson Agonistes* is thus clearly an act of iconoclasm against the idolatrous Philistines and cannot in itself be adduced as proof of Samson's degeneration.[34] The Chorus gloats over the Philistines, "Drunk with Idolatry" (1670), "Chanting thir Idol" (1672), who call upon themselves their own destruction. They see that the Philistines have hardened their hearts:

> So fond are mortal men
> Fall'n into wrath divine,
> As thir ruin on themselves to invite,
> Insensate left, or to sense reprobate,
> And with blindness internal struck.
> (1682–86)

In their idolatrous state and apparent victory, the Philistines are in fact the objects of a greater divine victory, subject to the wrath of God.

The authorities who execute the regicides and exhume Cromwell think that they have triumphed; they see the dismembered and desecrated bodies as grounding the renewed power of the monarchy. The regicides themselves answer with a reversal of the discourses of treason and martyrdom. But *Samson Agonistes* suggests another reading of such spectacles, that in reality God has given the victors over to idolatry and delusion. In their gruesome and excessive revenge, the royalists expose the rotten underpinnings of their power, including the idolatrous cult of the royal martyr. But the regicides can only call for the apocalyptic judgment of Samson's violent iconoclasm.

## IV

YET THE iconoclastic violence with which *Samson Agonistes* ends remains ambiguous. *Samson Agonistes* is not a simple threat to the royalists, a call to once again take up arms when God gives the word. The Israelites are self-enslaved and Samson's act of violence does not set them free. Nor is Samson an unambiguous martyr. Indeed, the Israelites appropriate the spectacle to create a new cult of martyrdom, linked with the enemies they abhor. The supreme irony about the violence with which *Samson Agonistes* ends is that Samson's act of iconoclasm against the Philistines enhances the tendencies toward idolatry in his own people.



From the beginning the Israelites seem in danger of making Samson's strength an idol, that is, an object of veneration separate from its divine source. Samson himself is obsessed with his past strength, his heroic deeds. The Chorus likewise tells of the great deeds of "that Heroic, that Renown'd, / Irresistible *Samson*" (125–26) without mentioning the reason for which they were done (to deliver Israel) or their divine source. Manoa similarly reminisces about

> That invincible *Samson*, far renown'd,
> The dread of *Israel's* foes, who with a strength
> Equivalent to Angels' walk'd thir streets,
> None offering fight.
>
> (341–44)

Manoa's lament over the loss of that strength is telling: "O ever failing trust / In mortal strength!" (348–49). The misplaced trust is underscored by the contrast with Samson's later words, "My trust is in the living God" (1140).

In this context, the dangers of Manoa's proposed ransom are illuminated. Separated from, or no longer laboring in, his divine mission to deliver Israel, Samson would become both idle and idol, a kind of national relic. There are ironic, unconscious puns in Manoa's concern to have Samson at home rather than laboring for the Philistines: "Better at home lie bedrid, not only idle, / Inglorious, unemploy'd, with age outworn" (579–80). As Manoa explains to the Chorus, he wants to set Samson up as a kind of icon:

> It shall be my delight to tend his eyes,
> And view him sitting in the house, ennobl'd
> With all those high exploits by him achiev'd,
> And on his shoulders waving down those locks,
> That of a Nation arm'd the strength contained.
>
> (1490–94)

Manoa's desire to retain the image of Samson's strength, the physical icon, would make Samson idle/idol. And yet Manoa ironically reiterates his belief that God has not permitted Samson to regain his strength only "to sit idle with so great a gift" (1500). Manoa focuses on the visible icon, divorcing the strength from its divinely mandated meaning.



Samson himself resists the temptation to be idle/idol, refusing to go home with Manoa:

> To what can I be useful, wherein serve
> My Nation, and the work from Heav'n impos'd,
> But to sit idle on the household hearth,
> A burdenous drone; to visitants a gaze
> Or pitied object, these redundant locks
> Robustious to no purpose clust'ring down,
> Vain monument of strength.
>
> (564–70)

But precisely why Samson refuses Manoa's offer is less clear. Often adduced as a sign of his regeneration, this speech actually evinces self-consciousness and refusal of shame; Samson does not want to be "to visitants a gaze."

Samson insists in his encounter with Harapha on the divine source of his strength, of which his uncut hair is simply a pledge, not an icon:

> My trust is in the living God who gave me
> At my Nativity this strength, diffus'd
> No less through all my sinews, joints and bones,
> Than thine, while I preserv'd these locks unshorn,
> The pledge of my unviolated vow.
>
> (1140–44)

Yet Samson's struggle is uneven, and in the final spectacle he ambiguously calls only upon his own strength: "such other trial / I mean to show you of my strength" (1643–44).

Whether Samson has again disregarded or in fact internalized the divine source of his strength in the final violent display, the Chorus and Manoa do not trouble over the distinction. In the last 200 lines of the poem, the focus is on Samson's last act as an act of personal revenge. Ironically, in their words God bears witness to Samson rather than vice versa: "[He] to his faithful Champion hath in place / Bore witness gloriously" (1751–52). The adulation of Samson by his countrymen extends beyond his death. Manoa will take the body home:

> there will I build him
> A Monument, and plant it round with shade

> Of Laurel ever green, and branching Palm,
> With all his Trophies hung, and Acts enroll'd
> In copious Legend, or sweet Lyric Song.
> (1733–37)

The divine source of the victory is absent in the proposal to build a monument to Samson: "Thither shall all the valiant youth resort, / And from his memory inflame thir breasts / To matchless valor, and adventures high" (1738–40). The acts of strength are separated from the divine mission of deliverance, the image separated from its divine source. The monument to enshrine Samson's relics is disturbingly close to Dalila's view of her future, linked with, even an extension of, Philistine idolatry.[35] Manoa and the Chorus set up a cult to venerate Samson, not actual worship, but dangerously linked with the cult Dalila imagines for herself.



*Samson Agonistes* does not so much make Samson a martyr as it shows how his fellow Israelites do so. The closure invoked by the Chorus is not closure for the reader, who knows that Israel does not "take hold" upon this occasion. Northrop Frye comments on the aftermath of the Samson story: "In the Book of Judges, the account of Samson is immediately followed by another story about the Danites in which, after appearing in a most contemptible light as idolaters, thieves, and murderers, they vanish from history."[36] *Samson Agonistes* makes the use of violence radically ambivalent; the Hebrews are self-enslaved and Samson's act does not set them free. The supreme irony is that Samson's act of iconoclasm makes him a kind of idol for his own people.

## V

MILTON had clearly at one time believed that Cromwell was a chosen instrument of God to free the English people from bondage. Praising Cromwell in *The Second Defense*, Milton writes: "For while you, Cromwell, are safe, he does not have sufficient faith even in God himself who would fear for the safety of England, when he sees God everywhere so favourable to you, so unmistakably at your side" (*CPW* 4:670). Milton's words to Cromwell seem lavish panegyric, yet that panegyric also clearly guides and instructs. By praising Cromwell for not taking the kingship, Milton warns him against it. Cromwell has "assumed a certain title very like that of father of your country," while "the name of king you spurned from your far greater eminence, and rightly so" (*CPW* 4:672). For Cromwell to take on the name of king would be to repeat the civil idolatry he had just overthrown: "For if, when you became so great a figure, you were captivated by the title which as a private citizen you were able to send under the yoke and reduce to nothing, you would be doing almost the same thing as if, when you had subjugated some tribe of idolators with the help of the true God, you were to worship the gods that you had conquered" (*CPW* 4:672). Milton here uses idolatry as a suggestive analogue to stigmatize kingship. But, as Richard Hardin has persuasively argued, Milton and others opposed as idolatrous the ceremonies of both church and state: Hardin points out that Milton rejects the distinction between *latria* (divine worship) and *dulia* (service owed to men) in his attack on civil idolatry.[37] From his early antiprelatical tracts through *Eikonoklastes* and *The Readie and Easie Way*, Milton depicts the king as false icon and the "deifying" people as prone to civil and religious idolatry.





Despite Cromwell's technical refusal of the crown, the Protectorate increasingly took on the power and many of the trappings of monarchy. After Cromwell's death, in a lavish lying-in-state at Somerset House, he was at last (in effigy) crowned. The lying-in-state and funeral were closely modeled after those final ceremonies for James I, the last English monarch (thanks to Cromwell) to have had the luxury of dying in his bed. Peter Mundy describes the regal splendor of the display at Somerset: "First, his coffin (wherin I thinck hee was at that tyme) which was of pretious wood, ritchly garnished with iron worcke, all guilt. Afterwards in the roome therof lay his effigies royally apparelled, with a crowne on his head and a scepter in his hand; the rest of the ornaments, as trophies, banners, scutcheons, etts., all very ritch and of excellent worckmanship" (*Travels*, 103). *The True Manner of the most Magnificent Conveyance of his Highness Effigies* (1658) reports "multitudes of all sorts of people coming dayly to behold [the effigy]."[38] But the lavish display was also resisted, if the disaffected republican Edmund Ludlow is to be believed: "This folly and profusion so far provoked the people that they threw dirt in the night on [Cromwell's] escutcheon that was placed over the great gate of Somerset-house."[39]

The regal funeral that the Protectorate gave Cromwell was itself an ambiguous spectacle, rich with ironies. John Evelyn describes the ceremony: "He was carried from *Somerset-house* in a velvet bed of state drawn by six horses houss'd with the same: the Pall held-up by his new Lords: *Oliver* lying in Effigie in royal robes, and & Crown'd with a Crown, Scepter, & *Mund*, like a King" (*Diary* 3:224). The funeral procession itself was lavish, in Peter Mundy's words, "severall companies of mourners, great personages, banners, standards of kingdoms, mighty streamers (all silk), silver and gold trumpetts, drummes intermixed," with even Cromwell's horse decked in "a trapping of red velvett, soe thick and ritchly embrodered with gold and silver" (*Travels*, 104). In the displays of death, if not in life, Cromwell was treated as a de facto monarch.

But the response to the display was ambivalent. John Evelyn comments that "it was the joyfullest funerall that ever I saw, for there was none that Cried but dogs, which the soldiers hooted away with a barbarous noise, drinking & taking *Tabacco* in the streetes as they went" (*Diary* 3:224). Abraham Cowley sees extravagance: "Much more cost bestowed than either the dead man, or indeed Death itself could deserve." To him, such extravagance, "much tumult, much expence, much magnificence, much vain-glory," is a form of idolatry: "The Herse was Magnificent, the Idol Crowned."[40] Quaker Edward Burrough even more vehemently condemns the adulation of the effigy as idolatry: "Is all this (said I) but to see a dead invented Image of Wood or wax, arrayed and decked with some foolish Inventions? Said my spirit, Oh abominable! Oh Idolatry! Oh folly and vanity!" For Burrough, the supreme irony is that the former iconoclast has been made an idol: "What for him! Alas for him! who was once a great Instrument in the hand of the Lord to break down many Idolatrous Images and grievous Idols . . . and have they now made an Image of him?"[41]



The lavish lying-in-state and funeral tried to control the memory of Cromwell, to project an image through display. But it did not accomplish its intended effects. Not only were at least some immediate observers cynical, disapproving, or dismayed, but the lavish spectacle did not help Oliver's son. Rather than legitimating Richard as a royal figure, turning the Protectorate into a hereditary monarchy, the most lasting effect of the spectacle on Richard seems to be that it placed him in a precarious and embarrassing state of debt.[42] Even at the moment of its power, the spectacle did not wholly succeed.

Among the civil servants who marched together in the long procession that carried Cromwell's effigy from Somerset House to Westminster were said to be John Dryden, Andrew Marvell, and the blind Latin Secretary, John Milton.[43] Milton did not record his attitude to the later Cromwell, with the exception of a pointed reference in *The Readie and Easie Way* to the restoration of liberty after "a short and scandalous night of interruption." But it seems safe to conclude, with Austin Woolrych, that disillusionment had set in.[44] In *The Readie and Easie Way* (unlike *The Second Defense*) Milton speaks out sharply against the rule of a single person. And he again sees kingship as an unwarranted "deifying" to which the backsliding people are notoriously prone.

The complex ironies and ambiguities of *Samson Agonistes*, then, may well reflect the ambiguities of Milton's own attitude toward Cromwell, the other regicides, and the English people in the 1660s and 1670s. The spectacles of execution and exhumation represent the tragedy of the nation as a whole, ever-harkening back to Egypt. The mute display of body parts continued to attest to the power, if not the justice, of the monarchical cause, and, from the republican point of view, the failure of the English people.

Cromwell's head remained on its post until 1685. Yet the cult of martyrdom of the regicides did lead to a bold if ill-fated uprising of a small band of fifth monarchists in January 1661, underscoring the contestatory nature of the spectacle of punishment and the need for a supplement to the display. To that story (in chapter 5) we will return.

# *Paradise Lost* and the Politics of Joy

> The joy was universal; and whosoever was not pleased at heart, took the more care to appear as if he was; and no voice was heard but of the highest congratulation, of extolling the person of the king, admiring his condescensions and affability, raising his praises to heaven, and cursing and detesting the memory of those villains who had so long excluded so meritorious a prince, and thereby withheld that happiness from them, which they should enjoy in the largest measure they could desire or wish.
>
> Earl of Clarendon, *Life*

THE EARL of Clarendon's disillusioned view of the acclaim that greeted the returning Charles II indicates that the celebration may have been a more complex interaction than it appeared. Royalist spectacle included not only displays of punishment—the executions or exhuming of traitors that we have been examining—but a positive spectacle of celebration, acclamation, and joy. In the first of two chapters on the royal triumph, I want to examine how the people themselves functioned as vehicles of power, how their very joy was politicized. Joy was the spectators' role in the theater of triumph, and while many no doubt experienced pleasure and liberation, the very mode of the celebration marked renewed obedience and subjection to the restored monarchy.[1]

In the pageantry and panegyric accompanying the return and coronation of Charles, joy was a defining characteristic of a restored golden age, an entire mythology by which the monarchy was idealized and legitimated.[2] The flowing of wine and widespread celebration were said to attest to the golden age returned with the Stuart monarchy, a powerful rewriting and recuperation of the millennial hopes of the revolutionaries. In the Restoration, joy was itself a mode of power, a consent to the new regime and to its forms.

Milton's epic rendition of the fall is thus a bold rewriting of and challenge to what Raymond Williams has called the "structure of feeling," through which royalist ideology was instantiated and lived.[3] *Paradise Lost* redefines joy as internal, private, domestic, and linked with obedience to a divine monarch; bacchic celebration marks not the return of the golden age, but the fall. The postlapsarian state is inevitably marked by woe, and attempts to restore joy on earth are perverse, misguided, and even Satanic. In telling its story of woe, *Paradise Lost* challenges a central tenet of royalist ideology in Restoration England, the return of the golden age on earth, the restoration of joy.



## I

Celebrations began on May 1, 1660, when the newly convened Parliament, overwhelmingly royalist in sentiment, declared England a monarchy and invited Charles to return. London was jubilant; according to Samuel Pepys, it was "the happiest May-day that hath been many a year to England" (*Diary* 1:122). The May Day celebration was in itself significant, since such long established festival days, encouraged by earlier Stuart kings, were banned during the Interregnum. As Leah Marcus has shown, the earlier Stuart kings traditionally fostered sports and pastimes as a kind of "escape valve," a control over somewhat volatile festivities that could shade over into disorder, even challenge and subversion.[4] The *Book of Sports*, issued by James I in 1618 and reissued under Charles in 1633, caused a furor even though it merely mandated that the traditional festivities be allowed, not that they be required. The very forms of the May Day celebrations for Charles II thus signaled adherence to the new regime.

Pepys goes on to describe a scene of extravagant excess: "Great joy all yesterday in London; and at night more bonefires then ever and ringing of bells and drinking of the King's health upon their knees in the streets," which, he adds, "methinks is a little too much" (*Diary* 1:122). This is a public, communal, highly visible joy—separated from any individual persons. *Mercurius Publicus* similarly describes the country's collective joy: "This Country, as if they had received new life, and full reparations for their former losses already, hath endeavoured to make good their part of the joy for the happy change in these Nations, each place the King hath been proclaimed hath strived to out-do the other in cost and gallantry in the performance of it."[5] Again, what was important was the public communal response, the visible joy. In the town of Purley, the people were "almost ravished with joy" and after hearing a sermon, "shewing the great cause of joy we have, and the lawfulness of pomp and jollity upon such an occasion," they erected a scaffold from which they shot off vollies of gunpowder, threw out five or six dozen spice loaves, drank eight hogsheads of beer and much wine, and wound up with a bonfire, which "gave testimony of [their] joy to six or seven counties."[6]

Such visible excess—drinking beer, open celebration—defied by its very nature the Interregnum regime. Thomas Rugg reports that in Leicestershire, Sir Henry Hudson roasted a "fat ox" to celebrate: "The towne and country at length grew to such emulation of eatch other in the eternizing the memory of this joyfull day that after the ox was eaten they accounted him happy that could but carry away either one of the ribs of the ox or the least shiver of the bones to treasur up as reliques." He goes on to describe the King's merrymaking at Hyde Park: "After the banquett his Majesty was pleased to make himself mery in throwinge amongst the soldiers neats tongues, west hamms, English gammons, oringes and leamons and the like. Great fierings, much company, great joy. Vale! Vale!" (*Diurnal*, 180). The joy was deliberately excessive and unique, pointing to the uniqueness of the king's return. *England's Triumph* (1660), which describes the "joyfull expressions" of the celebrations, concludes: "But no History can shew a president of such transcendent joy as was at the proclaiming *Charles* the Second."[7]



The citizens of London evinced their joy—and hence their loyalty—by their active participation in, and even financial sponsorship of, royal pageantry—the royal entry into London in 1660 and the coronation triumph almost one year later. In chapter 4 we will explore the "triumph" in its complex imitation and uses of Roman conquest. But the Roman triumph is also a celebration and was thus one central mode of representing and interpreting the widespread and potentially unruly public rejoicing at the return of the king. The Stuart triumph was grounded, even dependent, upon the citizens' enthusiastic and public display of joy.

A contemporary Dutch print of Charles's departure from Scheveningen (Fig. 9) shows a scene of much excitement and frenzied activity in which, indeed, the people are as much on display as Charles. The farewells included speeches from Dutch dignitaries, massive crowds, cannon fire, feasting, and merrymaking. James Heath recounts in *The Glories and Magnificent Triumphs of . . . Charles II* (1662) the Dutch response to Charles: "Your Majesty might have observed in the Countenance of all our People, the joy they had in their Hearts to see amongst them a Prince cherished of God, a Prince wholly miraculous, and a Prince that is probably to make a part of their quietness and felicity."[8] In Heath's view, the Dutch "shared as much felicity and joy [in Charles] and as truely manifested it as any other nation whatsoever."[9]

FIGURE 9 Charles II departing from Scheveningen for Dover in 1660, from a contemporary Dutch print. *By permission of the Trustees of the British Museum.*

Figure 10 Charles II entering into London in 1660, from a contemporary print. *By permission of the Trustees of the British Museum.*

Huge mobs also greeted the king as he arrived in England. Peter Mundy observes of the entry into and progress through London: "Of spectators, if I shold say fifteen hundred thousand I shold not much erre, accompting from Blackheath to Whitehall, the feilds, highwaies and hedges, covered waies, covered with people; the trees laden with boies, the streets thronged, the stages, stales [stalls], windowes, full (some even on the roofes)" (*Travels*, 118). The royal procession itself was a lavish and lengthy spectacle. A contemporary print (Fig. 10) shows the long processional winding into the gates of the city, where the scattered waving spectators would be replaced by thronging crowds.





Charles II proved himself a master of the dramaturgy of royal power. Much like Queen Elizabeth, and unlike his more aloof father and grandfather, Charles was highly responsive to the people as he passed through London, in the words of the Venetian resident, "raising his eyes to the windows looking at all, raising his hat to all and consoling all who with loud shouts and a tremendous noise acclaimed the return of this great prince so abounding in virtues and distinguished qualities of every sort" (*CSPV* 32:155). Having arrived at Whitehall, Charles maintained this visibility, "showing himself at every moment to the people who press impetuously forward to offer their devotion to their sovereign. He takes all his meals in public and by his royal presence affords his people the utmost consolation and enjoyment" (*CSPV* 32:155). The king played to his subjects, eliciting the joy that constituted the very power it celebrated.

At the coronation a year later, Thomas Rugg similarly writes of the "great joy and acclamations and shouts which the people gave as his Majesty passed" (*Diurnal*, 176). The lavish triumphal arches, which I will more fully discuss in the context of the Roman conquest, were explicitly said to represent the subjects' joy. John Ogilby introduces his lavish edition, *The Entertainment of His Most Excellent Majestie Charles II* (1662), by asserting that London, "participating in the greatest share of that inexpressible Happiness," has taken "the occasion of His *Majesties* Coronation, to express their Joy with the greatest Magnificence imaginable."[10] Occasional verses asserted that the arches represent a more permanent, internal joy. Hence *Festa Georgiana* (1660):

> for within
> Our hearts should Pageants of joy be seen,
> They are the sacrifices which we owe
> To such transcendent good, and blisse,
> To such surpassing joy as this.[11]

And John Dryden reaffirms in his *To His Sacred Majesty, a Panegyrick on his Coronation:* "We add not to your glory, but employ / Our time like Angels in expressing joy" (*Works* 1:35).

This overwhelming joy is linked with the return of the golden age, a motif that draws largely upon classical typology: hence Charles is linked with the Roman Augustus as in Dryden's *Astraea Redux:* "Oh Happy Ages! Oh times like those alone, / By Fate reserv'd for great *Augustus* Throne!" (*Works* 1:31). Images of Charles as Messiah, less frequent, also highlight the return of the golden age in biblical terms.[12] The masque figures in the coronation arches praise Charles as

> King of Peace,
> Who the Stars so long foretold,
> From all Woes should us release,
> Converting Iron-times to Gold.[13]



More prosaically, *The Jubilee* rejoices that after "Protector and Rump / Did put us in a dump," joy has again returned: "The golden times are come that we / Did one day think we ne'er should see."[14] Londoners hence evince joy as a mode of receiving the monarch, attesting to their loyalty and perhaps obviating questions of a less than loyal past.

Yet early celebrations recalled woes of the "Protector and Rump" to enhance present joy. Aurelian Cook would write in his 1685 biography of Charles II that at the return of the king "never was so much Joy heap'd together in *England.* It seem'd as if all the Melancholly of the former years was purposely designed to introduce and heighten the so extravagant gladness of that great Day, that some were ready to wish for a Renovation of the Civil Wars, that they might have that day repeated to them over again."[15] Joy was heightened by remembrance of woes past.

Lavish celebration of the restoration of monarchy was thus joined with, indeed incorporated, execration of the old regime. *The Parliamentary Intelligencer* reports that the proclamation of Charles as king was "received by the people with the loudest shouts, most joyful acclamations that enlarged hearts could send forth."[16] But the same account goes on to report on "an antick that night": "The Solemnization of the Funeral of a certain Monster they called *The Commonwealth,* represented by an ugly, misshapen body without an Head, but with a huge insatiable belly, and a prodigious Rump. The deformed Corps attended by Friends in Vizards, instead of mourners, was carried to the grave, and buried without expectation of Resurrection."[17]

Thomas Rugg likewise reports that in Lincolnshire the celebration—"the makinge bonefiers for joy [that] his Majesty was proclamed"—includes an attack on the Protectoral state arms: "They tooke downe the States armes and the yonge men draged them up and downe the streets and caused[d] the beadles of the towne to whip them, the[n] pissed and sh[it] on [them], and them burnt in their bonefiers" (*Diurnal,* 84). On June 11, 1660, the Venetian resident concludes his report of the people's "enjoyment" of the king with the observation that "for three days and three nights they have lighted bonfires and made merry, burning effigies of Cromwell and other rebels with much abuse" (*CSPV* 32:155). Joy was heightened not only by remembering, but by displaying and abusing the symbols of the old regime. Early celebrations incorporated punishments resonant of the grisly scaffold scenes that would follow.





The occasional verses celebrating the Restoration similarly depicted the monarchy as bringing joy after woe, as in Samuel Pordage: "The freest subject was before a slave; / We had all lost, but now our Joys renew, / And we have all again in having you." [18] Liberty is linked with both joy and obedience to the Stuart monarch. Rachel Jevon writes in *Exultationis Carmen:* "Hence, hence sad sorrows, and all past annoys, / Let nought approach You but tryumphant Joys." [19] Joy is depicted as release from the inhibitions of the previous rule, freedom from the constraints of power. Thus *Festa Georgiana* celebrates

> Those days return'd when we beguil'd
> Our time with harmlesse mirth, before the paines
> Rebellion brings, were crept into our veines,
> Before that *May* poles were thought gods,
> Or King and Parliament at od[d]s.
> Before Lawn sleeves were judg'd unholy,
> Before 'twas thought a sin to seem but jolly.
>
> (6)

In this verse, revolution becomes underhanded "rebellion" that has "crept" into their very veins: the increasing exaggeration of the rules—May Poles as gods, lawn sleeves as unholy, finally, it being a sin even to be jolly—conveys the intolerance and rigidity from which the monarchy frees the people. The king frees his subjects to return to their "harmlesse mirth" and to the traditional pastimes and festivities, a general state of being jolly.

Yet focus on what the previous powers prohibited obscured the extent to which the people were being channeled back into traditional forms of obedience. It is significant in this regard that *Festa Georgiana* goes on to link drinking, joy, and expressions of loyalty:

> The Products of the Sack flows in our veines:
> That cleares our bloud, and makes it good, and that shall teach us sing,
> With tides of joy, exalted notes to our new Crowned King.
>
> (7)

"The Products of the Sack," presented and received as liberation, serve to "teach" loyalty to the new rulers. Drinking sack, indeed being jolly, was as much mandated by the new regime as it was prohibited by the old.

Joy was thus not (or not only) a private, spontaneous emotion, but a politicized construct, the shaping of the bodies and minds of loyal subjects. Thus *Festa Georgiana* links obedience to the king with a distinctive mode of joy:

Tis your merry, merry soules,
Who take freely their bowles,
That still are as constant as fate
Whilst our dull-headed sots
Are construing of plots
To ruine the Church and the state,
Then let us be merry, and drink full cups round,
For to day, for to day, for to day, our King's Crown'd.
(8)



While "dull-headed sots / Are construing of plots," loyal subjects are freely passing the sack. In *The Claret Drinker's Song*, "A friend and a bottle is all my design—/ He's no room for treason that's top-full of wine."[20] The king's subjects expressed and participated in a joy that embodied and signified their devotion.

In the early Restoration, visible, public joy demonstrated loyalty or obedience on the part of the subjects, munificence on the part of an official elite that financially sponsored the festivities, and benevolence on the part of the approving king. The people were themselves part of the show, as *Anglia Rediviva* (1660) attests:

No sex, nor age
But throngs to act their Parts, as on a stage,
Of Homage to their Prince.

And yet very trope of theater indicated potential instability and was also a source of anxiety:

And all her children (Monsters she not ownes,
Though such there be, that with unnaturall frowns,
Or false smiles greet the Triumph of this Day)
With full consent of Heart and tongues do pay
Their Pray'rs, and loyall duty on their knee.[21]

In its very denials, the panegyric discloses anxieties about true feelings behind the show of joy.

And such public joy, even when sincere, could be a source of disorder. Potential excess or misappropriation of joy is evident in contemporary accounts. Philip Henry records with explicit disapproval the local celebration upon the coronation of Charles II: "King crowned, great joy, much sin, the Lord pardon. 'Twas a very wett evening, which prevented something of God's Dishonour."[22] Burnet comments that "with the restoration of the king, a spirit of extravagant joy spread over the nation, that brought on with it the throwing off the very professions of virtue and piety; all ended in entertainments and drunkenness" (*History*, 60). Pepys's account of the coronation celebrations vividly shows its excess: "We drank the King's health and nothing else, till one of the gentlemen fell down stark drunk and there lay speweing. And I went to my Lord's pretty well. But no sooner a-bed with Mr. Sheply but my head begun to turne and I to vomitt, and if ever I was foxed it was now—which I cannot say yet, because I fell asleep and sleep till morning—only when I waked I found myself wet with my spewing" (*Diary* 2:87). Pepys then concludes, apparently without irony: "Thus did the day end, with joy everywhere."

The court seemed aware that the vehicle of celebration could exceed or even be separated from the loyalty to which it should attest. In August 1660, Charles II issued a royal proclamation directed against those who "spend their time in Taverns, Tipling-houses, and Debauches, giving no other evidence of their affection to Us, but in drinking Our health, and Inveighing, against all others, who are not of their own dissolute temper; and who, in truth, have more discredited Our Cause, by the licence of their Manners and Lives, then they could ever advance it by their affection or courage."[23] There were obvious ironies in such a proclamation from the court of Charles II (a subject to which I will return). But the point of the proclamation warrants underscoring: joy is a necessary but not sufficient sign of loyalty; the means might exceed or even undermine the end.

And court records for the early 1660s show signs that for all the show of "universal" joy, there were some, perhaps many, who remained "not pleased at heart." A number of persons were charged in the Middlesex quarter sessions for seditious words, and their comments about the restored king resist the pageantry and panegyric of public joy. Some evinced the wrong kind of joy. On May 11, 1660, for instance, Edward Medburne, a glazier of Wapping, was indicted "for speaking certaine treasonable words against the King's Majestie, hee the said Medburne saying that if hee mett the King hee would run his knife into him to kill him, and that hee did not care though he were hanged for it himselfe, and did wish that the King and Generall Monk were hanged together, and that hee did not care if hee were the hangman himselfe, and that he would spend that day five shillings for joy" (*MCR* 3:303).

In July 1660, the Middlesex justices indicted the headborough at Stepney for allowing the escape from prison of one William Sparkes, charged "for being distempered with drinke, and for assaulting and strikeing of Thomas Jenings, and for speaking irreverent and unmannerly and uncomely words concerning the Kinges Majestie *vizt.* 'that the King was a poore and beggerly King' " (*MCR* 3:305). Here drink leads to disorder, disloyalty, and assault on a loyal subject. A second indictment relating to the escape elaborated on the charges against the prisoner: "The said William Sparkes having spoken desperat and dangerous words against the King, to witt, saying that His Majesty was a beggerly King, and that the morning following, meaning the Day of Thanksgiving for his deliverance and restoring of him to his kingdoms, would be the best day that ever the King should have" (*MCR* 3:306). The form that these seditious words took in the early 1660s is significant: there was resistance to the seeming "voluntary" day of thanksgiving and a bold if inarticulate reminder of the truly impecunious state of the young man being restored to the throne: Charles indeed was—or at least had been—a rather "beggerly King."



Behind the May Day celebrations at the return of the king were other charges brought against less than joyful citizens. On May 15, 1660, Dorothy Phillips was called "to answer for reviling of our Soveraign Lord King Charles, saying that he is a bastard" (*MCR* 3:303). On May 23, a shoemaker, Edward Jones, and his wife, Alice, were called to answer "for speaking these words of the Kinges Majestie on Munday the 22nd of May last, 'It was the King's time now to raigne, but it was upon sufferance for a little time, and it would be theres agine before itt be long' " (*MCR* 3:304). A 1660 deposition from York provides another vivid example of resistance in the alleged words of one Margaret Dixon: "What! is there not some Englishman more fit to make a King then a Scott? There is none that loves him but drunk whores and whoremongers. I hope hee will never come into England, for that hee will sett on fire the three kingdomes as his father before him had done. God's curse light on him. I hope to see his bones hanged at a horse tayle, and the doggs runn through his puddins."[24] The rhetorical violence and fervor of these words show that Charles II was not universally popular or welcomed. And, as we shall see, the invective already included an insult that would become particular to this court: "There is none loves him but drunk whores and whoremongers." The ceremonies and displays of state were resisted, despite the official rhetoric of universal joy.

Others threatened violence (however ineffectually) against the new king: on May 26, 1660, Richard Cheltham was indicted "for treasonable words, *vizt*, for sayeinge three monthes since that he hoped to meete the Kinge at the Gallows" (*MCR* 3:304). The threats for which William Fenne was indicted two months later were more elaborate: "For speaking severall words against the King and Queen's Majesties about five weekes last past, *vizt*, that he hoped to wash his hands in the King's blood; and heere is an old rusty sword, I wish it were up to the hilt in his heart; and that the Queene was a whore; and said that, if the King were in the roome, he would runne a sword that was there upp to his heart" (*MCR* 3:306). If the blustery threat to run a sword into the king was considered dangerous and liable to prosecution, resistance to royalist rhetoric was equally subversive to a monarchy that ruled more by hegemony than by force. Mockery, even blunt speaking about the king and the court, could be prosecuted, and the recurrence and patterns of the charges show the gap between the public rhetoric of universal joy and the inarticulate rumblings of discontent.



Charges of sedition recurred throughout the 1660s in Middlesex. In January 1661, Jane Blunstone was indicted "for speaking these dangerous and treasonable wordes against the honour of the King his Crowne and dignity, *vizt.* the Queen is the Great Whore of Babilon and the King is the son of a whore and the Duke of Yorke is a rogue and such like wordes" (*MCR* 3:309). Mary Green was charged in September 1663 "for speaking these wordes, A pox on all the Kings and she did not care a t[urd] for never a Kinge in England, for she never did lie with any" (*MCR* 3:327). In a sedition case in York in May 1662, one Tristram Hewbanck testified that "a little while before the coronation hee heard Walter Crompton, of Sunderlandwick, gent., say hee hoped the Kinge would never bee crowned, for hee was a bastard. And hee hath severall times seene him [Crompton] clap his hand on his horses buttocks and say, 'Stand up, Charles the third by the grace of God.' "[25] While a modern audience might appreciate the wry humor of naming one's horse Charles III, in the seventeenth century such mockery dangerously undercut the idealized representations of the monarchy. The court records also show recurrent allusions to one particular royal fault, succinctly put by one Andrew Dereew, called to answer in July 1664 "for saying 'The King keeps whores' and then drinking a health to the King and all whores" (*MCR* 3:339).

Even in the early years of the Restoration, then, outside the realm of offical discourse one can find genuine subversion, sought out and punished by the state. Joy was backed by the threat of punishment. But to focus on the censorship and punishment of sedition is to see state power as functioning solely through repression; I have been arguing that such power also functions by eliciting, even producing, a positive display of joy and celebration. As under the earlier Stuarts, festival freedoms were in themselves a sign of submission to royal authority. Although the participants no doubt experienced a sense of joyous liberation, that experience was also fostered as a form of social control. And, as with James I and Charles I, the new court seemed willing to reward poets who represented and praised the new joys. Monarchical power was articulated not only in the spectacles of punishment or in the surveillance and indictment of treasonous words and deeds, but also through the joy and celebrations of the king's loyal subjects.

## II

It was not John Milton's style to say that he "did not care a t[urd] for never a Kinge in England." Nor, to my knowledge, did he own a horse. But his epic poem is as much opposed to the royalist rhetoric of universal joy as are the discontented rumblings that appear in the court records from 1660 onward. In telling its story of woe, *Paradise Lost* resists a central tenet of royalist ideology in Restoration England, the return of the golden age on earth, the restoration of joy. Redefining joy and woe, the poem challenges the hegemonic discourse of praise used to represent the power of Charles II. The poem redefines joy as internal, private, domestic; lavish celebration is a perversion of true joy, linked with Satan and threatening the true poet. Milton's Eden, despite the use of similar key terms—joy, bliss, love—is defined against the Augustan golden age used to celebrate the Tudor and Stuart monarchies. Joy and love are less external, visible actions than they are internal modes of discipline, and attempts to regain an immediate, sensuous, public joy are misguided, perverse, and even Satanic.



*Paradise Lost* responds to false restoration in its story of the loss and true restoration of joy:

> Of Man's First Disobedience, and the Fruit
> Of that Forbidden Tree, whose mortal taste
> Brought Death into the World, and all our woe,
> With loss of *Eden*, till one greater Man
> Restore us, and regain the blissful Seat.
>
> (I.1–5)

Repeated use of the word "restore" signals a spiritual restoration which counters and defines by contrast that of the Stuart monarchy. Yet *Paradise Lost* also presents a monarch whose power is represented and mediated not only in direct punishment of his enemies but through the joy of his subjects in heaven and on earth. If Restoration pageantry and panegyric elicit joy as loyalty and obedience to the restored king, joy in *Paradise Lost* articulates obedience to a divine monarch. Milton reworks and employs the strategies that he challenges in their current political context.

*Paradise Lost* represents for the reader not only true heavenly joy, but its defining opposite, in the loss and perversion of joy with Satan. Milton's Satan, as critics have often noted, is no mere traditional devil, beyond human comprehension, but a character endowed with acute psychological qualities.[26] I want to trace how, bereft of heaven, Satan suffers not so much from physical as from psychological torment and thus serves to confirm by contrast heavenly joys. Satan himself sees heaven as a place of joy, and his farewell to heaven uses language of joy: "Farewell happy Fields /

Where Joy for ever dwells" (I.249–50). Joy in heaven is public, almost equated with the place itself. The landscape of hell is, in contrast, woeful. In other words, the poem mediates divine power by showing not a hell of grisly eternal punishment (contrast Dante's *Inferno*, for instance), but, as has been noted in other contexts, an inner state of misery, soon to become fully internalized—"myself am Hell" (IV.75).[27]





Hell in *Paradise Lost* is thus characterized as a place of woe as much as of pain. Satan views not only the "great Furnace" (I.62) of hell flames, but "sights of woe, / Regions of sorrow, doleful shades" (I.64–65), and he is condemned "To waste Eternal days in woe and pain" (II.695). In their exploration of hell, the other fallen angels pass through "many a dark and dreary Vale" (II.618) and "many a Region dolorous" (II.619), a geographic extension of their own inner woe. Hell is largely described in terms of psychological states, even when the landscape itself is being described and even before Satan leaves the geographical locale only to discover a hell within him.

The fall in *Paradise Lost* is represented as the result of a Satanic plan to restore his own lost joy by triumphing over Adam and Eve through force or fraud; in 1667, such false restoration would be a figure for other false restorings of joy. Satan's plan is an imperial mission to destroy Adam and Eve, launched in hell explicitly to disturb divine joy and regain joy for himself:

> This would surpass
> Common revenge, and interrupt his joy
> In our Confusion, and our Joy upraise
> In his disturbance.
>
> (II.370–73)

The plan immediately produces a kind of perverse joy: "The bold design / Pleas'd highly those infernal States, and joy / Sparkl'd in all thir eyes" (II.386–88).

Indeed, the destructive and narcissistic nature of Satanic joy might best be seen in the incestuous "joy" he has taken with Sin, as she recounts their prior relationship:

> Thyself in me thy perfect image viewing
> Becam'st enamor'd, and such joy thou took'st
> With me in secret, that my womb conceiv'd
> A growing burden.
>
> (II.764–67)

Satan's false joy shows how joy can be perverted, used for tyrannical and self-serving ends; but the poem seems designed not only to expose joy on earth as inevitably implicated in power, but to imagine the possibility of a true heavenly joy opposed to false imitations.

Defined by woe, Satan paradoxically affirms the power against which he rebels. Once out of hell, Satan finds that inner woe replaces the woe and external punishment of hell: "Me miserable! which way shall I fly / Infinite wrath, and infinite despair? / Which way I fly is Hell; myself am Hell" (IV.73–75). Satan is now "only Supreme / In misery; such joy Ambition finds" (IV.91–92). *Paradise Lost* uses woe to show sin as self-punishing; although it has long drawn readers' sympathy, Satan's confession actually seems designed to validate divine rule.[28]





Ironically, the joys of paradise make Satan even more miserable, since they only remind him of the lost joys of heaven they reflect. Satan cannot enjoy Eden, a place of "Vernal delight and joy, able to drive / All sadness but despair" (IV.155–56), and he compulsively reminds himself of his loss of joy: "With what delight could I have walkt thee round, / If I could joy in aught" (IX.114–15). If the garden increases Satan's woe, the sight of Adam and Eve makes him feel even worse, since they embody the joys whose loss he can only lament:

> Sight hateful, sight tormenting! thus these two
> Imparadis't in one another's arms
> The happier *Eden*, shall enjoy thir fill
> Of bliss on bliss, while I to Hell am thrust,
> Where neither joy nor love, but fierce desire,
> Among our other torments not the least,
> Still unfulfill'd with pain of longing pines.
> (IV.505–11)

The loss of joy replaces physical torment as Satan's punishment: viewing Adam and Eve is a "sight tormenting," his "pain" of longing, depicted as a torment. The language of physical punishment—pain, torment—is striking and significant in this passage. Milton wants to show that Satan receives not arbitrary and excessive divine punishment, but self-punishment with woe.

Edenic happiness is framed throughout *Paradise Lost* by the Satanic threat that will soon destroy it:

> Ah gentle pair, yee little think how nigh
> Your change approaches, when all these delights
> Will vanish and deliver ye to woe,
> More woe, the more your taste is now of joy.
> (IV.366–69)

Satan is obsessed with taking away their joy: "Live while ye may, / Yet happy pair; enjoy, till I return, / Short pleasures, for long woes are to succeed" (IV.533–35). Punished by lack of joy, by the pain of longing for joy, Satan's joy becomes utterly destructive: "Save what is in destroying, other joy / To me is lost" (IX.478–79). *Paradise Lost* links Satan's woe with his disobedience, Adam and Eve's joy with their obedience to a true monarch. Satan is no liberator; Adam and Eve will be miserable, as Satan is himself.

The reader's first view of Adam and Eve in *Paradise Lost* is from a God's-eye point of view, showing an Eden characterized by joy and love, poised between Satanic woe and the joy of heaven:

> On Earth he first beheld
> Our two first Parents, yet the only two
> Of mankind, in the happy Garden plac't,
> Reaping immortal fruits of joy and love,
> Uninterrupted joy, unrivall'd love
> In blissful solitude.
> (III.64–69)

Given the context of the golden age restored with the king, this picture has important political resonances. God gives his subjects true joy—joy linked with true obedience.[29] The differences between this joy and royalist renditions of the golden age are striking: this is a private, domestic joy inseparable from Adam and Eve's labor—the "fruits of joy and love" Adam and Eve reap are both figurative and literal. And while most important in the celebration of joy in the Restoration was that it be seen, be a public display, here only the eye of God beholds. The private joy recalls other earlier spectacles refigured by Milton as an inner state, with only God as witness.

The "happy garden" is a temporary paradise, its joy a reflection of heavenly joy. Once lost, the paradise cannot be restored externally on earth: it will come only in the millennium, from the presence of God, as Christ foresees that he:

> Then with the multitude of my redeem'd
> Shall enter Heav'n long absent, and return,
> Father, to see thy face, wherein no cloud
> Of anger shall remain, but peace assur'd,
> And reconcilement; wrath shall be no more
> Thenceforth, but in thy presence Joy entire.
> (III.260–65)

We will see that Christ's apocalyptic triumph, which restores joy in the presence of God, contrasts with the traditional Roman conquests—and their contemporary renditions in Stuart England. God the Father responds with a vision of true restoration: "As in him perish all men, so in thee / As from a second root shall be restor'd, / As many as are restor'd, without thee none" (III.287–89). In *Paradise Lost*, true joy and restoration come only in the direct presence of God.

Milton's God thus also rules by restoring joy. Such joy will come after long tribulation, when Christ's true eschatological triumph, unlike Satan's, will install a golden age of joy and love:

> New Heav'n and Earth, wherein the just shall dwell
> And after all thir tribulations long
> See golden days, fruitful of golden deeds,
> With Joy and Love triumphing, and fair Truth.
> Then thou thy regal Sceptre shalt lay by,
> For regal Sceptre then no more shall need,
> God shall be All in All.
>
> (III.335–41)



Golden age panegyric here is recuperated in scriptural terms with the triumph of Christ. The joy and love of Christ's eschatological victory do not participate in the visible material splendors, external excess, and revelry of earthly empire.

Indeed, the vision goes beyond monarchy, positing the dissolution of monarchy, as the will of God becomes all-encompassing. Joy triumphs in Milton's vision: monarchy itself is ultimately rejected when it is no longer needed, when the divine will is fully internalized. After the defeat of the angels in the war in Heaven, the Father again points to a final eschatological joy when "Earth be chang'd to Heav'n, and Heav'n to Earth, / One Kingdom, Joy and Union without end" (VII.160–61). To this true version of restored joy the angels respond "with a shout / Loud as from numbers without number, sweet / As from blest voices, uttering joy" (III.345–47). The representation of heaven in Book III concludes with a stress on joy: "Thus they in Heav'n, above the starry Sphere, / Thir happy hours in joy and hymning spent" (III.416–17). God rules in Milton's heaven not through coercion and force but through joy as a mode of power.

While this stress on the restoration of joy is notable, the picture of heaven throughout the poem highlights joy as its central and defining characteristic. After the exaltation of the Son, Milton significantly uses terms of joy: "Under his great Vice-gerent Reign abide / United as one individual Soul / For ever happy" (V.609–11). In Milton's heaven, joy is occasioned by a God who gives over power to his Son:

> They eat, they drink, and in communion sweet
> Quaff immortality and joy, secure
> Of surfeit where full measure only bounds
> Excess, before th' all bounteous King, who show'r'd
> With copious hand, rejoicing in thir joy.
>
> (V.637–41)

Such "communion sweet" shows bounty and abundance but not excess; they drink, as it turns out, "immortality and joy." The stress here is emphatically on the measure, bounds. But possible divergence between external and internal joy is suggested in heaven as well: "All seem'd pleas'd, all seem'd, but were not all" (V.617). Joy even in heaven can be faked, can be unstable.



Milton's Eden, then, is made even more poignant as a transient reflection of heavenly joy. The garden is characterized by joy, happiness, bliss, "for blissful Paradise / Of God the Garden was, by him in the East / Of *Eden* planted" (IV.208–10). The landscape itself is blissful, "A happy rural seat of various view" (IV.247). That the blissful landscape is a figure for the bliss of its inhabitants is made clear in Adam and Eve's own articulation of their inner joy. Adam's first speech praises their happy state:

> Sole partner and sole part of all these joys,
> Dearer thyself than all; needs must the Power
> That made us, and for us this ample World
> Be infinitely good, and of his good
> As liberal and free as infinite,
> That rais'd us from the dust and plac't us here
> In all this happiness.
>
> (IV.411–17)

Adam values their happiness—Eve the dearest of "all these joys"—and such happiness leads him directly to praise of God. Yet from this first speech the grounding of their obedience in joy shows both its strength and its potential weakness.

What God the Father has pointed to as their "reaping immortal fruits of joy and love" (III.67) becomes in Adam's more mundane terms the task of pruning:

> But let us ever praise him, and extol
> His bounty, following our delightful task
> To prune those growing Plants, and tend these Flow'rs,
> Which were it toilsome, yet with thee were sweet.
>
> (IV.436–39)

The task in itself is significant. Given the characteristic abundance of the Restoration golden age, it is striking that Adam and Eve's job is to prune away, to avoid excess. The garden symbolizes not only their joy, but their potential excess. The narrator repeatedly urges Adam and Eve to enjoy their "fill," but not to go beyond their limits. Adam and Eve's pruning—a distinctive, even odd rendition of paradise—curbs the abundance of the garden as a mode of self-discipline. Adam's own articulation of his joy is crucial; and, at this early point, there is only a slight suggestion that his joy in Eve may, like the garden, become excessive.

Eve's first speech likewise articulates her joy in Adam, showing both the strength and potential vulnerability of her obedience: "I chiefly who enjoy / So far the happier Lot, enjoying thee / Preëminent by so much odds" (IV.445–47).[30] Eve has both internalized and subtly revised the words of the divine voice that promised "him thou shalt enjoy / Inseparably thine" (IV.472–73). Yet this affirmation precedes Eve's more ambivalent account of her enjoyment of her own image:

> I started back,
> It started back, but pleas'd I soon return'd,
> Pleas'd it return'd as soon with answering looks
> Of sympathy and love; there I had fixt
> Mine eyes till now, and pin'd with vain desire,
> Had not a voice thus warn'd me.
>
> (IV.462–67)

Eve insists upon her happiness: "God is thy Law, thou mine: to know no more / Is woman's happiest knowledge and her praise" (IV.637–38). But this speech claiming no further desire for knowledge immediately precedes her questioning of Adam regarding celestial matters; their joy is threatened not only from without but, it seems, from within.

Adam's account of his creation to Raphael also stresses—notably and characteristically—his predominant joy in Eve. Adam feels joy from his first creation, "all things smil'd, / With fragrance and with joy my heart o'erflow'd" (VIII.265–66), and such joy leads him to seek and show homage to a divine author, feeling himself to be "happier than I know" (VIII.282). Yet without Eve Adam is not happy, even in the happy garden, and he questions his creator: "In solitude / What happiness, who can enjoy alone, / Or all enjoying, what contentment find?" (VIII.364–66). Adam articulates his lack specifically in terms of joy—a concept not found in the Genesis account.[31] Given Eve as companion, Adam finds the consummation of their marriage "the sum of earthly bliss / Which I enjoy" (VIII.522–23). But the very marital joy which sustains Adam in his obedience to God threatens, if overvalued, to undermine that relationship. Hence Adam is rebuked for his admission that while he is "in all enjoyments else / Superior and unmov'd" (VIII.531–32), he feels "weak / Against the charm of Beauty's powerful glance" (VIII.532–33). Joy defines Adam's relationship with God and with Eve. Such joy makes their obedience seem natural, but it also raises a potential vulnerability: if happy, then obedient, but what then if unhappy?

Joy and obedience are again linked as the narrator, observing the happy first couple, depicts the fall as desire not for knowledge but for increased joy: "Sleep on, / Blest pair; and O yet happiest if ye seek / No happier state, and know to know no more" (IV.773–75). Raphael tells Adam, "Meanwhile enjoy / Your fill what happiness this happy state / Can comprehend, incapable of more" (V.503–5). Happiness itself is presented as part of Adam and Eve's human limits, so that Raphael warns Adam, "joy thou / In what he gives to thee, this Paradise / And thy fair *Eve*" (VIII.170–72). The locating of Adam's joy in Eve is both well grounded and potentially unstable.



As in the Restoration pageantry and panegyrics, then, joy in *Paradise Lost* is inseparable from obedience. Raphael advises: "That thou art happy, owe to God; / That thou continu'st such, owe to thyself, / That is, to thy obedience; therein stand" (V.520–22). Or, he elaborates: "Myself and all th' Angelic Host, that stand / In sight of God enthron'd, our happy state / Hold, as you yours, while our obedience holds" (V.535–37). Raphael warns Adam and Eve that Satan

> now is plotting how he may seduce
> Thee also from obedience, that with him
> Bereav'd of happiness thou mayst partake
> His punishment, Eternal misery.
> (VI.901–4)

Edenic joy is backed by the threat of punishment if they eat of the forbidden tree: "From that day mortal, and this happy State / Shalt lose, expell'd from hence into a World / Of woe and sorrow" (VIII.330–33). Adam and Eve, like the reader of the poem, are given the example of Satanic disobedience and woe: "And some are fall'n, to disobedience fall'n, / And so from Heav'n to deepest Hell; O fall / From what high state of bliss into what woe!" (V.541–43). Misery is, like joy, used to induce obedience to a divine sovereign.

In the fall in *Paradise Lost*, Milton boldly employs language of joy that would have had political resonances in Restoration England. Satan's initial tempting of Eve in her dream focuses on joy. Satan flatters Eve as one "in whose sight all things joy" (V.46) and he offers the fruit to increase her happiness: "Here, happy Creature, fair Angelic *Eve*, / Partake thou also; happy though thou art, / Happier thou may'st be" (V.74–76). Satanic joy makes an impression on Eve. The fall becomes a bacchic celebration: Eve is "hight'n'd as with Wine, jocund and boon" (IX.793). Like Satan, Eve determines to give Adam the fruit only after she becomes jealous of his possible joy without her, fearing that "*Adam* wedded to another *Eve*, / Shall live with her enjoying, I extinct" (IX.828–29). In offering the fruit to Adam, Eve again uses language of joy, arguing that "bliss, as thou hast part, to me is bliss, / Tedious, unshar'd with thee, and odious soon" (IX.879–80) and urging, "Thou therefore also taste, that equal Lot / May join us, equal Joy, as equal Love" (IX.881–82). Eve feels "new Hopes, new Joys" (IX.985) and she weeps "for joy" (IX.990) when Adam joins her. Adam too uses the language of joy, albeit to place Eve above joy or woe: "from thy State / Mine never shall be parted, bliss or woe" (IX.915–16). Such language is not to be found in Genesis or in traditional accounts of the fall.

Adam and Eve's fallen, temporary joy thus strikingly recalls Restoration panegyric, joy, and bacchic celebration. Adam and Eve promise themselves not only wisdom and godhead, as in the Genesis account, but the "joy and love" that marked their golden days. And, notably, Adam and Eve become intoxicated: "As with new Wine intoxicated both / They swim in mirth" (IX. 1008–9). Their new supposed golden age transforms joy as obedience into joy as lust, and Adam's sense is inflamed "With ardor to enjoy thee" (IX.1032). Joy, which earlier characterized their chaste domestic life and labor, now becomes physical sexual "enjoyment"—making visible their disobedience.



Adam and Eve's fall is represented as a perverse and misguided attempt to enhance their own happy state—self-seeking bliss, intoxication with wine, and sexual lust. But the bacchic celebration represents for Adam and Eve a fall from, not a return to, paradise. Adam and Eve's disobedience brings false joy soon followed by woe. Milton's rendition of the fall thus challenges and subverts royalist rhetoric of the golden age restored with Stuart monarchy. Adam and Eve lose true joy because of disobedience to the true king; their drunken revelry, reminiscent of Restoration celebrations, is transient, perverse, and self-destructive. In *Paradise Lost* attempts to imitate or restore the true heavenly golden age are deluded, fallen, or even Satanic.

## III

In this context, it is significant that the blind narrator of *Paradise Lost* explicitly opposes the tumult of bacchic celebration:

> Standing on Earth, not rapt above the Pole,
> More safe I Sing with mortal voice, unchang'd
> To hoarse or mute, though fall'n on evil days,
> On evil days though fall'n, and evil tongues;
> In darkness, and with dangers compast round,
> And solitude.
>
> (VII.23–28)

The narrator places himself—blind, "fall'n on evil days," surrounded with dangers—in what has been generally recognized as a Restoration milieu.[32] But as his song goes on to oppose the "barbarous dissonance" of Bacchus, the poem deploys very specific and resonant political figures. The drunken revelry that ensued upon the proclamation of Charles's kingship and at such events as his return and coronation were quite literally presented as the bacchic celebration of the golden age.



Bacchus, the god of wine and revelry, was prominently featured in the Restoration celebrations. In the coronation triumph, Bacchus reigned on the fourth arch in the Garden of Plenty (Fig. 11). The visual representation is underscored by Ogilby's explanatory verse in *The Entertainment:* "Over the *Postern*, on the *South*-side of the Entrance is *Bacchus*, a Youth in a Chariot drawn by *Tigres;* the Reins, Vine-Branches; his Mantle a *Panther's* Skin; his Crown, of *Grapes*, and Ivy; a *Thyrsus* in his left Hand; a *Cup* in his right" (143). Plenty welcomes the king:

> Great Sir, the Star, which at Your Happy Birth,
> Joy'd with his Beams (at Noon) the wond'ring Earth
> Did with auspicious lustre, then, presage
> The glitt'ring Plenty of this Golden Age.
>
> (165)

And this golden age is explicitly dominated by Bacchus:

> *Ceres* and *Pales*, with a Bounteous Hand,
> Diffuse their Plenty over all Your Land;
> And *Bacchus* is so Lavish of his Store,
> That Wine flows now where Water ran before.
> Thus Seasons, Men, and Gods their Joy express;
> To see Your Triumph, and our Happiness.
>
> (165)

The bacchic celebration at the coronation of the king was characterized by plenty, lavishness, flowing wine, excess.

The people seemed ready enough to express their joy through Bacchus's lavish store. A celebration in Scotland in 1661 made literal the iconography of the Restoration triumph. Hence, Thomas Rugg describes the "Joy in Scotland" at the coronation: after the magistrates attended a sermon "for joye of his Majestys coronation in England," and the young lords and ladies "expressed their joy by several sorts of dances," a display is set up at the town square:

> After they had refreshed themselves the Lord Provost with the magistrates, etc. eatch of them haveinge a whit batton in his hand, went to the Cross, where were the representation of vineyard, and under a large vine Bacchus bestridinge a hogshead of wine accompanied by Silenus and about a halfe a score Bachides. In this posture, Bacchus proclamed to all a liberty to frolick themselves for the space of 12 houers, with all sorts

FIGURE 11 Bacchus in his chariot. Detail from the fourth coronation arch, from Ogilby, *Entertainment* (1662). *By permission of the Houghton Library, Harvard University.*

of mirth imaginable, which was noe sonner pronounced but streames of wine poured out from the conduits and the magistraits begane his Majestyes health. (*Diurnal*, 179–80)

The liberty to frolic that Bacchus proclaims leads seemingly inexorably to expressions of loyalty, to the drinking of his Majesty's health. In the celebrations that greeted the return of the monarchy, joy was linked with festive, excessive celebration, "liberty to frolick" that by its very form repudiated the old regime.



In this political context, Milton daringly appropriates and reverses the Bacchus myth to pass judgment on his contemporaries and legitimate his own position, while poignantly registering a sense of the danger he faces. He appeals to a divine muse, Urania, for protection:

> But drive far off the barbarous dissonance
> Of *Bacchus* and his Revellers, the Race
> Of that wild Rout that tore the *Thracian* Bard
> In *Rhodope*, where Woods and Rocks had Ears
> To rapture, till the savage clamor drown'd
> Both Harp and Voice; nor could the Muse defend
> Her Son. So fail not thou, who thee implores:
> For thou art Heavn'ly, shee an empty dream.
> (VII.32–39)

Milton's depiction of himself as Orpheus in *Paradise Lost* is not an escape from politics but a bold challenge to the ideology of Restoration power.

Such a challenge is even more specific and extensive than has been previously recognized.[33] In Milton's text "universal joy" becomes the "barbarous dissonance / Of *Bacchus* and his Revellers," a "savage clamor" that threatens the true poet. Milton not only passes judgment on his contemporaries, but he reflects the danger he himself faces, recalling the death and dismemberment of the poet Orpheus by the maddened bacchante revelers whose advances he had spurned. Orpheus becomes an emotionally powerful figure for the regicides and for Milton's own precarious situation in the early Restoration. As we have seen, doubling the joy and celebrations is the drama of the scaffold, the grisly and horrific hangings, beheadings, and quarterings of the regicides; the exhuming and desecration of Cromwell, Ireton, and Bradshaw. The figure of the dismembered, beheaded Orpheus would have been particularly moving and resonant in 1667, given the harrowing fate that Milton himself had just narrowly escaped.

The Orpheus figure is one that had long haunted Milton. In "Ad Patrem," Milton refers to the power of Orpheus's song, which "held streams spellbound and gave ears to the oak-trees and moved lifeless phantoms to tears."[34] In "Lycidas," Milton registers the gruesome death of Orpheus as, in the words of one critic, "a nightmare of senseless destruction which even the Muse is powerless to prevent."[35] In Milton's early masque the central temptation posed by Comus, son of Bacchus and Circe, demonstrates both the appeal and the dangers of the bacchic mode.[36] More politicized references to Bacchus are found in Milton's late prose tract, *The Readie and Easie Way*, in which royalist pamphleteers are "tigers of Bacchus, fanatics of not the preaching but the sweating-tub, inspir'd with nothing holier than the venereal pox" (*CPW* 7:452–53). As he eloquently resists the seeming inexorable rush toward monarchy, Milton explicitly echoes the biblical prophet Jeremiah, but his words also implicitly recall Orpheus as the classical poet who had the power to move trees and stones: "Thus much I should perhaps have said though I were sure I should have spoken only to trees and stones; and had none to cry to, but with the Prophet, *O earth, earth, earth!* to tell the very soil it self what her perverse inhabitants are deaf to" (*CPW* 7:462–63). In the epic poem, the Orpheus figure becomes a powerful means for opposing the joy of the Restoration celebrations and for providing a countermeasure. Orpheus, we should recall, was not simply a victim of horrifying violence. His song had power to restore the age of gold.



## IV

MILTON'S epic thus not only tells of the loss of paradise but points to the true golden age, restored on earth only in part as internalized self-discipline. Adam and Eve's bacchic celebration is a perversion and loss of joy, and, when they grow sober, is followed by a world of woe. Significantly, Adam and Eve are miserable even before they are judged by the Son: unlike the Genesis account, their disobedience here brings almost immediate woe and loss of joy. Their misery is represented as self-induced, consequent upon disobedience, not an arbitrary external punishment:

> They sat them down to weep, nor only Tears
> Rain'd at thir Eyes, but high Winds worse within
> Began to rise, high Passions, Anger, Hate,
> Mistrust, Suspicion, Discord, and shook sore
> Thir inward State of Mind, calm Region once
> And full of Peace, now toss't and turbulent.
> (IX.1121–26)

Adam and Eve's inner misery, described in terms from the natural world—rain, wind, storm—reflects the "natural" woe ensuing from disobedience.

Sorrow thus becomes the keynote of the postlapsarian human condition in *Paradise Lost*. Adam and Eve's joy in God's presence is lost. Adam laments: "How shall I behold the face / Henceforth of God or Angel, erst with joy / And rapture so oft beheld?" (IX.1080–82). The Son coming down to judge Adam and Eve asks: "Where art thou *Adam*, wont with joy to meet / My coming seen far off?" (X.103–4). The judgment is largely given in terms of additional woe: to the woman, "Thy sorrow I will greatly multiply / By thy Conception; Children thou shalt bring / In sorrow forth" (X.193–95), and to the man, "Curs'd is the ground for thy sake, thou in sorrow / Shalt eat thereof all the days of thy Life" (X.201–2). Such woe is more than a powerful counterstatement to the Restoration ideology of a return to joy; it is also used to mediate divine authority in Milton's poem.

Satan's handing over the kingdom of earth to Sin and Death and returning to hell in triumph in Book 10 is, as we will see in chapter 4, a bold rewriting and subverting of the Restoration triumph. I want to explore here the remarkable extent to which this triumph is specifically depicted as a restoration of joy. "With joy / And tidings fraught" (X.345–46), Satan returns to hell, only to gain further joy in reuniting with Sin and Death and their impressive creation of an arched bridge over chaos: "Great joy was at thir meeting, and at sight / Of that stupendous Bridge his joy increas'd" (X.350–51). Satan returns to hell precisely to restore joy: "them to acquaint / With these successes, and with them rejoice" (X.395–96). He reveals himself suddenly to "joy / Congratulant" (X.457–58) and, recounting his conquest over Adam and Eve, offers a parody golden age or millennium: "What remains, ye Gods, / But up and enter now into full bliss" (X.502–3). But a divine ruler exposes Satan's "joy" as false and deluded by transforming the fallen angels into a swarm of hissing serpents who emit not joy but "A dismal universal hiss, the sound / Of public scorn" (X.508–9). Satan is not allowed to joy, and the ritual is repeated annually "to dash their pride, and joy for Man seduc't" (X.577). The Satanic restoration is revealed as false, transient, and perverted—a pointed figure for the contemporary political scene.

Satan's false joy is immediately juxtaposed to Adam and Eve's true, if limited, restoration. Adam is "miserable of happy!" (X.720) and laments the "fleeting joys / Of Paradise, dear bought with lasting woes!" (X.741–42). Acknowledging divine justice, Adam finds himself "miserable / Beyond all past example and future, / To *Satan* only like both crime and doom" (X.839–41). Initiating reconciliation, Eve now claims more misery, as she had earlier claimed more joy:

> On me exercise not
> Thy hatred for this misery befall'n,
> On me already lost, mee than thyself
> More miserable.
>
> (X.927–30)

Marital obedience and guidance are first reinstated as help in woe: Adam urges that they "strive / In offices of Love, how we may light'n / Each other's burden in our share of woe" (X.959–61). And, if they earlier obeyed out of joy, Adam and Eve now obey to mitigate woe:

> they forthwith to the place
> Repairing where he judg'd them prostrate fell
> Before him reverent, and both confess'd
> Humbly thir faults, and pardon begg'd, with tears
> Watering the ground, and with thir sighs the Air
> Frequenting, sent from hearts contrite, in sign
> Of sorrow unfeign'd, and humiliation meek.
> (X.1098–1104)



Repenting their disobedience, Adam and Eve now find "new hope to spring / Out of despair, joy, but with fear yet linkt" (XI.138–39). Woe, like joy, is used to bring obedience.

In sharp contrast to contemporary political discourse, the final books of *Paradise Lost* demonstrate how paradise—or joy—can be restored on earth. But that God the Father sends Michael to restore a tempered and internal joy to Adam and Eve also shows the final link between joy and obedience in *Paradise Lost*, as Milton deploys the very strategies that he contests in their contemporary political applications. Adam is shown his true misery—"What misery th' inabstinence of *Eve* / Shall bring on men" (XI.476–77). Michael's account of human history is a story of woe: "O miserable Mankind, to what fall / Degraded, to what wretched state reserv'd!" (XI.500–501). But defined against this woe are divine restorations such as the covenant with Noah: "Whereat the heart of *Adam* erst so sad / Greatly rejoic'd, and thus his joy broke forth" (XI.868–69).

In contrast to Satan's false restoration, an eschatological golden age is restored when "Earth / Shall all be Paradise, far happier place / Than this of *Eden*, and far happier days" (XII.463–65). The millennial vision of earth as paradise restores Adam's joy. "Replete with joy and wonder" (XII.468), he queries: "Whether I should repent me now of sin / By mee done and occasion'd, or rejoice / Much more, that much more good therof shall spring" (XII.474–76). Angelic prophecy looks ahead to a millennial golden age: "New Heav'ns, new Earth, Ages of endless date / Founded in righteousness and peace and love, / To bring forth fruits Joy and eternal Bliss" (XII.549–51). Through faith in this spiritual, eschatological state of joy, Adam regains a kind of limited joy on earth. Contrasted to, indeed replacing the happy garden is the paradise within: "then wilt thou not be loath / To leave this Paradise, but shalt possess / A paradise within thee, happier far" (XII.585–87).

Satan's hell within is a paradise lost; Adam and Eve lose the physical paradise, and can only reinstate it within the individual conscience: "a paradise within thee, happier far." The paradise within is a temporary, limited instantiation of that future age in which "God will be all in all." And yet the turn to the paradise within is not escapist but a deliberate alternative to the external, bacchic joy of the fall in *Paradise Lost*—and of the Restoration court in Milton's England. The joy within is not a final end, but a precondition for the golden age on earth to which the poem nonetheless looks forward.



## V

In 1697, the bacchic mode could still be used positively by the poet-laureate, John Dryden, in his *Alexander's Feast:*

> Bacchus, ever fair and young
> Drinking joys did first ordain;
> Bacchus' blessings are a treasure,
> Drinking is a soldier's pleasure;
>   Rich the treasure,
> Sweet the pleasure,
> Sweet is pleasure after pain.

But the bacchic mode had become a source of discontent with the court itself. Popular perception, recorded in diaries, letters, and court records, is of a court that has taken on the vices of Bacchus—debauchery, drunkenness, whoremongering. Such concern can be traced in Pepys's diary; in August 1661, he is already worrying about the vices of the court: "Court things are in very ill condition, there being so much aemulacion, poverty, and the vices of swearing, drinking, and whoring, that I know not what will be the end of it but confusion" (*Diary* 2:167). The following May, Pepys describes the public "joy" at the arrival of Charles's new queen, Catherine of Braganza, as hollow and indifferent: "At night all the bells in the towne rung, and bonefires made for the joy of the Queenes arrivall, who came and landed at Portsmouth last night. But I do not see much thorough joy, but only an indifferent one, in the hearts of people, who are much discontented at the pride and luxury of the Court, and running in debt" (*Diary* 3:83). The scene contrasted sharply with the celebrations upon the arrival of the king just two years earlier; the material forms of public joy here remained—bells, bonfires—but the hearts of the people were now more exposed in their actual indifference.

"Pride and luxury," of course, were only part of the grievances many people felt against the court after even as short a time as two years. Charles had found it impossible to satisfy the many and conflicting economic, ecclesiastical, social, and political demands of his subjects. Yet I would argue that the motif of bacchic joy is in itself unstable, readily enough used to critique as well as to praise the court. On Christmas Day, 1662, Pepys hears a sermon by Bishop Morley, "long and reprehending the mistaken jollity of the Court for the true joy that shall and ought to be on these days" (*Diary* 3:292). In October 1665 Pepys's friend talks of the "wantonness of the Court and how it minds nothing else," of how "the king doth spend most of his time in feeling and kissing [his mistresses] all over their bodies in bed" (*Diary* 6:267). Pepys's concerns with a "sad, vicious, negligent court" (*Diary* 6:426) are echoed by others, notably John Evelyn, who in 1666 sees the recent plague, fire, and war with the Dutch as divine judgments on "our prodigious ingratitute, burning Lusts, disolute Court, profane & abominable lives" (*Diary* 3:464).



It may now seem unlikely that Charles's dalliances with a string of royal mistresses brought on plague, fire, and war, or even that such behavior had the deleterious political effects feared by some contemporaries. But the excesses of the court were notorious, and disillusionment had set in by 1667. The bacchic mode, as subjects ranging from Milton to the unruly Middlesex commoners realized, was inherently unstable. The very tools of royalist ideology could be turned against the court in the time of England's merry monarch.

# Milton and the Roman Triumph

Their Souls and Vestments glitter'd both that day
Joying him home the twenty nineth of *May*.
Fresh glories did the *Coronation* shew
The glorious *Prince* hath made his *Subjects* so.
The *Triumphs* of the *Antients* mean appear,
If we compare them with our *Splendour* here.

Carew Reynell, *The Fortunate Change*

THE ENTRY of Charles II into London in May 1660 and the coronation one year later displayed the "triumph" of monarchical power in a distinctively Roman mode.[1] We have seen that the public joy of the spectators affirmed their renewed obedience to the king in the theater of triumph. I now want to look more precisely at the nature and complexities of the king on display as Roman conqueror. In splendor and conspicuous material glory, these triumphs imitated and (allegedly) outwent their Roman models. Yet the conquest by force was inherently unstable and ill-suited to Charles, who had not won a military victory; indeed, Cromwell himself seemed more aptly praised as a Roman conqueror. The victorious Roman general was therefore supplemented with a model of Christian conquest through patience in suffering, and Charles was rewritten as a truly glorious king who conquers hearts and minds.

Despite his deep, even iconoclastic distrust of the spectacle, Milton in *Paradise Lost* not only undercuts but outgoes contemporary political uses of the Roman triumph in the parody splendors of hell and the truly glorious triumphs of heaven; the epic reflects the appeal, as well as the dangers of the triumphal mode. In *Paradise Regained* and *Samson Agonistes*, the triumph on earth is more clearly rejected as a temptation and sign of impenitence. Milton's three major poems not only rebuke the triumphs of the Stuart monarchy, but, as we shall see, provide an ambivalent commentary on the Romanized and regal Cromwellian Protectorate.

## I



In imitation of the Roman generals and emperors who celebrated military victories by entering into the city regally dressed in purple and riding a chariot, with a procession of musicians, captives, trophies, and spoils of conquest, monarchs in Europe from the fifteenth to the seventeenth centuries widely celebrated coronations and other state occasions with triumphs.[2] Jonathan Goldberg and Stephen Orgel have traced the Roman mode under the early Stuart kings.[3] Cromwell too, as we shall see, was celebrated in the language of Rome. In 1661, the Roman triumph served to recuperate for the monarchy the prestige and authority of the classical past, to mediate and legitimate the positions of king and people by uniting them against a common enemy. Royal virtues and loyal hearts were embodied in material glories, the lavish displays of architecture, clothing, pageantry, and drama.

The coronation triumph of April 1661 was a theatrical spectacle that encompassed much of the city: lavish display, splendid clothing, admiring spectators, architectural wonder, drama, music.[4] The Venetian resident recounts that "His Majesty's coronation has been accomplished this week, so desired by his subjects, with all possible splendour and decorum, no one sparing his money to make it exceptional and memorable for ages to come, and it was certainly the most conspicuous solemnity that has ever been seen in this realm" (*CSPV* 32:286). In its lavish excess the coronation was said to outdo Roman models. Henry Beeston queries rhetorically: "And where's the *Roman*, or the *Greek Parade*, / Can *march* with *Glorious Tuesdays Cavalcade?*"[5]

The glory of the king's estate was represented through material excess of the lavish cavalcade. Observers emphasize the glittery, expensive surfaces, the clothing, and the architecture. James Heath, who records the display in *The Glories and Magnificent Triumphs* (1662) lest "any of these scattered rayes, and refractions of this Monarchs Glory should be dimmed or disappear in the obscurity of time," focuses on the material glories of the show: "It is incredible to think what costly cloathes were worne that day, the cloaks could hardly be seen what silke or sattin they were made of for the gold and silver laces & embroydery that was laid upon them; the like also was seen in their foot-cloathes."[6] Heath concludes with a theatrical trope: "All the world that saw it, could not but confess, that what they had seen before was but solemn mummery to the most *August*, noble and true glories of this great day" (208). The effect upon the spectators was to produce joy, admiration, and wonder, as Heath writes: "Infinite and innumerable were the acclamation and shouts from all the parts as his Majestie passed along, to the no less joy then amazement of the spectators, who beheld those glorious personages that rid before and behind his Majesty" (208).



Pepys concurs in the motif of incomparability. On the monarchical procession he comments: "So glorious was the show with gold and silver, that we were not able to look at it—our eyes at last being so much overcome with it" (*Diary* 2:83); similarly, after the coronation, he observes: "Now after all this, I can say that besides the pleasure of the sight of these glorious things, I may now shut my eyes against any other objects, or for the future trouble myself to see things of state and shewe, as being sure never to see the like again in this world" (*Diary* 2:88). Heath protests after his long and detailed description that the show cannot be described: "Indeed it were in vain to attempt to express this Solemnity, it was so far from being utterable, that is almost inconceivable" (207).

The glories of the coronation triumph were further circulated by printed word and image. A contemporary engraving by R. White (Fig. 12) shows Charles II on horseback, crowned, in splendid robes, and holding his scepter; in the background, the triumphal procession passes by thronging onlookers on its way to the coronation at Westminster. The entire triumph was reproduced in John Ogilby's copiously annotated and lavishly illustrated *The Entertainment of His Most Excellent Majestie Charles II.*[7] Rival books, like rival shows, were mere "mummery."

Culminating the pageantry were four elaborate Roman arches that created and reinforced ideals of monarchy, mythologizing Charles II as Roman conqueror. The Venetian ambassador describes the scope of the proceedings: "[The King] proceeded in solemn cavalcade to Whitehall, attended by all the peers, grandees and officials of the realm, richly attired, traversing the whole city which was decorated in the most delightful manner, a number of triumphal Arches being set up in the streets at which they have laboured for many months" (*CSPV* 32:286). In their representation of traditional military conquest over a foe, the triumphal arches offered a dual display: the king was mythologized as Augustus, Aeneas, and Neptune, but underlying and supplementing the eulogies were the punished bodies of his defeated foes, linked with Satan, disorder, chaos, destruction, hell, and the scatological. The shame, like the glory, was linked with and said to go beyond the classical past. The triumph visually presented both an ideal with which to identify and an alien against which the king and people could be united. Praise and execration were not two separate ceremonies, but dual aspects of the same display.[8]

In the triumphal arches the citizens of London did not conceal past re-

FIGURE 12 Charles II on horseback, his coronation procession in background (c. 1661). *By permission of the Trustees of the British Museum.*

bellion; rather they used the mode of triumph to publicize and demonize republicanism, heightening the shame through visual display. As the king approached the first arch, a woman impersonating Rebellion demanded the stage: "Stand! Stand! who'ere You are! this Stage is Ours." Rebellion is incomparable in her visual monstrosity: "A Woman personating *Rebellion*, mounted on a *Hydra*, in a Crimson Robe, torn, Snakes crawling on her Habit, and begirt with Serpents, her Hair Snaky, a Crown of Fire on her Head, a bloody Sword in one Hand, a charming Rod in the other" (13). Attended by Confusion, "in a deformed Shape, a Garment of several ill-matched Colours, and put on the wrong way; on her Head, Ruines of

FIGURE 13 Decollated heads, one resembling Cromwell. Detail from the first coronation arch, from Ogilby, *Entertainment* (1662). *By permission of the Houghton Library, Harvard University.*

Castles, torn Crowns, and broken Scepters in each Hand" (13), Rebellion blocked the king's passage and revealed her Satanic lineage: "I am Hell's daughter, *Satan's* eldest Childe, / When I first cry'd, the Pow'rs of Darkness smil'd" (41). But she was dismissed from the stage by the two "stately Ladies," Monarchy and Loyalty:

> To Hell, foul Fiend, shrink from this glorious light,
> And hide thy Head in everlasting Night.
> Enter in safety, Royal Sir, this Arch,
> And through Your joyful Streets in Triumph march.
> (42)

The threat of rebellion was both deployed and contained through the mode of the triumph, allowing the citizens to distinguish treason from themselves and to demonstrate their loyalty.

Treason was represented in the first arch not only by these human figures, but by paintings that Ogilby reproduces in *The Entertainment.* On the north side was a "Trophy with decollated Heads," (Fig. 13), severed heads on spikes representing Cromwell and other regicides as traitors who go beyond all classical precedents. Over the painting is the motto *Ultor a Tergo Deus*, which Ogilby cites as out of Horace: "God's Vengeance Rebels at the Heels pursues." Underneath the heads is written *Ausi Immane Nefas, Ausoque Potiti*, which Ogilby identifies as from Virgil's *Aeneid* 6: "All dared bold crimes and thrived in what they dared" (21–22). As we have seen earlier, visual representations displayed in graphic physical detail Cromwell's punishment and fate—as with the executed regicides and unlike Charles I. The heinousness of crime and punishment is underscored by the ignominious display. Indeed, the painting exaggerates reality, multiplying the number of heads and making them startlingly animated, with eyes open and placid gazes. If Charles's severed head was avoided, Cromwell's was prominently displayed.



A second painting on the arch likewise enhanced Cromwell's unnatural crime: "The *King*, mounted in calm Motion, *Usurpation* flying before him, a Figure with many ill-favoured Heads, some bigger, some lesser, and one particularly shooting out of his Shoulder, like *Cromwells;* Another Head on his Rump or Tayl" (28). In this grotesque Hydra-Rump figure, the display once again reified past treason in a convenient scapegoat whom the king could now conquer. The king is flanked by his deified royal ancestors; mounted calmly, albeit with sword raised, the king drives the grotesque figure into a monstrous, flaming mouth of hell. Cromwell's severed head again appears, growing unnaturally out of a monster, marked not by dignity, or even tragedy, but degradation and shame, an unseemly and grotesque body. In the visual displays the incomparable glories were supplemented by incomparable crimes and punishments.

The panegyric that interpreted and responded to the pageantry extended the trope of incomparability from the splendid display to the king's own virtues. For Samuel Pordage, the monarch himself excels Caesar as much as the arches supersede their Roman types:

> Aspiring Pyramids that touch the skie
> Under his vaster Fame and Glory lie;
> No *Caesar* e're deserv'd to triumph so,
> Triumphal Arches are too mean and low
> When th' arched vault of the bright spangled frame,
> Cann't bound the Eccho of his mighty Name.[9]

*To the King, Upon His Majesties Happy Return* (1660) posits Charles's glory as beyond Caesar's: "Where Caesar could no further Glory win, / There is the scene, where Yours does but begin."[10]

Yet for all the extravagance of the pageantry, the accompanying panegyric discloses an uneasiness with the Roman model and with the king being thus eulogized.[11] Force would recall the darker side of the Roman caesars, the ending of the republic, the potential for tyranny as well as liberty. Roman emperors—even Augustus—were by no means unqualified models of liberty versus autocracy. Hence, differences from and improvements upon the Roman model were much stressed; present imitations not only outdid but contrasted with their Roman antecedents.



Charles II was pointedly praised for bringing the virtues without the vices of the Roman conquerors. *To the King, Upon His Majesties Happy Return* praises Charles for conquering himself:

> You might possess by Armies, and by Fleets,
> All where the Sun doth rise, or where he sets;
> But You a nobler Conquest have design'd
> The placing limits to Your greater minde.[12]

In a move beyond display to inner virtues, the poet praises self-conquest as primary, the "nobler Conquest" for which Charles is given the title not of imperator but "*King of greatest Pow'r and greatest Peace.*" Likewise, Thomas Higgins stresses how Charles's conquest by virtue differs from and surpasses his classical models:

> Had conquering Rome but such a Monarch seen,
> One with your vertue, and your right beside,
> With freedom's name she ne'er had couzen'd bin,
> And Brutus had not so untimely dyed.[13]

The conquest of hearts allowed the panegyrists both to praise Charles in the Roman mode and to warn him against its potential excesses.

The arches themselves were removed from the historical particulars, and, even in defiance of fact, showed Charles II defeating Cromwell. But the panegyric was obsessed with the one historical fact that might undermine this whole elaborate edifice of praise, that Charles II had in fact been defeated by Cromwellian troops at Worcester.[14] Thus some, like Samuel Pordage, assert that Charles deliberately avoided the conquest of his own people:

> Heav'n wisely knew if you had had successe,
> And your Victorious sword had more imbrew'd
> In English blood, your Triumph had bin lesse,
> And bodies had, rather than minds, subdu'd.[15]

For the author of *Epinicia Carolina* (1660), "Had You that time o'ercome in fight / That very Name had spoil'd the shew," since even Roman conquerors were sometimes better off not triumphing:

*Caesar* in *triumph*, when he led
Great *Pompy's* children, lost more praise,
Then *Victory* did Trophies raise.[16]

Charles's very defeat could be rewritten to go beyond the sometimes ambiguous triumphs of the Roman emperors.

And at the same time, the negative side of the Roman mode was used to stigmatize the victorious Cromwell as a tyrant. In 1661 an illustration in Richard Perrinchief's *The Syracusan Tyrant or the Life of Agathocles* shows Cromwell, "Tyrannus," standing in Roman armor between figures of "Perfidia" and "Crudelitas," and being crowned with a wreath of serpents.[17] As late as 1684, John Nalson's *A True Copy of the Journal of the High Court of Justice* reproduces an earlier print (Fig. 14) that satirizes Cromwell in the Roman mode.[18] In the illustration, Cromwell, in armor but with wolflike hands and legs, rides in a chariot driven by the Devil and drawn by fire-breathing griffins. Cromwell holds upon the point of his sword a scale in which a bunch of feathers labeled "Liberty" outweigh the crown, church, scepter, and orb; his left claw rests upon the crown. The sword-spoked wheels of the chariot crush beneath them the bodies of the beheaded Charles I and of Justice.

Here the mode of Roman conqueror evinces tyranny and oppression. Background images link Cromwell with predatory animals destroying innocent victims: Amity, a naked cherub, is chained and in a cage; wolves pursue a flock of sheep; a hawk pounces upon a dove escaping from a cage. Nalson's accompanying verse explains this decidedly nonheroic conquest:

See the sad Trophies of our Civil Wars,
The fatal period of Intestine Jars.
Behold th' insulting Monster; with what Pride,
Mounted on high, she does in triumph ride.

Three "weeping Beauties," manacled and crowned women who ride in the chariot, represent the three British nations who wear "inglorious Shackles" under Cromwell. The Roman mode aptly shows, in Nalson's words, how "Scepters, Crowns, Religions, Justice, Laws, / Became the Triumphs of the *Black Old Cause*."

It should by now be apparent that the mode of Roman triumph, used to praise Charles II throughout his reign, was not unequivocal. The figure of Roman conqueror could be used to praise or attack. But others contended that Charles did, in fact, conquer in defeat. Thus *To the King, Upon His Majesties Happy Return:* "The lesser conquest was to You deny'd, / That by the greater it might be supply'd."[19] Or, Thomas Higgins: "Nor did your fortune make your Glory lesse. / You were unconquer'd, when your troops

FIGURE 14 Cromwell in Roman chariot driven by the Devil, from Nalson, *A True Copy of the Journal of the High Court of Justice* (1684). *By permission of Rare Books and Special Collections, the Pennsylvania State University Libraries.*

did yield; / And won renown, although you lost the field."[20] Charles's apparent defeat paves the way for a better conquest, so that Samuel Pordage praises him paradoxically:

> Tis not by bloody Arms, or dreadful War
> (Those helps to lesse beloved Monarchs are)
> That he must conquer and assume his right;
> The splendor of his conquest shines more bright:
> Peace brings him in, Olive his Temples binds,
> And his great virtues conquer hearts and minds.[21]



"A Glorious Conqueror without a fight," Charles's glory is more, not less, for having been defeated at Worcester.[22]

Victory through defeat was able to incorporate the glorious martyr, an image that had troubled and threatened to undermine Cromwellian panegyric. The glory of Roman conquest for Charles II was supplemented by the glory of Christian conquest through suffering. Parliament's promise to make Charles I a "great and glorious king" was widely and bitterly repeated after his execution.[23] But now the son could regain the glory of his martyred father. The links between father and son that we traced in chapter 1 recurrently foreground the glory of martyrdom.

And yet Charles II recuperates the Roman mode as well. At the end of Charles's reign, Aurelian Cook represents him in a greater kind of triumph: "He did not leap on Shore with his Sword in his Hand, by way of Compulsion, but he was saluted with the free and unanimous Voice of three great Nations. As he had no other real enemies but his own Country, so in this he appeared *more than Conqueror*, that he vanquish'd the very minds of his enemies. Never was such a Triumph seen at *Rome*."[24] The differences between this triumph and the Roman mode made Charles II more truly glorious, a conqueror over the hearts and minds of men.

## II

In his Restoration poetry, Milton grappled with the royalist spectacles of power, not only the displays of punishment, but the positive and celebratory mode of the Roman triumph. In *Paradise Lost*, the Roman conqueror is parodied in Satan as general and emperor of hell, obsessed with material and gaudy glory, and deceitfully conquering an innocent foe; but the Roman mode is then revised and outdone in Christ who triumphs in and through his reflection of divine glory.[25] In *Paradise Regained* the Son rejects the false glory of Roman conquest in order to attain a more complete spiritual conquest and true glory; and in *Samson Agonistes*, the Hebrews are marred not by their thirst for violence but by their vainglory as they continually slip from divine to human conquest. Milton both exposes the problematics of spectacle and transforms that spectacle into a spiritual triumph whose true audience is divine.

In the figure of Satan, *Paradise Lost* critiques the Roman triumph as a mode liable to appropriation, mimicry, and perversion. Satan, as a kind of manipulative Caesar, regains and consolidates his power by staging unearned and illegitimate triumphs, false and tawdry imitations of heavenly glory. Satan's false glory embodies the danger and the appeal of the Roman forms. Satan, whose original aim had been "to set himself in Glory above his Peers" (I.39) remains obsessed in defeat by glory he sees as linked with martial deeds, public acclaim, and visible display. His first speech characterizes the failed rebellion as a "Glorious Enterprise" (I.89); he insists that "that strife / Was not inglorious, though th' event was dire" (I.623–24). While Satan acknowledges that God has proved more powerful, he will not play the role of captive, honoring the conqueror: "That Glory never shall his wrath or might / Extort from me" (I.110–11).



"Glorying" in *Paradise Lost* becomes a sign of Satanic pride. Satan continues defiant despite acknowledging "all our Glory extinct" (I.141); he and Beelzebub are soon "glorying to have scap't the *Stygian* flood" (I.239). Surveying the might and numbers of the reassembled angels, Satan's heart "distends with pride, and hard'ning in his strength / Glories" (I.572–73). Yet the only true "glory" which Satan retains is the visual remnant of heavenly light:

> his form had yet not lost
> All her Original brightness, nor appear'd
> Less than Arch-Angel ruin'd, and th' excess
> Of Glory obscur'd.
>
> (I.591–94)

Satan's darkening reflects a loss of divine glory, so that he is later unrecognized and rebuked by heavenly forces: "That Glory then, when thou no more wast good, / Departed from thee" (IV.838–39).[26]

Cut off from the divine source of true glory, Satan moves to false imitation through triumphal display. Book 1 closes with an elaborate building project that resembles the classical Doric arches used to celebrate a triumph. A "Fabric huge" rises, "built like a Temple, where *Pilasters* round / Were set, and Doric pillars overlaid / With Golden Architrave" (I.713–15). Satan stages in hell a display of lavish magnificence by which his power is both celebrated and constituted. Hell imitates the architectural glories of heaven in the lavish Roman and monarchical architecture of Pandemonium:

Not *Babylon*
Nor great *Alcairo* such magnificence
Equall'd in all thir glories, to inshrine
*Belus* or *Serapis* thir Gods, or seat
Thir Kings, when *Egypt* with *Assyria* strove
In wealth and luxury.

(I.717–22)





By building Pandemonium, Satan and the fallen angels reconstruct heavenly glory in material terms—wealth, luxury, visual magnificence. And from the spectators, as in monarchical displays, comes admiration and wonder: "the hasty multitude / Admiring enter'd" (I.730–31).

The war council that opens Book 2 exposes the false glory of wrongful conquest. "Exalted" on his throne, Satan argues that their recovery will be especially glorious: "From this descent / Celestial Virtues rising, will appear / More glorious and more dread than from no fall" (II.14–16). The fallen angels sit, "designing or exhorting glorious war" (II.179). After the war council, having volunteered to expand the infernal empire through conquest of God's newest colony, Satan is by "transcendent glory rais'd / Above his fellows" (II.427–28). Satan's ongoing quest for glory continues, and while that glory is now associated not with martial deeds as such but with deceit, it is nonetheless figured as a conquest. Arriving on earth, Satan claims that "Honor and Empire with revenge enlarg'd, / By conquering this new World, compels me now / To do what else though damn'd I should abhor" (IV.390–92). As he prepares to tempt Eve, he revels in the glory:

To mee shall be the glory sole among
Th'infernal Powers, in one day to have marr'd
What he *Almighty* styl'd, six Nights and Days
Continu'd making.

(IX.135–38)

Milton forcefully registers the dangers of glory linked with Roman conquest in the figure of Satan.

Milton's most significant undercutting of the Roman triumph is his representation of the fall as a Satanic conquest of Adam and Eve resulting in a triumphal return into hell (which we earlier explored as a false restoration of joy). In what I would argue is the epic's closest figure for the contemporary political scene, Satan hands over the kingdom of earth to Sin and Death, returning to hell in a parodic imitation of the Roman triumph.[27] The poem, like the coronation triumph itself, displays the anti-triumph, grotesque and parodic, linked with the scatological. Satan's moment of apparent glory is turned to shame.

Returning to hell, Satan is welcomed by Sin and Death and their perverse creation of an arched bridge over Chaos. Satan now embraces his postfall name "for I glory in the name, / Antagonist of Heav'n's Almighty King" (X.386–87). He assures his "fair daughter and thou son and grandchild both" that they

> Amply have merited of me, of all
> Th' Infernal Empire, that so near Heav'n's door
> Triumphal with triumphal act have met,
> Mine with this glorious Work.
>
> (X.388–91)

The infernal bridge linking earth and hell is reminiscent of the classical arches celebrating a victorious Roman triumph—or their Stuart counterparts: "Over the foaming deep high Archt, a Bridge / Of length prodigious" (X.301–2). Satan, like Charles II, is about to celebrate his victory by a triumphal entrance. The Roman arches are now placed in hell, or rather connect hell to earth, and Satan's "glorious work" has been to conquer Adam and Eve through fraud and deceit. Satan's is a tawdry and false glory.

But that Satan's triumph is soon undercut and the expected celebration thwarted reveals the deceit and shame behind the facade of monarchical glory. Satan returns to hell disguised as a plebeian angel, ironically, like the foot soldier who rode beside the triumphing general to remind him of his mortality. He reveals himself only gradually:

> At last as from a Cloud his fulgent head
> And shape Star-bright appear'd, or brighter, clad
> With what permissive glory since his fall
> Was left him, or false glitter.
>
> (X.449–52)

Satan announces his new empire and his intention "to lead ye forth / Triumphant out of this infernal Pit / Abominable" (X.463–65). The arches provided by Sin and Death, he assures them, will "expedite your glorious march" (X.474). But the glory of triumph is turned to shame. Expecting to hear the "universal shout and high applause" that greets the conquering triumphator, Satan instead hears "from innumerable tongues / A dismal universal hiss, the sound / Of public scorn" (X.507–9). Satan gets no honor, no celebration, no glorious spectacle. The other angels who wait "sublime with expectation when to see / In Triumph issuing forth thir glorious Chief" (X.536–37) see instead "a crowd / Of ugly Serpents" (X.538–39). As the audience itself turns serpentine, the "applause they meant, / Turn'd to exploding hiss, triumph to shame" (X.546–47).

In the swarming, monstrous bodies of Satan and his followers, *Paradise*

*Lost* presents a display of the grotesque body that exceeds the shaming of earlier triumphs. The grotesque, cartoonlike images of Satan, "a monstrous Serpent on his Belly prone" (X.514) and of hell "thick swarming now / With complicated monsters, head and tail, / Scorpion and Asp" (X.522–24) parallel and go beyond earthly triumphal displays of the shamed, defeated foe. Satan as a mimic Roman conqueror, seemingly powerful, has actually been part of a divine triumph all along. In representing Satan's greater shame and God's greater conquest, Milton uses the very strategy of incomparability to rebuke royalist displays.



## III

Milton thus challenges contemporary royalist spectacle in the figure of Satan as Roman conqueror in *Paradise Lost*, dramatizing fully the complexities of evil, its visual and theatrical appeal as well as its underlying danger and perversion of true heroism. But the poem is not simply iconoclastic, undercutting and satirizing the display. Rather, Milton deconstructs Satan's triumph only to replace it with a greater and truly glorious divine triumph. In his much-puzzled-over Romanized heaven, Milton sets up God the Father and the Son as true conquerors, truly glorified, a model from which Satanic and earthly imitations deviate. Milton can thus imagine a purified triumph that rebukes contemporary political displays. But he can also show the power of that false imitation, the complicating ambiguities of spectacles in hell, in heaven, and on earth.

Divine glory in *Paradise Lost* is frequently imaged in terms of light, an inherent virtue of the divine, separate from and a rebuke to the gaudy, glittery displays of hell.[28] Angels praise the Father "invisible / Amidst the glorious brightness where thou sit'st" (III.375–76). Christ visibly reflects the Father as "the radiant image of his Glory" (III.63), "most glorious, in him all his Father shone" (III.139). The angels are marked by glory in terms of light. Satan comes upon Uriel a "glorious Angel" (III.622), and Raphael appears to Adam a "glorious shape . . . another Morn / Ris'n on mid-noon" (V.309–11). Abdiel reminds Satan that God has created them "in thir bright degrees, / Crown'd them with Glory, and to thir Glory nam'd / Thrones, Dominations, Princedoms, Virtues, Powers" (V.838–40).

Adam and Eve likewise evince glory in their reflection of the divine:

> Two of far nobler shape erect and tall,
> Godlike erect, with native Honor clad
> In naked Majesty seem'd Lords of all,
> And worthy seem'd, for in thir looks Divine
> The image of thir glorious Maker shone.
>
> (IV.288–92)

Given the elaborate displays that marked the glories of earthly monarchy, it is striking that Adam and Eve show true majesty, true glory, in their very nakedness which alone can image the divine. Hence, as he meets Raphael, Adam is:

> without more train
> Accompanied than with his own complete
> Perfections; in himself was all his state,
> More solemn than the tedious pomp that waits
> On Princes, when thir rich Retinue long
> Of Horses led, and Grooms besmear'd with Gold
> Dazzles the crowd, and sets them all agape.
> (V.351–57)



Theirs is a private, domestic scene—no gaudy display, no spectators.

The Edenic state implicitly critiques the gaudy pomp of earthly monarchy, a sentiment found throughout Milton's prose. Some of his harshest words in *The Readie and Easie Way* (1660) pointed to the civil idolatry of monarchy: "A king must be ador'd like a Demigod, with a dissolute and haughtie court about him, of vast expence and luxurie" (*CPW* 7:425); a king will "set a pompous face upon the superficial actings of State, to pageant himself up and down in progress among the perpetual bowings and cringings of an abject people, on either side deifying and adoring him for nothing don that can deserve it" (*CPW* 7:426). In his *History of Britain* (published in 1670 but probably written much earlier), Milton emphasizes the hollowness of Roman triumphs: "*For that Cittie in reward of vertue was ever magnificent: and long after when true merit was ceas't among them, lest any thing resembling vertue should want honour, the same rewards were yet allow'd to the very shadow and ostentation of merit*" (*CPW* 5:68). Milton evinces in poetry and prose a distrust of the ceremonious spectacle, including the glories of triumph.

Indeed, the desire to be on display, to establish one's own glory apart from God's, is a significant factor in the fall in *Paradise Lost.* Adam and Eve rightly praise the glories of divine creation. Eve questions, "for whom / This glorious sight, when sleep hath shut all eyes?" (IV.657–58), and they extol "thy glorious works, Parent of good, / Almighty, thine this universal Frame, / Thus wondrous fair; thyself how wondrous then!" (V.153–55). But the desire to be thus praised is precisely the temptation Satan offers Eve:

> Fairest resemblance of thy Maker fair,
> Thee all things living gaze on, all things thine
> By gift, and thy Celestial beauty adore
> With ravishment beheld, there best beheld
> Where universally admir'd.
> (IX.538–42)

The fall itself evinces the dangers of the display as Eve returns (metaphorically) to gazing upon her own image and Adam errs in "overmuch admiring" (IX.1178). Eve's desire for a "glorious trial" (IX.961) apart from God brings "guilt and dreaded shame; O how unlike / To that first naked Glory" (IX.1114–15). True glory comes not in display but in imaging the divine.

The war in heaven shows similar vainglorious displays, linked now with conquest. The rebel angels aspire "to glory . . . Vain-glorious" (VI.383–84). Satan insists that the strife should be called "the strife of Glory" (VI.290). And he alone takes on the role of Roman triumphator: "High in the midst exalted as a God / Th' Apostate in his Sun-bright Chariot sat / Idol of Majesty Divine" (VI.99–101). Christ, in contrast, is not a general leading his troops; that role belongs to Michael. Christ does not even fight but is sent out by the Father, "that the Glory may be thine / Of ending this great War" (VI.701–2).





Yet triumph and spectacle are nonetheless crucial to divine glory in *Paradise Lost.* John Rumrich is theologically correct when he writes of *Paradise Lost* that "while Satan suffers defeat in attempting to establish his own glory apart from God, the Son suffers martyrdom in the course of his glorification of God."[29] But such martyrdom is not represented in Milton's epic. Rather, the glory of the Son in *Paradise Lost* depends much more upon spectacle and conquest than on the suffering and martyrdom we do not see. Christ in the war in heaven evinces conquest, triumph, and glory.[30] The chariot Christ drives "from the right hand of Glory where he sat" (VI.747) is a spectacle that goes beyond spectacle, countering false imitations.

Precisely at the center of *Paradise Lost*, then, Christ rides into battle in a triumphal chariot, whose very appearance will defeat the rebel angels:

> forth rush'd with whirl-wind sound
> The Chariot of Paternal Deity,
> Flashing thick flames, Wheel within Wheel, undrawn,
> Itself instinct with Spirit, but convoy'd
> By four Cherubic shapes, four Faces each
> Had wondrous, as with Stars thir bodies all
> And Wings were set with Eyes, with Eyes the Wheels
> Of Beryl, and careering Fires between.
> (VI.749–56)

Michael Lieb astutely explains the effect as "the experience of overwhelmingness," a mode that he traces to Ezekiel.[31] But such "overwhelmingness" also counters, in our context, the incomparability motifs of royalist panegyric. This is a spectacle that goes beyond and defies all spectacle; it is virtually impossible to visualize, in Lieb's words, a "vision that overwhelms those who are ironically to be cut off from 'blessed vision.'"[32] The "overwhelmingness"—flaming chariot, wheels within wheels, four-fold faces, stars, and eyes—blends classical and Hebrew chariots in a spectacle that surpasses the gaudy and trivial displays without as well as within the poem.

In this bold revision of the triumph, Milton's Christ gains true glory from the faithful angels and from God. Christ himself predicts victory through spectacle alone: "Matter to mee of Glory, whom thir hate / Illustrates, when they see all Regal Power / Giv'n me to quell thir pride" (V.738–40). "Grieving to see his Glory" (VI.792), the rebel angels are only hardened. But when Christ changes to terror "His count'nance too severe to be beheld / And full of wrath bent on his Enemies" (VI.825–26), the sight alone drives out the rebel angels. And Christ is praised in strikingly triumphal language:



> Sole Victor from th' expulsion of his Foes
> *Messiah* his triumphal Chariot turn'd:
> To meet him all his Saints, who silent stood
> Eye-witnesses of his Almighty Acts,
> With Jubilee advanc'd; and as they went,
> Shaded with branching Palm, each order bright,
> Sung Triumph.
>
> (VI.880–86)

For his conquest, Christ rides "Triumphant through mid Heav'n" (VI.889) and is received "into Glory" (VI.891). In Christ's triumph in heaven, Milton forcefully critiques the gaudy, theatrical displays of the Stuart court and imagines as alternative a paradoxical spectacle against spectacle.

If in his expulsion of the rebel angels, Christ not only undercuts but surpasses the Roman conquerors, his second triumph is even more revisionary—not a battle at all, but a creation. Milton depicts Christ's creation of the earth as a conquest over Chaos, followed by a triumphal procession. Christ rides into Chaos as "The King of Glory in his powerful Word / And Spirit coming to create new Worlds (VII.208–9). Praised by the angels as "greater now in thy return / Than from the Giant Angels" (VII.604–5), Christ rides in royal triumph back to the Father:

> Up he rode
> Follow'd with acclamation and the sound
> Symphonious of ten thousand Harps.
>
> (VII.557–59)

Such a triumph goes beyond the most "incomparable" of earthly renditions. The scope of the triumph extends to all heaven and earth, as the "Planets in thir station list'ning stood, / While the bright Pomp ascended jubiliant" (VII.563–64). The *Io triumphe* is replaced with greater Psalmic praise:

Open, ye everlasting Gates, they sung,
Open, ye Heav'ns, your living doors, let in
The great Creator from his work return'd
Magnificent.

(VII.565–68)



Christ returns to the Father, with "glorious Train ascending" (VII.574), exceeding all earthly models in a triumph that incorporates biblical and classical, heaven and earth.

Such triumphs look forward to an even greater eschatological triumph over evil. Captive kings in the triumphal procession are replaced with all of evil, as Christ prophesies that "I through the ample Air in Triumph high / Shall lead Hell Captive maugre Hell, and show / The powers of darkness bound" (III.254–56). The display includes the shamed body of his defeated foe in a final triumph:

Then to the Heav'n of Heav'ns he shall ascend
With victory, triumphing, through the air
Over his foes and thine; there shall surprise
The Serpent, Prince of air, and drag in Chains
Through all his Realm, and there confounded leave;
Then enter into glory.

(XII.451–56)

Here Christ excels the victorious Roman conqueror, the parody conquests of Satan, and all earthly imitations. *Paradise Lost*, for all its ultimate theological dependence upon "patience and heroic martyrdom," counters the displays of the Stuart state not by iconoclasm but by boldly revised counter-spectacle, including the grotesque body of the shamed and defeated foe.

Early responses to *Paradise Lost* recognized precisely the "overwhelmingness" or incomparability of Christ as conqueror—and of Milton as author. Andrew Marvell's tribute to the sublimity of *Paradise Lost* is well known:

Where couldst thou words of such a compass find?
Whence furnish such a vast expence of mind?
Just Heav'n thee like *Tiresias* to requite
Rewards with Prophesie thy loss of sight.

(*LR* 5:86)[33]

But even more focused on the overwhelming spectacle of triumph is Samuel Barrow's poem, which, like Marvell's, was placed as preface to the 1674 edition of *Paradise Lost:* "O what leaders in war he has brought forth! what arms! what songs he sings, and what dire battles on the trumpet! Celestial armies! and Heaven in conflict!" (*LR* 5:88). For Barrow, the Son's chariot overwhelms both the rebels and the reader:



> But at the same time the symbols of the Messiah gleam in the heavens; and the living chariots, the arms worthy of God, and the wheels grate terribly, and the raging lightnings of the wheels burst out in fierce flashes, and the flames quiver, and real thunders mixed with flames resounded in the hollow sky. . . . Yield, you Roman writers; yield, you Greeks, and those whom recent or ancient fame has celebrated. Whoever reads these lines will think that Homer sang only of frogs, Virgil only of fleas. (*LR* 5:88–89)

The incomparability of the poem specifically answers royalist panegyric and pageantry, challenging and replacing earthly display with divine.

## IV

IF IN *Paradise Lost* Milton rebukes the gaudy triumphs of earthly monarchy and imagines a purified divine mode, in his final two poems he more fully presents the dangers of the Roman conquest—and the vainglorious triumph on earth. In *Paradise Regained*, Rome is "great and glorious" (IV.45), characterized by its "Statues and Trophies, and Triumphal Arcs" (IV.37). But it is also characterized by the moral and political corruption of Tiberius and the servitude of its people. The emperor is "old, and lascivious, and from *Rome* retir'd" (IV.91); Rome is linked with sexual excess, tyranny, autocracy, and persecution.[34] It is in this context of false glittery display masking corruption that Satan offers to the Son Roman conquest.

Satan holds up Roman conquest principally as a means of gaining earthly admiration and glory, like Julius Caesar, who "the more he grew in years, the more inflam'd / With glory" (III.40–41). The Son's answer rebukes popular, earthly glory—"For what is glory but the blaze of fame, / The people's praise, if always praise unmixt?" (III.47–48)—and posits true glory as heavenly:

> This is true glory and renown, when God
> Looking on th'Earth, with approbation marks
> The just man, and divulges him through Heaven
> To all his Angels, who with true applause
> Recount his praises.
>
> (III.60–64)

In rejecting the earthly state "where glory is false glory" (III.69), the Son seems to rule out earthly conquest altogether:

> They err who count it glorious to subdue
> By Conquest far and wide, to overrun

> Large Countries, and in field great Battles win,
> Great Cities by assault.
>
> (III.71–74)

Such conquest leads to the vainglory and even idolatry of triumph, as the conquerors "swell with pride, and must be titl'd Gods, / Great Benefactors of mankind, Deliverers, / Worship't with Temple, Priest and Sacrifice" (III.81–83).





But, as in the earlier epic, the Son rejects the false only to gain true conquest, triumph, and glory.[35] "Victory and Triumph" (I.173) come to the Son of God for his private, emotional, spiritual triumph—without audience, without the cheering crowds, without record. At the end of *Paradise Regained*, Satan brings to his crew "Joyless triumphals of his hop't success" (IV.578) and holds "in Hell / No triumph" (IV.623–24). The conquest is won by words and will, not weapons; and the glory comes not with lavish display or admiring crowds but from an angelic hymn before the Son simply goes home: "Hail Son of the most High, heir of both worlds, / Queller of Satan, on thy glorious work / Now enter, and begin to save mankind" (IV.633–35). *Paradise Regained* not only rebukes but also reconstitutes the Roman triumph.

Although *Samson Agonistes*, the companion poem to *Paradise Regained*, depicts a literal overthrow of a Philistine triumph, its relation to the Roman mode is similarly complex. As Nicholas Jose has compellingly argued, Milton's Philistines are remarkably Roman in their triumph over Samson.[36] Samson is "thir Captive, and thir triumph" (426); their celebration of Dagon over the conquest of Samson takes place in an arched temple complete with "Sacrifices, Triumph, Pomp, and Games" (1312) and resembling nothing so much as a Roman triumph. Both Dalila and Harapha are concerned with earthly glory, Dalila claiming to have been persuaded "how glorious [it was] to entrap / A common enemy" (855–56) and Harapha regretting that he was not able to fight Samson: "So had the glory of Prowess been recover'd / To *Palestine*, won by a *Philistine* / From the unforeskinn'd race" (1098–1100).

Yet the Israelites too are concerned with glory, and, in the end, oddly Romanized. Much of their reaction to Samson's fallen state laments the loss of Samson's and their own glory. To the Chorus, Samson represents an incomparable turn of fortune's wheel: "By how much from the top of wondrous glory, / Strongest of mortal men, / To lowest pitch of abject fortune thou art fall'n" (167–69). For the Chorus Samson is "the glory late of *Israel*, now the grief" (179). While they recognize that Samson was elected to achieve "some great work, [God's] glory" (680), they do so only while protesting his degradation: "So deal not with this once thy glorious Champion, / The Image of thy strength, and mighty minister" (705–6). The

Chorus recognizes divine glory but nonetheless continually slips back into concern with Samson's or their own glory or shame.





Manoa too focuses not on divine but on his own and Samson's glory. He asks the Chorus to point out "your once gloried friend, / My Son now captive" (334–35) and laments how, "Glorious for a while" (363), Samson has now become his "Foes' derision" (366). Manoa believes that God "will not long defer / To vindicate the glory of his name / Against all competition" (474–76). Yet that God has been "Disglorified, blasphem'd, and had in scorn / By th' Idolatrous rout amidst thir wine" (442–43) distresses Manoa primarily as it reflects badly upon his own family:

> Which to have come to pass by means of thee,
> *Samson*, of all thy sufferings think the heaviest,
> Of all reproach the most with shame that ever
> Could have befall'n thee and thy Father's house.
> (444–47)

Manoa remains, even more than the Chorus, focused on the shame brought not to God but to himself.

Samson likewise vacillates between concern for divine glory and his own. Initially focused on his own shame, as we saw in chapter 2, he later insists that God's dishonor is "my chief affliction, shame, and sorrow" (457) and asserts his faith in a divine conquest:

> He, be sure,
> Will not connive, or linger, thus provok'd,
> But will arise and his great name assert:
> *Dagon* must stoop, and shall ere long receive
> Such a discomfit, as shall quite despoil him
> Of all these boasted Trophies won on me,
> And with confusion blank his Worshippers.
> (465–71)

But, paradoxically, Samson's faith in God as a kind of Roman conqueror who can take care of himself drives him to near despair and desire for death: "My race of glory run, and race of shame, / And I shall shortly be with them that rest" (597–98).

Samson's own ambiguous state of mind does not alter the conquest that the God of Israel gains over his enemies at the end of *Samson Agonistes*. But the Chorus and Manoa, perhaps like Milton's own countrymen, give to the human conqueror the praise that belongs to the divine. The Chorus wishes as Samson goes off that he might go "to what may serve [God's] glory best" (1429). But after the catastrophe they focus on the human glory. Manoa wants to know "what glorious hand gave *Samson* his death's wound?" (1581). And the Chorus sees a spectacle of personal revenge:

> O dearly bought revenge, yet glorious!
> Living or dying thou hast fulfill'd
> The work for which thou wast foretold
> To *Israel*.
>
> (1660–63)



While the Chorus recognizes that God "to his faithful Champion hath in place / Bore witness gloriously" (1751–52), the glory remains largely Samson's. The Chorus misplaces the glory from divine to human, and they fail to see the suffering and repentance that distinguishes Samson from a simple figure of martial conqueror. Their focus remains on earthly glory. Indeed, the monument for Samson that Manoa envisions with "Laurel ever green, and branching Palm, / With all his Trophies hung, and Acts enroll'd / In copious Legend, or sweet Lyric Song" (1735–37) is characteristically Roman. Manoa and the Chorus provide an ironic commentary on the Romanizing tendencies of even the chosen people of Israel—or of England.

## V

MILTON's uses of the Roman triumph in his Restoration poetry reflect the complexities and ambiguities of a mode used to praise and attack not only the Stuart kings but Oliver Cromwell himself. We looked briefly at Restoration uses of the Roman conqueror to attack Cromwell as tyrant. But it is important to recognize that Cromwell too was praised in the Roman mode. Significantly, Cromwell did not present himself as Roman conqueror, but rather attributed his martial victories to divine providence and God's glory.[37] But the figure of Augustus Caesar might have seemed particularly apt for Cromwell, who helped ensure peace after civil war and gained his power through military prowess. While Cromwell's initial victories were over incongruous foes—Charles I and the English people—his victories in Ireland and Scotland could be used to praise him as Roman conqueror. The iconography of Cromwell in the 1650s was predominately martial, perhaps for the obvious reason that he did not take the crown and could not be represented on the throne. An engraving by W. Faithorne (Fig. 15) shows a heroic Cromwell ("Olivarius Britannicus Heros") in complete armor atop a rearing horse. An expansive battle scene fills the background. Portraits of Cromwell show him as a martial, even Roman, figure.

Yet Cromwellian panegyric in the 1650s tried to project a new kind of triumph, not only Christianizing the Roman triumph, but developing a

FIGURE 15 Cromwell on horseback, in full armor, with battle in background (1656). *By permission of the Houghton Library, Harvard University.*

kind of republican mode against royalist models. In Marvell's *Ode*, Cromwell assumes the part of Roman conqueror, first ambiguously in relation to Charles I, when "*Caesars* head at last / Did through his Laurels blast," and then more clearly in relation to foreign foes:

> A *Caesar* he ere long to *Gaul*,
> To *Italy* an *Hannibal*,
> And to all States not free
> Shall *Clymacterick* be.[38]

But for Marvell, Cromwell's triumph is evinced not in gaudy display but in enhancing the Commonwealth, as he "forbears / His fame to make it theirs." For Thomas Sprat, Cromwell was not self-seeking in triumph: "Others by thee did great things do, / Triumph'st thy self, and mad'st them triumph too."[39] Payne Fisher's *Veni, Vidi, Vici* (1652) depicts Cromwell's victories over the Irish and the Scots as in themselves an incomparable triumph: "Cast your eyes then upon our conducting General, whose heroick acts (exceeding even the utmost limits of belief) to the present age proclaime their own triumph, and amaze succeeding generations with their greatness."[40]

Yet Cromwellian panegyric discloses anxiety by the very traits it praises. Hence Thomas Sprat's *To the Happie Memory of the Most Renowned Prince* (1659): "Thou fought'st not to be high or great, / Not for a Scepter or a Crown, / Or, Ermyne, Purple, or the Throne."[41] While asserting that "We can no less than Romane *Trophies* glory; / Admire our *Cromwell*," *Veni, Vidi, Vici* nonetheless praises Cromwell for not seeking praise:

> Blest *Hero*, whose uprightness all commands,
> Whose joy in vertue more than triumph stands,
> Thou scorn'st the people's suffrage, or their praise,
> Those airy cracks cannot thy *Trophies* raise.[42]

Cromwell allegedly does not seek the earthly glory that was the end of the Roman triumph.

Milton's 1652 sonnet, "To the Lord General Cromwell," works to keep the focus on divine providence and divine glory, away from the vainglorious display.

> Cromwell, our chief of men, who through a cloud
> Not of war only, but detractions rude,
> Guided by faith and matchless Fortitude,
> To peace and truth thy glorious way hast plough'd,
> And on the neck of crowned Fortune proud
> Hast rear'd God's Trophies and his work pursu'd,

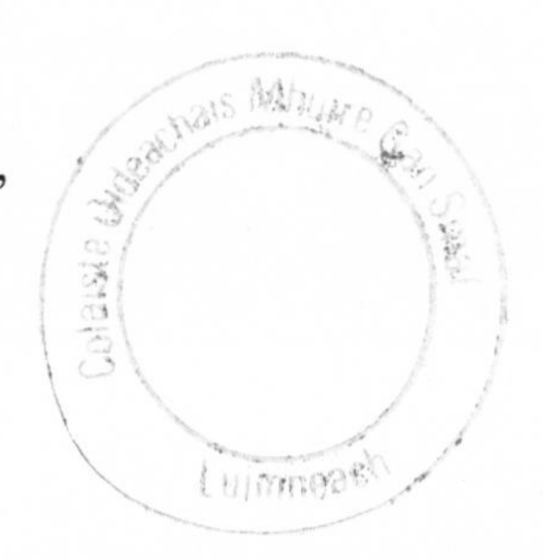

While Darwen stream with blood of Scots imbru'd,
And *Dunbar* field resounds thy praises loud,
And *Worcester's* laureate wreath.[43]

Milton's sonnet shows both the power and the equivocations of the figure of Roman conqueror. In relation to Marvell's *Ode*, the absence of visual spectacle is striking. It is difficult to visualize either Cromwell, who is represented in terms of his faith and fortitude, or his opponents, who appear as "crowned fortune" or in the fields or stream "with blood of Scots imbru'd." The sonnet transforms the Roman triumph—the admiring crowds, the lavish display of the conqueror—into a spiritual conquest that images the divine.



But Milton sees the conquest by force as incomplete: "yet much remains / To conquer still; peace hath her victories / No less renown'd than war."[44] Tension remains between Cromwell's activism and the providential mode.[45] Although Milton's Cromwell acts not out of personal ambition but to rear "God's Trophies" and "his work" pursue, the praise nonetheless goes to Cromwell himself, whose way is "glorious." In his *Second Defense*, Milton further qualifies the figure of Roman conqueror, commending Cromwell in that "Commander first over himself, victor over himself, he had learned to achieve over himself the most effective triumph, and so, on the very first day that he took service against an external foe, he entered camp a veteran" (*CPW* 4:668).

The tensions within the Roman mode when applied to Cromwell (as with Charles II) made it available for attack as well as praise, and in 1661, the exhuming seemed to Cromwell's enemies a fitting anti-triumph for a false and tyrannical ruler. *Short Meditations on . . . the Life and Death of Oliver Cromwell* (1661) traces Cromwell's rise to power as the ambitious maneuvering of a Caesar: "The Generalissimoship soon procured to be conferred on him, then had he liberty and opportunity like *Caesar* from a General to be made an Emperor." Cromwell's tyrannical rise to power, according to this tract, appropriately ends with the anti-triumph of Tyburn: "But the Corps of him whose aspiring minde could never be satisfied hath now no other Tombe but a Turf under *Tyburn*, and no other Trophie but the Situation of the common place of Execution circumfering him, *So let all the Kings Enemies perish O God.*"[46]

The iconography of the disinterment also undermined Cromwell as martial figure. A 1661 portrait (Fig. 16) shows Cromwell in armor and holding a truncheon, framed by a shrouded corpse (presumably his own) hanging from the gallows and by three severed heads (his own and those of Ireton and Bradshaw) atop Westminster. Below is Cromwell's coat of arms and the less than honorific title, "Oliverus Cromwell, Rex Independentium, Angliae Tyrannus." Cromwell's tyranny is allegedly answered in

FIGURE 16 Portrait of Cromwell in armor, his hanging body and decollated head in background (1661). *By permission of the Trustees of the British Museum.*

the anti-triumph of Tyburn. The conqueror is no longer glorious but shamed and degraded. Hence, in *Justa Sive Inferiae Regicidarum or Tyburn's Revels* (1661), Cromwell welcomes the sledge as a Roman chariot and the gibbet as a crown:

> Imagination prompt'd me to be King,
> 'Tis easie work, I have it in a string.
> Here's a triumphant Chariot without wheels,
> Not subject to mad Fortune's giddy reels,
> And here's three standing Crowns, whose massy weight
> Will break the neck to this curst politick pate.[47]

To some, perhaps many, of Milton's contemporaries, Cromwell was a tyrant whose false vainglories were fittingly answered in the "triumphant Chariot" at Tyburn.

The ambivalences of the Roman mode in Milton's three major poems, often ignored or explained away in the interests of theological orthodoxy, reflect the ambivalences of the figure of Roman conqueror in Interregnum and Restoration England. The poems show not only Milton's distrust of the vainglorious Stuart kings, from whom he would have expected nothing better, but his disillusionment with the royalized Cromwell and the subservient people who had turned from God's glory to their own.

# *Paradise Regained* and Venner's Uprising

> A thing that never was heard of, that so few men should dare and do so much mischief. Their word was, "King Jesus, and the heads upon the gates." Few of them would receive any Quarter, but such as were taken by force and kept alive; expecting Jesus to come here and reign in the world presently, and will not believe yet but their work will be carried on, though they do die.
>
> Pepys, *Diary* 2:10–11

THE SPECTACLES of state, both the celebrations and the punishments we have been tracing, evoked perhaps the most memorable reaction not from the admiring crowds but from a radical sect of nonconformists who chose to differ forcefully. On January 9, 1661, a small group of fifth monarchists, led by wine vintner Thomas Venner and seeking revenge for the deaths of the regicides, rose up in arms.[1] Venner and his men apparently hoped to overthrow the current government, "to take down their Masters, those regicides quarters" from London Bridge, and to install the reign of the saints and King Jesus.[2] That Venner and his men were inspired by the very punishment designed to warn against treason underscored the need for a supplement to the spectacle. Indeed, government officials now responded with not only a new display of force but a significant shift from display to surveillance and discipline, from destruction of bodies to the production of speech. Widely publicized and displayed in print and (in pieces) on London Bridge, the spectacle of punishment enabled an official discourse of treason that was used to legitimate increasingly repressive measures against religious dissenters of all kinds.[3]

As it depicts the use of force as a Satanic strategy to which the Son of God does not succumb, Milton's *Paradise Regained* appears to support, or at least to complement, official discourse on fifth monarchism. But Milton's representation of the wilderness temptation is more complex and tenacious. *Paradise Regained* rebukes the use of force only to provide an alternative model for dissent, an internal discipline that answers and counters new government strategies of coercion and control.



## I

By the 1650s, the most militant and extreme millenarians in England had come to be known as fifth monarchists, distinguished primarily by their willingness to use force to bring about the kingdom of God and their precise specifications of the nature of this kingdom.[4] The fifth monarchy would follow the defeat of all earthly monarchy and lead to the reign of Christ himself on earth. An unsympathetic contemporary, Quaker George Fox, disparages the fifth monarchy men "whoe lookt for Christ's personall comeinge in [16]66: & some of them did prepare themselves when it thundered & rained & thought Christ was comeinge to sett uppe his kingedome."[5] Fifth monarchists attempted to ascertain the precise time of Christ's kingdom, as Ephraim Paggitt reports in his *Heresiography* (1662): "Months, weeks, daies, and half-times, and such like Chronology alwaies past away their mad hours of meeting and then they departed home as full of rancour against Magistry, as if they were set apart to that Diabolical work and went thither on purpose to recruit their venome."[6] Paggitt goes on to point to the central biblical texts on which such radical eschatology was based: "The Prophesies of Daniel, the book of Revelations, and their most abstruse and difficult texts were the common Theams & subject of their inspired, or rather possessed brains."[7]

In the obscure prophecies of Daniel and Revelation, then, the fifth monarchists (like other, less extreme, millenarians) found symbols of the earthly monarchies that must be defeated for Christ to begin his reign, legitimating immediate violent action. One crucial text is the prophecy of the stone in Daniel:

> Thou, o king, sawest, and behold a great image. . . . This image's head was of fine gold, his breast and his arms of silver, his belly and his thighs of brass. His legs of iron, his feet part of iron and part of clay. Thou sawest till that a stone was cut out without hands, which smote the image upon his feet that were of iron and clay, and brake them to pieces . . . and the stone that smote the image became a great mountain, and filled the whole earth. (Daniel 2.31–35)

Gold, silver, iron, and clay were interpreted as the four world monarchies that Christ's kingdom would ultimately succeed. For the fifth monarchists, this was a kingdom to be brought in by the saints' own use of force. William Aspinwall in *A Brief Description of the Fifth Monarchy* (1653) paraphrases Daniel in insisting on a kingdom gained by force: "This new Monarchy or stone cut out of the Mountaine without hands, shall crush and break in pieces all the other four Monarchies, *Dan* 2.34.45. which is inconsistent with Church-power."[8] The kingdom is to be brought not by faith alone but by the sword.





At the time of the regicide, millenarian fervor was widespread and many at first saw the prophecies of Daniel fulfilled in the execution of Charles I. Fifth monarchists and others identified Charles I with the little horn on the fourth beast and believed that the ensuing reign of the saints was about to usher in the reign of King Jesus. According to Aspinwall: "It is said, *That judgment was given to the saints, and they executed judgment on the little horne*, Dan. 7.22.26. which was fulfilled 1648."[9] Although Milton did not identify with the extreme millenarians and fifth monarchists in their belief that the virtues necessary for government were found only in a regenerate minority of saints, he did employ eschatological prophecies in his defense of the regicide in *Eikonoklastes*: "*To bind thir Kings in Chaines, and thir Nobles with links of Iron*, is an honour belonging to his Saints; not to build *Babel* . . . but to destroy it, especially that spiritual *Babel;* and first to overcome those European Kings, which receive thir power, not from God, but from the beast; and are counted no better then his ten hornes" (*CPW* 3:598).[10]

Fifth monarchists reached the height of their power in 1653 at the time of the Barebones or Nominated Parliament under Cromwell; but this Parliament proving ineffectual, it was soon dissolved and replaced by a Protectorate that for the disillusioned saints resembled, once again, Daniel's beasts. In 1657, Thomas Venner and his men planned an uprising against the apostate Oliver Cromwell.[11] Thwarted and imprisoned for a time, Venner upon his release immediately returned to plotting, now against the newly restored Charles Stuart.

On January 9, 1661, Venner and his men armed themselves with muskets, blunderbusses, pistols, and armor and set about bringing in the kingdom. Setting up their sentry outside St. Paul's, these men challenged the passersby to say who they were for. When one passerby was unlucky enough to reply that he was for King Charles, Venner's men responded that they were for King Jesus, underscoring the point by shooting him dead. This action brought out the city's citizen militia, and the Lord Mayor himself with his troops. Pepys awakened on January 9 to find "people running up and down in Mr. Davis's house, talking that the Fanatiques were up in armes in the City"; in the streets he found "everybody in arms at the doors . . . the streets full of traine bands, and great stories what mischief these rogues have done" (*Diary* 2:9). Eventually even General Monck and the Duke of York arrived with an entire regiment of troops and horse. The fifth monarchy men, numbering probably no more than forty, nonetheless managed to terrorize London for three days, retiring at night to a nearby wood and charging into the city in broad daylight. Their numbers were greatly overestimated and exaggerated, Pepys reporting that they were thought to be "at least 500." The rebels surrendered only after they had killed about a dozen men, and most of them had been killed or seriously wounded, leading Pepys to conclude: "A thing that never was heard of, that so few men should dare and do so much mischief" (*Diary* 2:10).

Even by seventeenth-century standards, Venner was a lunatic. But his uprising provided the government with an opportunity to link political subversion with religious enthusiasm. Disingenuously or not, the civic authorities both greatly overestimated Venner's force and continued to "discover" new plots throughout the 1660s and 1670s, strengthening the case for enforcement of religious conformity.[12] Seen by its participants as a fulfillment of scriptural prophecy, the uprising looked to the government like just plain treason, the seeds of which allegedly lay in freedom of conscience and the right to worship outside the Church of England.

In *A Door of Hope* (1661), Venner explained and tried to justify his rebellion by drawing on such characteristic millenarian themes as the fulfillment of the Daniel prophecies. *A Door of Hope* asserts that Charles II is the latest example of the ungodly monarchies, stemming from Nimrod and running through "the *Assyrian*, *Persian*, *Grecian*, and *Roman* Monarchies." Venner and his men identify themselves with the stone of Daniel 2, "called of God, and *cut out without hands*" to rise up on God's behalf against the self-styled Roman rule of the Stuart monarchs.[13] In chapter 4 we explored the Romanizing of the restored monarchy in detail, but it is worth noting here that the monarchy's own mode of self-representation made it vulnerable to the deployment of biblical prophecy on the demise of worldly (in this case Roman) empire. That the king had been widely praised as a new Augustus and his return represented as a Roman triumph ironically fitted the restored regime into the empire threatened by biblical prophecies.

The immediate government response to Venner's uprising was a public trial and execution, a display of treason much like the punishment of the regicides. And again the accused refused to confess to the crime. Indicted for murder and treason, Venner gave "an extravagant and bottomless discourse about the fifth monarchy" and declared his innocence on the grounds that "twas not he, but Jesus led them."[14] Even in the process of being hanged, drawn, and quartered, Venner and his chief accomplice, Hodgkins, used the public forum to justify their cause. Clarendon writes that "at their deaths (there being ten or a dozen executed) [they did not] make the least show of sorrow for what they had attempted."[15]

*The Last Speech and Prayer, with other passages of Thomas Venner* (1661), modelled upon *The Speeches and Prayers* of the earlier regicides, shows Venner's resistance to the display of justice, although it does not make him a martyr. Urged to confess his "great fault and wickedness," Venner responds, "There must be conviction before there can be confession, which I cannot find in my own conscience."[16] On the ladder, with the rope about his neck, Venner affirms his cause: "What I did was from the Word of the Lord, you ought to believe that the *Fourth Monarchy* is come, and that it is the duty of the people of God to looke for liberty" (5). His final prayer is strikingly lucid, considering the demonization to ensue: "Oh Good Lord; I am coming to thee; Oh Lord, forgive me; Oh Lord, comfort me; into thy hands Oh Lord I commit my spirit: at which words he was turned off the Ladder, and having hang'd the space of a quarter of an hour, he was cut down and quartered according to his Sentence" (8). Venner's words of faith contest and undercut the spectacle of treason.



As with the regicides, the government displayed the bodies (or body parts) of Venner and Hodgkins, who alone received the full sentence of hanging, drawing, and quartering. The punishments of Venner and Hodgkins preceded those of the others, as Peter Mundy reports: "Eleven heads were set on London Bridge, soe that at present there were twenty one heads stuck on poles and set over the gate that leadeth unto Southwarcke: the quarters of Venner and Hoskins distributed over other gates" (*Travels*, 130).

Yet there were crucial differences in this crime and punishment, when set alongside that of the regicides. Venner was not made a martyr, but rather was universally denounced in lavish and extravagant terms by both civil authorities and other dissenters wishing to distance themselves from his violence. Venner's treason was not simply displayed, but used to justify the institution of searches, seizures, imprisonment, and the banning of nonconformist meetings. Civic officials circulated both the crime and punishment, making visible the threat of nonconformity as sedition. Venner became part of a broader discourse legitimating more pervasive if less violent measures of government control.

Printed accounts were supplemented by illustrations of a fully armed, threatening Venner. One portrait (Fig. 17) shows Venner in armor and wearing a helmet; in one hand is a halberd, in the other a book inscribed *Biblia in Manu Et Diabolum in Corde*. The left of the picture indicates Venner's hypocrisy with the words *Pietas et Paupertas Simulata*. On the right, at an angle, another print is imposed on the portrait, depicting a nonconformist meeting, *Conventicula Curiosa*, the fanaticism of which is shown by a woman dancing naked before the congregation of men and women. The more threatening the images of Venner that circulated, the more pressing the need for religious conformity.

The spectacle of punishment was thus supplemented by official dis-

Figure 17 Portrait of fifth monarchist Thomas Venner in battle dress (1661). *By permission of the Trustees of the British Museum.*

courses that magnified the threat of the uprising and the providential deliverance. And indeed, the threat had to be magnified given that only two dozen or so men were involved. *Londons Glory, Or, The Riot and Ruine of the Fifth Monarchy Men* describes the uprising as "the grand and notorious piece of impudence in an Act of horrid and Malitious treason against our Soveraign Lord the King and Kingdom, far surpassing the Gunpowder-treason, or Oliver the late usurping Tyrant, or red Dragon."[17] *The Last Farewel to the Rebellious Crew of Fifth Monarchy Men* labels the event "the Barbarest insurrection that ever hapned in any Kings Government . . . the Greatest peece of impudence and grandest plot of treachery." As such, the perpetrators will be made a spectacle of punishment for present and future: "Lets leave them to the stash of the greatest stripes of punishments that [are] due for the reward of such unparalleled, rebellious, and notorious Traytors, that after ages may heare the story, and lay it as a pattern or sad spectacle before their eyes to take warning by."[18]





Other accounts insisted upon a widespread conspiracy. *An Advertisment as touching the Fanaticks late Conspiracy* claims that the fact that "they rose up (as you say) in several places of the City at once, signes a grand Conspiracy. But that they did so once and again, and upon several dayes too, demonstrates a grand Confederation and abetment."[19] The Venetian ambassador comments that "every one blesses the mercy of God for this miraculous escape as if these rascals had had their way the scene would have been terrible and no one would have escaped unhurt from their sacrilegious hands" (*CSPV* 32:240).

For many the violence pointed directly to the dangers of freedom of conscience. *Mercurius Publicus* insists that the "Rebellious Insurrection of the bloody Phanaticks in *London*" who were preparing "to murther us in our Beds" was part of a broader-based conspiracy: "the same bad Spirit . . . hath led these wild Sects all over *England*, since the Hedge was broken down (the Government of the Church) and multitudes of Religions as well as of men were swarming among us."[20] Liberty of conscience and religious toleration ultimately and perhaps inevitably result, according to this account, in rebels who "blaspheme the Son of God, by cutting our throats in the name of King Jesus" (17).

Opponents to toleration, then, had a vested interest in publicizing the very treasonous words they ostensibly aimed to suppress. Venner's words no doubt had more circulation in excerpts quoted by his opponents than in the original tract. The effect, if not the intent, of the tracts denouncing Venner was to display his words, much as his body was displayed, as a dire threat and warning. These tracts published the very treason they opposed so that all could see, as *An Impartial Narrative of the Late Rebellious Insurrection* puts it, that "though their number (thanks be to God) be very small, yet their malice and blood thirstiness is not easie to be equalled."[21] Having published the threat, *An Impartial Narrative* can then go on to urge its readers to "confess his Majesty the most merciful Prince in the world to afford these bold Hypocrites such Liberty for their pretensions of having *Tender Consciences;* and they the most ingrateful Rebels under Heaven for so monstrously abusing His Clemencie to destroy him and all his good Subjects" (19).



While Venner undeniably plotted and attempted a rebellion against the government, the official responses magnified the numbers involved far beyond the original uprising. The news of the uprising was quickly followed by a royal proclamation prohibiting unauthorized meetings and directing the militia to search houses and arrest suspicious persons. *An Impartial Narrative* asserts that the king has been forced, "these destructive Rebels having drawn it from Him" to set forth a proclamation "*Prohibiting all unlawful and seditious meetings, and Conventicles under pretence of Religious worship*" (26). Such meetings were seen as politically dangerous, as Baptists, Quakers, and fifth-monarchy men "under pretence of serving God do dayly meet in secret places at unusual times, having thereby frequent opportunities of a perfect correspondencie and confederacie, of which some evil effects have already ensued to the disturbance of the publique-Peace by Insurrection and Murther, and far worse may be still expected" (26).

What is striking here is that not only fifth monarchists but other dissenters—Congregationalists, Baptists, Quakers—came under suspicion. Persons assembling unlawfully, that is, attempting to worship God outside of the established church, were now subject to arrest; mayors, sheriffs, and constables were ordered to search all places where such meetings were suspected, arresting the inhabitants and forcing them to take the Oath of Allegiance. All nonconformists were linked with the fifth monarchists as politically dangerous, even treasonous. The Venetian ambassador comments that "since this [uprising] more strict visitation has been made and continues in all the houses of the reputed sectaries, arms being taken away and everything else likely to encourage the animosity they feel against the present government, which is now considering measures to prevent similar disorders" (*CSPV* 32:240).

Other nonconformists tried unsuccessfully to distance themselves from Venner. A number of prominent Congregationalist ministers, for instance, joined in denouncing the rebellion, which, they insisted, had been "falsely and most uncharitably charged on those (at least as the favorers of it) whom some will needs stile the Independent Party, [and] We therefore hold our selves Necessitated to make this true and sincere *Renuntiation* of and *Protestation* against so horrid a *Fact*, and *Principle* they were acted by, as both highly *Derogatory to Christ* and most *Pernitious to his Saints.*"[22] Baptists sent petitions to the king denying connections with Venner and protesting against the searches, seizures of goods, and imprisonment they were undergoing.[23] The Quaker response was exemplified by Thomas Ellwood's reference to "that mad prank of those infatuated fifth-monarchy men."[24] George Fox and other prominent Quakers condemned the use of physical force in a joint declaration.[25] But Philip Henry, soon to be ejected as a Presbyterian minister, rightly worried that Venner's uprising "may give occasion to those that seek occasion to restrayn our libertyes hitherto indulg'd."[26]



The uprising was thus used to group together and blacken various and differing sects. *An Advertisment* is typical in dismissing as pure hypocrisy the declarations of Baptists, Congregationalists, Quakers, and others who, professing loyalty to the monarchy, had denounced Venner's uprising: "Every wise man will read there, their combined multiplicity, confident audacity, and adjured secresy, palliated hypocrisy; the old way of deceiving the People save that it comes too soon upon them to rub a fresh sore, and lay a Trap before an open eye" (5). This tract argues that the suppressing of private meetings is wholly justified: "As for the *Suppressing of their private Meetings (wherein these things were first hatcht)* I shall rejoyce for the after prudence, as a lesse fear of evill; but, I should have been gladder of a former, for that had not only prevented such evill, but procured much good both to this Church and State" (5). Divine providence must be aided by active prevention and warning: "I do not mislike your charitable opinion, to hope that the rest of this furious Sect will be warned from their Fanatick principles, in a detestation of this their damnable exploit: Yet I must tell you, Conversion is only by the grace and mercy of God, but prevention must be by the prudence and justice of men" (5–6).

Venner's uprising marked the display of the executed regicides as a site of struggle that could generate defiance as well as consent. But this threat became, paradoxically, a means by which civil and ecclesiastical authorities extended their domain. In 1660, early negotiations for a religious settlement had held out some hope for the Presbyterians and even for more radical nonconformists; the king himself seemed tolerant and conciliatory toward religious dissent, if only to alleviate the burdens placed on loyal Roman Catholics. But Charles's gestures of toleration through the 1660s and 1670s were invariably countered by Parliamentary restrictions. Religious dissent was widely viewed as linked with political disorder and subversion; and in this linkage the spectacle of punishment and the deployment of treason were crucial tools.

The pattern of repression seen in the responses to Venner's uprising continued throughout the 1660s and 1670s.[27] In 1662, Parliament reimposed the Book of Common Prayer through the Act of Uniformity, resulting in the ejection of nearly two thousand ministers. In 1664, the Conventicle Act struck at the rank and file of nonconformity, making religious meetings illegal if more than five persons other than members of the household were present. A second Conventicle Act in 1670 significantly increased both the penalties for offenders and the financial rewards for informers. The culmination of uniformity was the Test Act of 1673, which required all holders of civil and military office to receive the sacrament according to the Anglican rite and to declare their disbelief in transubstantiation. Such measures filled the jails with nonconformist preachers who refused to be silenced. The Quakers, who refused to take any oaths, were also a particular target. If the spectacles of punishment, then, were relatively few in the 1660s, civil and ecclesiastical authorities soon moved to other, more extensive means of shaping the minds and consciences of the people.



## II

IN MILTON'S *Paradise Regained*, as Satan presents the kingdoms of the world, the Son of God must resist political shortcuts and the use of force, and must ascertain the true nature of his kingship and kingdom in a world in which Israel and the Roman people themselves are oppressed under tyranny, unable to speak freely, stigmatized and persecuted. The historical setting of *Paradise Regained*—Israel under the rule of the Emperor Tiberius—would have had particular force in the Romanized England of the 1660s and 1670s. The poem's central concerns with the nature and meaning of Christ's kingdom recall and comment upon the past and present concerns of the defeated republicans who had fought and hoped for the kingdom of God on earth.

One central issue in recent criticism of *Paradise Regained* regards the extent to which the work is quietist, representing a rejection of military force by a disillusioned revolutionary. Andrew Milner argues that the Son's rejections of Satan's political offers reflect Milton's own advocacy of temporary quietism in face of the collapse of the Commonwealth.[28] Michael Wilding also argues for quietism: "After the failure of the Good Old Cause and the re-establishment of the Stuart monarchy, Christ's kingdom was no longer seen by most of the Puritan sects as a military, political objective of this world, but as a moral objective of the spirit. . . . In *Paradise Regained* Milton explores this new spiritual paradise, this quietist rejection of the world, of earthly kingdoms gained by military means."[29] Joan Bennett objects to the quietist label, arguing that the poem posits a more activist renewal of individual liberty.[30] Although Christopher Hill sees the Son as rejecting contemporary politics in *Paradise Regained*, he likewise argues that "this is not a quietist doctrine. The kingdom of Christ is a kingdom of preaching, and its ultimate object is 'to conquer and crush his enemies.'"[31]

The relationship between *Paradise Regained* and fifth monarchy in general has not been unnoticed. Michael Fixler, in *Milton and the Kingdoms of God*, perceptively argues that *Paradise Regained* exposes mistaken Jewish messianism particularly as linked with contemporary apocalyptic materialism. According to Fixler, "Milton found in the delusions of his own time historical evidence that the kingdom of Christ could still be so misunderstood."[32] In Fixler's view, however, the brief epic rather straightforwardly rebukes fifth monarchist aspirations for a kingdom on earth. Although I agree with Fixler that millenarianism, and particularly the fifth monarchists, are central to *Paradise Regained*, I would argue that the poem shows a more complex and politically volatile response. *Paradise Regained* shows that the use of military force to (re)gain the kingdom is mistaken, even Satanically deluded. But Milton at the same time revises and redeploys the prophecies of Daniel and Revelation integral to millenarianism. This revision is not quietist but polemical; Milton's *Paradise Regained* provides a model by which the saints can internalize their warfare, can turn to new weapons in a spiritual battle that is nonetheless directed toward a similar goal, to vindicate King Jesus and the heads upon the gates.



From its opening lines, *Paradise Regained* focuses on expectations of the coming kingdom, as the narrator recalls the prophecy of John the Baptist:

> Now had the great Proclaimer with a voice
> More awful than the sound of Trumpet, cried
> Repentance, and Heaven's Kingdom nigh at hand
> To all Baptiz'd.
>
> (I.18–21)

Satan cannot recognize or assimilate the more spiritual meanings of prophetic signs, including the baptism of the Son, the descent of the Dove, and the heavenly voice that speaks. As Satan sees it, John the Baptist "pretends to wash off sin" (I.73), but actually intends to prepare the people to show the Son "honor as their King" (I.75). Similarly, he reads the "Sovran Voice" (I.84) that proclaims Jesus' sonship at his baptism as a sign that a monarchical God is about to promote his Son: "His Mother then is mortal, but his Sire, / Hee who obtains the Monarchy of Heav'n, / And what will he not do to advance his Son?" (I.86–88). Myopically concerned with earthly political power, Satan interprets the Son as a military Messiah, King Jesus about to commence his reign on earth:

> Ye see our danger on the utmost edge
> Of hazard, which admits no long debate,

But must with something sudden be oppos'd,
Not force, but well couch't fraud, well woven snares,
Ere in the head of Nations he appear
Their King, their Leader, and Supreme on Earth.
(I.94–99)



Significantly, it is Satan in Milton's poem who most fears and hopes to prevent the reign of King Jesus; fear of the military Messiah is itself a Satanic delusion.[33]

Milton's choice of a brief epic might lead the reader to expect, as does Satan, some kind of battle. By constructing the debate as a battle and placing it within the epic genre that typically treated battles, Milton is able to signal the difference between the physical force fifth monarchists such as Venner expected and the spiritual weapons of the Son's kingdom. And yet the genre signals as well that there is, nonetheless, conquest involved in this kingdom; the kingdom is not just a renunciation of force, but the implementing of a different mode of power (which may ultimately include force). God, like Satan, describes the Son's struggle with Sin and Death as his "great warfare" (I.158), and although his weapons, first developed in the wilderness temptation, will be "Humiliation and strong Sufferance" (I.160), he nonetheless will conquer: "His weakness shall o'ercome Satanic strength / And all the world, and mass of sinful flesh" (I.161–62).

The military means that appealed to the youthful Son are not so much rejected as supplanted by another kind of conquest. The Son thus explains that earlier:

victorious deeds
Flam'd in my heart, heroic acts; one while
To rescue *Israel* from the *Roman* yoke,
Then to subdue and quell o'er all the earth
Brute violence and proud Tyrannic pow'r,
Till truth were freed, and equity restor'd.
(I.215–20)

Given the predominantly Roman mode of the Restoration monarchy, the Son's words are particularly apt. And while the Son seems now to have rejected those means, he still speaks in terms of conquest: "Yet held it more humane, more heavenly, first / By winning words to conquer willing hearts, / And make persuasion do the work of fear" (I.221–23).

The disciples too expect a military Messiah who will restore the Kingdom: "Now, now, for sure, deliverance is at hand, / The Kingdom shall to *Israel* be restor'd" (II.35–36). These messianic expectations are, as Christopher Hill reminds us, the dreams of the English revolutionaries in the

1640s and 1650s—dreams, we might add, which are still flickering in Restoration England:[34]

> God of *Israel*,
> Send thy Messiah forth, the time is come;
> Behold the Kings of th'Earth how they oppress
> Thy chosen, to what height thir pow'r unjust
> They have exalted, and behind them cast
> All fear of thee; arise and vindicate
> Thy Glory, free thy people from thir yoke!
> (II.42–48)





But, of course, the disciples are disappointed; even though the kingdom is regained, they do not see it. While they expect a literal restoration, the kingdom to be conquered is the kingdom of the heart, to "make persuasion do the work of fear." *Paradise Regained* is about a different kind of restoration than that looked for by the revolutionaries in the 1640s and 1650s—or offered by Charles II in 1660. The fifth monarchists believed that they would free the kingdom by force from the Stuarts in 1649 and 1661. *Paradise Regained* significantly revises and yet reinstates that dream.

If the fifth monarchists, among others, drew on prophecies to justify immediate action, the first temptation in *Paradise Regained* shows the danger of literalizing prophecy and of acting precipitiously out of distrust in God's care for his chosen nation.[35] Satan attempts to get the Son to act before his time by perverting, first of all, his prophetic role, taking prophecies too literally. Satan tempts the Son to immediate action:

> But if thou be the Son of God, Command
> That out of these hard stones be made thee bread;
> So shalt thou save thyself and us relieve
> With Food, whereof we wretched seldom taste.
> (I.342–45)

Milton and others had used the figure of Israel in the wilderness as symbol of England in the civil war. Here the Son responds, alluding to God's care of Elijah and others, by rejecting the implied distrust: "Why dost thou then suggest to me distrust" (I.355). In the Son's denial of the ultimate efficacy of literal bread, the poem reproves those who look for the literal fulfillment of prophecy—or who distrust providence because of the external signs of seeming defeat.

Milton's choice of the temptation as the subject for regaining paradise enables him to present the earthly kingdoms as a temptation. To the gospel account Milton adds a significant component of military force: the most extended and elaborate of the temptations Satan offers the Son is that of the kingdoms of the world, immediate earthly power. Such power is strikingly and resonantly presented in terms of the Israelites' restoration and deliverance from their enemies, particularly from Rome. Satan attempts to get the Son to regain the throne of David, to free "*Judaea* now and all the promis'd land" (III.157), which "Reduc't a Province under Roman yoke, / Obeys *Tiberius*" (III.158–59), urging, "Zeal of thy Father's house, Duty to free / Thy Country from her Heathen servitude" (III.175–76).





Yet the kingdoms that Satan presents, a sonorous list of the ancient empires of Assyria, Babylon, Persia, and Greece, corresponds to what Renaissance commentators on Daniel—as well as the fifth monarchists—identified with Daniel's four monarchies or beasts.[36] And while the others show, in their splendor, luxury, violence, and decay, the beasts who "had their dominion taken away: yet their lives were prolonged for a season and time" (Dan. 7.12), Rome is flourishing. The worldly monarchies that threaten Israel are rapidly traversed by Satan: Nineveh and the Assyrian empire,

> built by *Ninus* old,
> Of that first golden Monarchy the seat,
> And seat of *Salmanassar*, whose success
> *Israel* in long captivity still mourns.
> (III.276–79)

Likewise, Satan surveys the Babylonian empire under Nebuchadnezzar:

> There *Babylon* the wonder of all tongues,
> As ancient, but rebuilt by him who twice
> *Judah* and all thy Father *David's* house
> Led captive and *Jerusalem* laid waste,
> Till *Cyrus* set them free.
> (III.280–84)

But the greater threat to God's chosen people is Rome: with Parthian might the Son can attain "Deliverance of thy brethren" (III.374), the ten lost tribes, "serving as of old / Thir Fathers in the land of *Egypt* serv'd" (III.378–79). Hence Satan urges:

> This offer sets before thee to deliver
> These if from servitude thou shalt restore
> To thir inheritance, then, nor till then,
> Thou on the Throne of *David* in full glory,
> From *Egypt* to *Euphrates* and beyond
> Shalt reign, and *Rome* or *Caesar* not need fear.
> (III.380–85)

From Satan's point of view, the chosen people are in literal bondage to Rome and need to be freed by force: the poem rewrites the fifth monarchist program as a Satanic temptation.

Several of the tracts that sought to demonize Venner and his followers had in fact drawn upon the wilderness temptation of Christ. John Clarke, in *The Plotters Unmasked, Murderers No Saints* (1661), writes: "Oh let not the Devil thus deceive you, by perswading you that you are Saints, and that you must rule the Kingdomes of the world and he must raign in you, and that you must come to it by breaking his Commands, by spilling of bloud, and robbing. What a snare hath the Devil got you into?"[37] Clarke goes to warn that they appear to have given in to the Devil's temptation: "You give just occasion to all to think, that the Devil hath given you a sight of the glory of the Kingdomes of the world, which hath tempted you to worship him, that you may obtain them, or else surely you would never shed blood to obtain them, and steal weapons to do it withal."[38] Similarly, *An Advertisment* argues that "if these kind of men were not so Satanically deluded, as indeed they are, they might plainly discerne that *Christs Kingdome* is not of this *World*, and therfore he neither calls, nor owns any such *Servants*, as shall adventure thus to fight for him, John. 18.36" (4).



Yet *Paradise Regained* is not a simple renunciation of force—past or present—against Rome or self-styled Roman conquerors. Force is renounced for the time being only because it is inappropriate and ineffectual. And this is so because the real threat to Israel is not any external empire but the Israelites themselves. Milton dramatically rereads the gospel temptation in this respect. While in the gospel accounts, the kingdoms are to be rejected because they are earthly and accepting them would be to accept power from Satan, here they are offered as a means for restoring Israel and rejected because the Israelites do not deserve to be restored. Such a position is a dramatic politicized redaction that implicitly rejects the fifth monarchists' use of force and yet does not condone in any way the existing regime.

The captive tribes, the Son insists, have "wrought their own captivity" (III.415) by falling away from God to worship idols and heathen deities and do not deserve freedom:

> Should I of these the liberty regard,
> Who freed, as to their ancient Patrimony,
> Unhumbl'd, unrepentant, unreform'd,
> Headlong would follow, and to thir Gods perhaps
> Of *Bethel* and of *Dan?* No, let them serve
> Thir enemies, who serve Idols with God.
>
> (III.427–32)

If the interpretation of Israel is paradigmatic of the chosen nation, the royalists in England have not so much triumphed as the republicans have enslaved themselves.

For this view of Israel, Milton had considerable Old Testament warrant. The Book of Kings continually ascribes the external defeats of the Israelites to their own apostasy. Hence, the defeat by the Assyrians comes because of Israel's covenant violation: "For *so* it was, that the children of Israel had sinned against the Lord their God, which had brought them up out of the land of Egypt, from under the hand of Pharaoh king of Egypt, and had feared other gods" (2 Kings 17.7). The destruction of Jerusalem by Nebuchadnezzar is likewise attributed to covenant violation, to the apostasy and evil of Israel under Manasseh so that God forsakes even the remnant: "And I will forsake the remnant of mine inheritance, and deliver them into the hand of their enemies; and they shall become a prey and a spoil to all their enemies" (2 Kings 21.14). The real threat to the chosen people is not their external enemies but their own apostasy. External subjugation or loss of liberty reflects internal.

Such a reading of Israel in subjection under Rome clearly points to other chosen nations under bondage to other self-styled Roman conquerors. It is also a self-validating mode of explaining the failure while at the same time continuing to justify the Good Old Cause. Milton's Son of God, as we have seen in chapter 1, is not the Christ of the passion, nor a clear exemplar of divine love. He speaks, rather, with the harsh and judgmental tones of the Old Testament prophets, with the voice of Jeremiah that Milton had himself assumed in *The Readie and Easie Way.* There Milton had drawn an explicit analogy between England poised on the verge of restoring the Stuart monarchy and Israel at her point of greatest crisis, just before the Jews actually returned to Egypt, forcing the old prophet to go with them to the land where he would die: "If, lastly, after all this light among us, the same reason shall pass for current to put our necks again under kingship, as was made use of by the *Jews* to return back to *Egypt* and to the worship of their idol queen, because they falsly imagind that they then livd in more plentie and prosperitie, our condition is not sound but rotten, both in religion and all civil prudence" (*CPW* 7.462).[39] But even in this late tract, Milton speaking in a prophetic voice does not give up all hope for the saving remnant.

If *Paradise Regained* critiques the hopes for a fifth monarchy, it does not point to loyalty to or even (as is often argued) quietist acceptance of the Restoration regime. *Paradise Regained* accumulates a series of no's—the Son seems determined not to do anything. And yet when the Son rejects earthly kingdoms once and for all, he defines his own kingdom using a strikingly millenarian text, the Daniel prophecy of the stone:

> Know therefore when my season comes to sit
> On *David's* Throne, it shall be like a tree
> Spreading and overshadowing all the Earth,
> Or as a stone that shall to pieces dash
> All Monarchies besides throughout the world,
> And of my Kingdom there shall be no end.
> (IV.146–51)



Critics seem not to have noticed what an unexpected and riddling answer the Son gives here. The Son does not, after all, reject the earthly kingdom, or the force that may be necessary to attain it.

The Son's answer is thus peculiarly compact and allusive. The "season" recalls the time given to the beasts in Daniel 7.12–14, who "had their dominion taken away: yet their lives were prolonged for a season and time." The tree is often identified without further explanation as Nebuchadnezzar's vision of a tree which "grew, and was strong, and the height thereof reached unto heaven, and the sight thereof to the end of all the earth" (Dan. 4.11). But this tree is a sign of impending doom. Nebuchadnezzar will go mad and eat grass like a beast. In appropriating the image of the tree, the Son both distinguishes himself from earthly kings and yet appropriates their power.

The tree that overshadows the earth also points to a specifically New Testament revision of Daniel:

> And [Christ] said, Whereunto shall we liken the kingdom of God? or, with what comparison shall we compare it? It is like a grain of mustard seed which, when it is sown in the earth, it is less than all the seeds that be in the earth: But when it is sown, it groweth up, and becometh greater than all herbs, and shooteth out great branches; so that the fowls of the air may lodge under the shadow of it. (Mark 4.30–32)

The parable of the mustard seed is both an allusion to and a repudiation of Daniel's tree. The kingdom is at first invisible; yet the Son is not saying that his kingdom has nothing to do with politics. He clearly indicates that his kingdom finally triumphs over other kingdoms, as the kingdom in Daniel "shall break in pieces and consume all these kingdoms, and it shall stand for ever" (Dan. 2.44).

Milton had used this image before. In *Eikonoklastes*, he argues that "Kings of this world have both ever hated, and instinctively fear'd the Church of God. Whether it be for that thir Doctrin seems much to favour two things to them so dreadful, Liberty and Equality, or because they are

Children of that Kingdom, which as ancient Prophesies have foretold, shall in the end break to peeces and dissolve all thir great power and Dominion" (*CPW* 3.509). Again in *Paradise Regained*, Milton sets Christ's kingdom against earthly monarchies and yet does not give up the political force of that kingdom. In *Paradise Regained*, Milton does not attempt to raise an army or even the national consciousness. His brief epic poem seems designed more to reinterpret and to tell the story than to change political structures. But it is crucial to see that the very way in which the Son rebukes the present use of force and points to a future kingdom indicts the present regime and provides an alternative.



Satan has been obsessed throughout the poem with ascertaining the time of and means to the coming kingdom. Scoffing at the Son's obscurity and poverty, Satan claims: "Great acts require great means of enterprise" (II.412). Satan particularly focuses on the means to the throne of David: "prediction still / In all things, and all men, supposes means, / Without means us'd, what it predicts revokes" (III.354–56). But unlike the fifth monarchists who wanted to delineate the precise details of the kingdom, the Son refuses to tell the means: "Means there shall be to this, but what the means, / Is not for thee to know, nor me to tell" (IV.152–53).

Yet the "means" to this kingdom are implicit in the poem's history of Israel—covenant history. The Son's choice of terms, "David's throne," recalls the covenant promise to David and hence points neither to quietism nor resignation nor, finally, to an other-worldly kingdom. Milton reads the temptations through Old Testament images; for the Books of Kings the problem is not the Assyrians nor the Babylonians nor any of these world empires, but the Israelites themselves, continually drawn into idolatry. When Satan tempts the Son with these kingdoms, the poem discloses that the external threat is not the problem. Covenant history entails divine action but depends on human action for the political and social transformation of society. In refusing political deliverance—such as that proposed by the fifth monarchists—the work indicts a people who have apostasized from covenant conditions. The fact that *Paradise Regained* seems to rebuke the use of force such as that deployed against the Restoration government paradoxically impugns that very government.

The final temptation both rebukes the apocalyptic hopes of instituting the kingdom by force and dramatically envisions the alternative. The last temptation of the Tower also seems directly relevant to the apocalyptic hopes of the revolutionaries—in 1649 and 1671. The assumption of invulnerability, recalling the fifth monarchists' assurance that not a hair of their heads would perish, is depicted in the poem as a Satanic temptation to presumption. Satan tempts the Son to cast himself down:

Now show thy Progeny; if not to stand,
Cast thyself down; safely if Son of God:
For it is written, He will give command
Concerning thee to his Angels, in thir hands
They shall up lift thee, lest at any time
Thou chance to dash thy foot against a stone.
(IV.554–59)



Resistance to Satan is again internalized, as the Son's will becomes one with the Father's: "Tempt not the Lord thy God; he said and stood" (IV.561).

The Son allows Satan to control his body throughout, but domination and coercion of the body are opposed to consent of the spirit. *Paradise Regained* does not end with the repudiation of force; rather, force is overcome or superseded by the Son's full internalization of the divine will. The Son does not deliver anybody, but he regains the kingdom. What is restored or regained in *Paradise Regained* is not an external paradise or rule; the Son simply returns home at the end. But this is not to say the kingdom is not a political entity or the kingdom would have no force. The construction of the self-disciplined subject is a model for the dissenters of the 1660s and 1670s. It is not an escape from politics, but a new mode of opposition, which ultimately defeats Satanic force: "But Satan smitten with amazement fell" (IV.562).

# Plague, Fire, Jeremiad, and *Samson Agonistes*

God hath (after your long and great Prosperity) of late begun his Controversie with you, partly in spiritual Judgements, partly in Temporall, among these, eminently in the Judgement of the *Plague*, whereby God turned the Bodies of thousands into their *Graves*, and into Dust; and of the *Fire* whereby he brought the top of your highest houses into your lowest *Cellars*, and turned them into ashes.

Thomas Dolittle, *Rebukes for Sin by God's Burning Anger*

In 1665 and 1666 two devastating calamities, the plague and the fire of London, provided the dissenting clergy with a site for divine spectacle that could counter and surpass the spectacles of the restored church and state.[1] The executions and exhumings of regicides and fifth monarchists after 1660 displayed the power of the monarchy; these later jeremiads in turn represented plague and fire as more pervasive and horrifying punishments from a divine hand. We have seen the conflicting impulses of Puritans (later, dissenters) to appropriate as well as to destroy the displays of state—the miscalculation of the effect of a *public* execution for Charles, the rewriting of the regicides as martyrs, the Romanizing of Oliver Cromwell, and Venner's forceful rejection of the regicides' punishment. In their jeremiads over plague and fire, dissenters found a powerful mode to interpret and appropriate a spectacle of misery, to posit divine punishment of the newly royalized nation.[2] But again the spectacle was a contested site, and the established clergy—especially with the fire—deployed the jeremiad mode to argue against the sin not of royalism but of rebellion. And others wanted to see behind the display of misery not their own sin or the hand of God but the hand of their defining others—the Roman Catholics.

Situated in relation to these jeremiads, Milton's *Samson Agonistes* does not depict a single authoritative prophetic voice. Rather, it dramatizes the resistance to the jeremiad mode by self-interested characters who, in the face of Samson's misery and apparent punishment, blame everything and everyone but themselves. Samson, flawed throughout, nonetheless recognizes his sin and the saving nature of divine chastisement. But the true tragic figure is the nation of Israel, marked by pride and verging dangerously on hardness of heart.



The tragedy of the elect nation remains figural and paradigmatic in *Samson Agonistes;* but in *Of True Religion* Milton again employs a jeremiad stance to warn the English people more directly against hardness of heart and the idolatry of popery. *Samson Agonistes* and *Of True Religion*, in conjunction with the indictment of the self-enslaved nation in *Paradise Regained*, provide Milton's final critique of England as a chosen nation that has failed to respond to divine chastisement—or favor.

## I

Contemporary letters, tracts, newspapers, sermons, diaries, and medical tracts cohere in their representations of the plague and fire as spectacles of misery. Nathaniel Hodge, a London physician, depicts the miseries of the plague—"Who can express the calamities of such times? The whole British nation wept for the miseries of her metropolis"—and goes on to detail such miseries: "In some houses carcasses lay waiting for burial, and in others persons in their last agonies; in one room might be heard dying groans, in another the ravings of delirium, and not far off relations and friends bewailing both their loss and the dismal prospect of their own sudden departure." The public view was as dismal as the private: "Some of the infected ran about staggering like drunken men, and fell and expired in the streets; while others lie half-dead and comatose, but never to be waked but by the last trumpet."[3]

A 1665 broadsheet (Fig. 18) visually represents the manifold miseries. Drawings of "Multituds flying from London by water in boats & barges" or "Flying by land" show the mass exodus from the infected city in which perhaps 100,000 people died. If the exodus itself was a spectacle, more horrifying were the burials, in which individual coffins were eventually replaced by "Carts full of dead to bury" and mass graves. Contemporary Thomas Gumble writes: "All the musick in the night was the sad sound (Bring out your dead) which, like dung, were thrown out into a cart, and tumbled into a pit without numbring."[4]

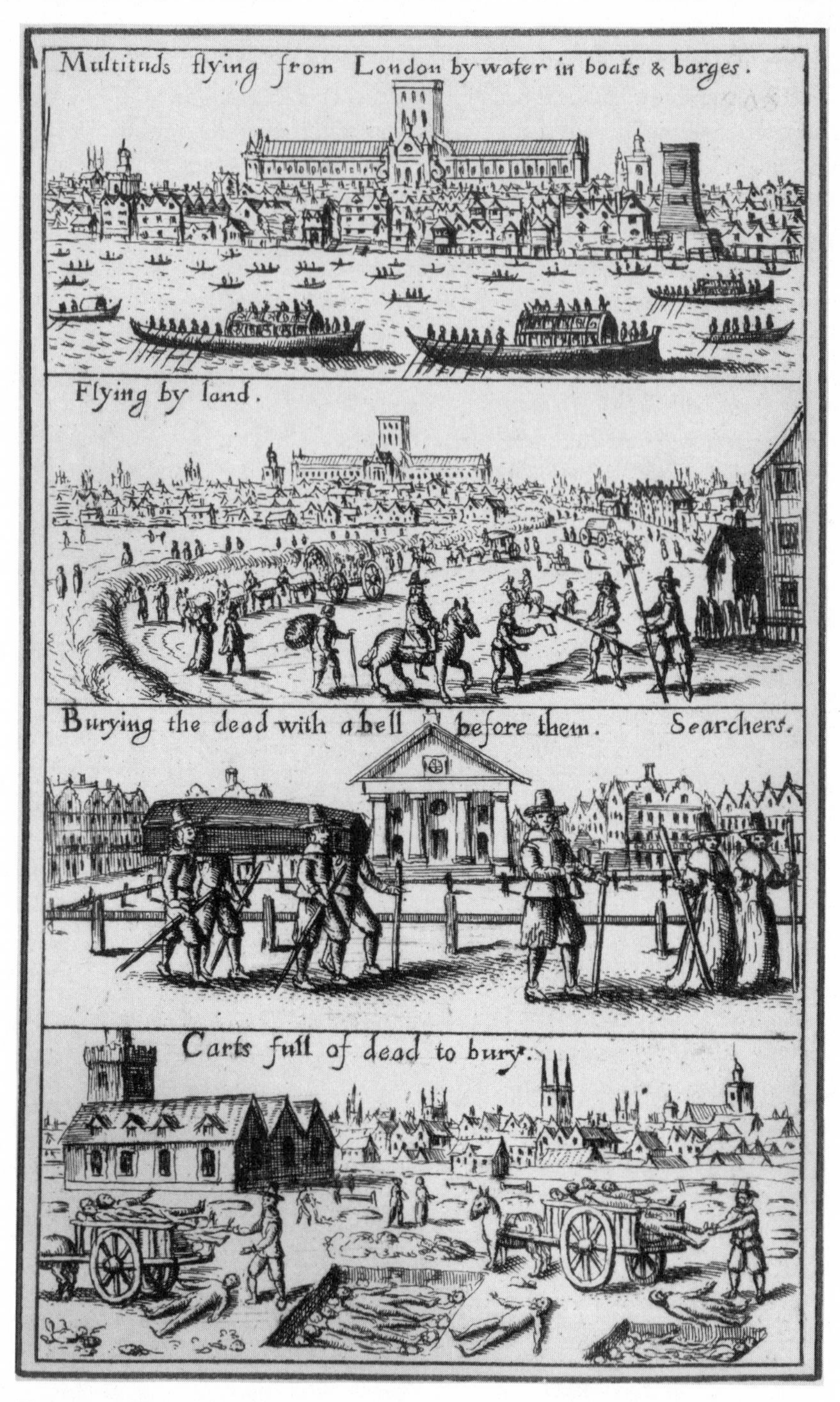


FIGURE 18 Broadsheet plague scene (1665). *By permission of the Master and Fellows, Magdalene College, Cambridge.*

John Evelyn records the equally dismal spectacle of the city in flames: "O the miserable and calamitous spectacle, such as happly the whole world had not seene the like since the foundation of it, nor to be outdon, 'til the universal Conflagration of it. . . . God grant mine eyes may never behold the like, who now saw above ten thousand houses all in one flame!" (*Diary* 3:453). The people are reduced to misery: "some under tents, some under miserable Huts and Hovels, many without a rag, or any necessary utinsils, bed or board, who from delicatness, riches, and easy accommodations in stately and well-furnished houses, were now reduc'd to extreamest misery and poverty" (*Diary* 3:457). The spectacles of misery replaced the theater of joy that we traced in chapter 4 as part of the ideology of the returning monarchy. And indeed the threat that such disasters posed to royalist ideology is noted by the Venetian ambassador after the fire: "The king's palace is not touched, but is possibly reserved to be the theatre of some dire spectacle, as cries are now heard on every hand that since the House of Stuart came to the throne England has never enjoyed felicity but has suffered from incessant miseries" (*CSPV* 35:77).

In tracts and sermons that lament in the manner of Old Testament prophets, urging repentance and threatening further judgment, the dissenting clergy shifted the agency of punishment from the human to the divine. The spectacles of misery were represented through the jeremiad mode as judicial punishment meted out by a divine sovereign who embodies right and law and the power to revenge. As both correlative and challenge to monarchical practice, God was depicted not as a king, but as judge in these tracts and sermons. Matthew Mead writes in *Solomon's Prescription:* "When I considered the sore Judgment wherewith we have been visited, which so evidentlie declares Wrath to be gone forth from the Lord against us, I thought it might be an Essay verie acceptable to God, and profitable to our selves, to do the best I could to make the voyce of the Rod Articulate."[5] Like the king, the divine sovereign left his mark on the vanquished offender; the punishment was spectacular, discontinuous, and asymmetrical.

Plague and fire thus took on the character of a penal ceremony, a public display of punishment by which the eclipsed and disobeyed power of the divine sovereign was reinstated. Indeed, plague and fire were punishments more widespread, repeated throughout the social body, more widely diffused than a solitary action on a scaffold. *London's Plague-Sore Discovered* (1665) explains:

> The Mighty God hath singled out our City
> For Wrath and Vengeance, casting off all Pitty;
> In every corner of our famous Town
> He sends his Arrows of Destruction down.[6]

Thomas Vincent represents a graphic scene of plague in *God's Terrible Voice:* "Now the Arrows begin to flie very thick about their ears, and they see many fellow sinners fall before their faces, expecting every hour themselves to be smitten; and the very sinking fears they have had of the Plague, hath brought the Plague and death upon many."[7] Similarly, in the great fire all of London became the scaffold, the burned houses replacing the punished or plague-stricken bodies.





Correlating visible punishment with invisible sins, dissenting clergy published the crimes that had brought on plague and fire and that all of England shared. Vincent in *God's Terrible Voice* points to extraordinary sins and judgment: "It was an extraordinary hand of God which brought the Plague, of which no natural cause can be assign'd . . . but that sin was grown to a greater height; and that a Fire should prevail against all attempts to quench it, to burn down the City, and that Judgment just following upon the heels of the other; what reason can be assigned, but that *Englands* sins and Gods displeasure hath been extraordinary" (64–65). Crime is no longer confined to the figure on the scaffold, but is England's sin. And hence the dissenting clergy can call for widespread repentance and reform in a powerful tool against the restored church and state.

The jeremiad speakers weep for and warn the people under the moral authority of Jeremiah, as in John Tabor's *Seasonable Thoughts in Sad Times:*

> O that my head a Fountain were, and I
> Could vent a stream of grief from either eye,
> Weep, and blot out of sin the crimson stain
> Whereby the Daughter of my People's slain![8]

And yet they too share in the guilt. Mead writes *Solomon's Prescription* so that "not onlie Gods Wrath, but the sin he scourgeth us for, and the duty he would drive us to, might be found in legible Characters" (Sig $A3_r$).

Displaying punishment and sin to urge confession, jeremiad speakers take on authority otherwise vested in ecclesiastical and civil institutions. Samuel Rolle, in his sermon on the burning of London, uses the language of juridical confession: "Now *England* hold up thy hand at the Bar and answer, Art thou guilty or not guilty of the great sin of incorrigibleness?"[9] *The Plague Checkt* views the bodily plague as sign of "a worse plague, the plague of the heart" and uses medical language to urge its readers to search themselves spiritually: "After you are dead you must have the searchers to view your bodies, be you who you will; be you searchers to your selves and your own Souls, and see to it that there be no Spiritual Feaver Spots, or Plague Spots upon you."[10] Vincent spells out the terms of reprieve or pardon: "God doth not only expect that Londoners should now acknowledge their sins, and humble themselves, and mourn for their sins; but also that they should turn from them, otherwise pardon, and healing, and his favour is not to be obtained" (167).

Given the oppressive ecclesiastical atmosphere, it is not surprising that most of the sins the dissenting clergy cited—lust, pride, sabbath breaking, swearing, dicing, immorality, drunkenness—are not explicitly political, although some did point to the lack of toleration and the ejection of faithful ministers. Yet the jeremiads over the plague and fire were powerful political tools for the dissenters who were preaching illegally and in a time of great crisis. As they cried out against the sins of the nation, these clergymen implicitly indicted the Restoration regime, looking to a higher authority to judge and punish the nation. That the sins indicted at such great length tended to be moral rather than explicitly political did not make the genre any less effective—or dangerous.



Yet the spectacles of plague and fire were, like the displays of state, contested sites, open to varied interpretation. If the dissenters dominated, especially during the plague, established clergy also deployed the jeremiad mode to interpret the plague and the fire as divine spectacle that reinforced the monarchy and church. The monarch himself responded to the disasters with proclamations for fasting. The proclamation on the fire, like the jeremiads, first publicized the spectacle of punishment: "A Visitation so dreadful, that scarce any Age or Nation hath ever seen or felt the like." The people were called to a "day of Solemn fasting and Humiliation, to implore the mercies of God, that it would please him to pardon the crying sins of the Nation, those especially which have drawn down this last heavy Judgment upon Us."[11] The site of punishment was deployed in a civil and ecclesiastical ritual.

In the printed version of his fast-day sermon, *Lex Ignea*, Anglican William Sancroft includes a print of the burning St. Pauls Cathedral (Fig. 19). Despite expectations that it would provide a safe haven, the cathedral was severely damaged and thus a vivid example of the horrors of the fire. Sancroft both visually represents the spectacular nature of the fire and underscores its crucial differences from other kinds of spectacle: "Have we any so hard-hearted amongst us, that can look upon so sad a Spectacle, as if they sate all the while in the Theater, or walkt in a Gallery of Pictures; little more concern'd, than at the Siege of *Rhodes*, or the Ruines of Troy?"[12] Sancroft continues the theatrical metaphor to warn against beginning "to con our part, when we are ready to be hist off the Stage, and Death is now pulling off our properties."[13] The theater of divine punishment demands an immediate response.

Those most explicit about the political causes of punishment were, in fact, Anglican clergy or other royalists. Some, like Edward Stillingfleet, blamed the judgments on ingratitude for the restoration of Stuart monar-

LEX IGNEA:

OR

The School of Righteousneſs.

A

SERMON

Preach'd before the KING,

*Octob.* 10. 1666.

At the SOLEMN FAST appointed

For the late

FIRE in *LONDON*.

By *WILLIAM SANDCROFT*, D. D.

Dean of S. *Pauls*.

Publiſhed by His Majeſtie's Special Command.

*London*, Printed for *R. Pawlett*, at the Bible in *Chancery-lane* near *Fleetſtreet*.

FIGURE 19 Title page to Sancroft, *Lex Ignea* (1666), with St. Paul's Cathedral in flames. *By permission of Rare Books and Special Collections, the Pennsylvania State University Libraries.*

chy: "Was this our requitall to *him* [God] for restoring our *Soveraign*, to *rebell* the more against Heaven? Was this our thankfulness for removing the *disorders* of *Church* and *State*, to bring them into our *lives?*"[14] Meditating on a fast day sermon over the fire, John Evelyn adds to the sin of "prodigious ingratitude" the sins of "burning lusts, dissolute court, profane and abominable lives" (*Diary* 3:26). Others looked back to the rebellion as cause of judgment. John Bell in *London's Remembrancer* (1665) sees apocalyptic judgment for the death of Charles I: "Our Rebellion extended to the height of Rebellion, even to the taking away the life of the best of Kings, his late Majestie of ever blessed Memory, whose blood doubtless doth uncessantly cry to the Lord for Vengeance."[15]



Contemporaries recognized the conflicting interpretations of the displays of plague and fire. Matthew Mead writes in *Solomon's Prescription* that although some "might be convinc't that sin in the general, was the cause of all our miseries, yet hardly that it was their sin, or their friends, but some bodies else that they don't love; and so shift it off to this or that Party, who they would have punish't, had they been in Gods stead" (10–11). One contemporary letter comments with acumen on the great fire that "though all see the same desolation, yet, by looking on it with different opinions and interest, they make different constructions as if the object were so."[16]

The correspondent goes on to explain that even the interpretation of the misery as punishment for sin is contested, "some thinking it a natural and bare accident, while others imagine it a judgment of God, and are as confident of it as if they saw the hand on the wall." And he then delineates the range of alleged sins: "The Quakers say, it is for their persecution. The Fanaticks say, it is for banishing and silencing their ministers. Others say, it is for the murder of the king and rebellion of the city. The Clergy lay the blame on schism and licentiousness, while the Sectaries lay it on imposition and their pride. Thus do many pretend to determine the sin aimed at in this punishment."[17] Like the punishments of state we have been tracing, the spectacle of divine punishment was both ambivalent and contested.

It was clear to contemporaries that the disasters could be read as threatening the monarchy. Dryden in *Annus Mirabilis* actually depicts the ghosts of the regicides rejoicing over the fire:

> The Ghosts of Traitors, from the *Bridge* descend,
> With bold Fanatick Spectres to rejoyce:
> About the fire into a Dance they bend,
> And sing their Sabbath Notes with feeble voice.
> (*Works* 1:93)

And so royalists were forced to resort to the strategy of the opposition, that is, to reread the spectacle or to find a counterspectacle as sign of a divine hand. Bishop Burnet, reflecting upon the period in his *History*, comments that with the "dreadful appearance" of the plague of 1665, "all the king's enemies, and the enemies of monarchy, said here was a manifest character of God's heavy displeasure upon the nation" (148). Burnet counters by pointing to an even greater divine spectacle, the providential restoration of the monarchy: "What all had seen in the year 1660 ought to have silenced those who at this time pretended to comment on Providence. But there will be always much discourse of things that are very visible, as well as very extraordinary" (148). Burnet's observation attests to the efficacy of spectacle, both visible and extraordinary, as an ongoing and contested mode of power.

But the jeremiads did not simply appropriate and contest in a divine mode the penal displays of state; they also radically reenvisioned the punishment itself as corrective rather than destructive, even as a sign of election. Hence, the metaphors used to describe the display shift from the juridical to the medical and familial: God shifts from judge to physician or chastising father. Matthew Mead combines medical and juridical language in *Solomon's Prescription:* "And once again, let me desire every Reader to place himself, as at the Bar of God, and so to passe a true judgment upon himself, and not to quarrel with the Physitian, instead of falling out with the disease" (16). Punishment is a multivalent sign and may indicate chastisement rather than destruction, divine love as well as wrath.

God as physician may wound to heal or as father may chastise to correct. Hence Mead looks on affliction as "a Medicine for a distempered Nation" and writes "in order to its kindlie working with us, to tell the nature, import, and use of it; and to give directions how it ought to be received" (Sig $A3_r$). *The Plague Checkt* urges its readers to pray that "God would remove his heavy stroake, true; but with all, that he would sanctifie it, and do us much good by it, knowing that Covenant affliction and Judgments sanctified, are better much better then common mercies" (49); the tract goes on to argue that, paradoxically, the worst punishment may be to have the punishment removed: "God punisheth most severely when he refuseth to punish. . . . The Physitian hath little or no hope of the Patient when he gives over the Cure, it may prove the greatest Judgment to have a Judgment removed" (50). By thus radically reenvisioning the punishment, the clergy could continue to critique the people, church, and state on behalf of a wrathful God—even when the spectacle of punishment was removed.

## II

In our earlier discussion of Milton's *Samson Agonistes*, we looked at the construction of Samson as martyr, the convergence of iconoclasm and idolatry in the chosen nation, with resonances for the martyrologies of the 1660s. But the tragedy intersects with other political discourses, and to focus only on the iconoclastic violence against the Philistines is to marginalize the punishment of the Israelites themselves. *Samson Agonistes* is marked not only by iconoclasm, but by jeremiad, divine punishment of an elect leader and of a chosen nation.[18]

The jeremiad paradigm of sin, punishment, repentance, and deliverance of the chosen nation recurs throughout the Book of Judges from which Milton takes the story of Samson. Judges receives its name from the leaders, *shopeṭim*, who deliver Israel from its foes between the death of Joshua and the beginning of monarchy. The children of Israel sin; God in anger gives them over to their enemies; Israel repents; God raises up a judge to deliver them.[19] *Samson Agonistes* extends the concerns of sin, punishment, and repentance to Samson, whose uneven, agonizing progress is clarified by the paradigm of the jeremiad.[20] Struggling throughout with pride and despair, Samson comes to a crucial understanding of his miseries as divine chastisement, sign of election and mercy; but it is an understanding that, I will argue, finally eludes the Chorus, with ominous resonances for Milton's own chosen nation.



As in the jeremiads we have been tracing, *Samson Agonistes* opens with a spectacle of misery. Samson laments his blindness, indignity, and defeat—but not, as yet, the sins that have caused them. Indeed, he implicitly blames and distrusts the hand of God, which he views as giving strength without sufficient wisdom: "Suffices that to mee strength is my bane, / And proves the source of all my miseries" (63–64). Samson focuses specifically on these miseries:

> To live a life half dead, a living death,
> And buried; but O yet more miserable!
> Myself my Sepulcher, a moving Grave,
> Buried, yet not exempt
> By privilege of death and burial
> From worst of other evils, pains and wrongs,
> But made hereby obnoxious more
> To all the miseries of life,
> Life in captivity
> Among inhuman foes.
>
> (100–109)

Samson laments not his sin but his misery, a position strikingly far from the jeremiad recognition of sin and chastisement that marks the book of Judges (and the contemporary discourses we have been tracing).

Samson's fellow Israelites are no more perspicacious. The entering Chorus sees the misery of the fallen Samson, but not the sin or the afflicting hand of God:

> Which shall I first bewail,
> Thy Bondage or lost Sight,
> Prison within Prison
> Inseparably dark?
>
> (151–54)[21]





And Manoa, exclaiming "O miserable change!" (340), distrusts the hand of God: "Why are his gifts desirable, to tempt / Our earnest Prayers, then, giv'n with solemn hand / As Graces, draw a Scorpion's tail behind?" (358–60). When Manoa turns from his own disappointment to God's treatment of Samson, he can see only unjust, excessive punishment:

> Alas! methinks whom God hath chosen once
> To worthiest deeds, if he through frailty err,
> He should not so o'erwhelm, and as a thrall
> Subject him to so foul indignities,
> Be it but for honor's sake of former deeds.
>
> (368–72)

Manoa sees only "frailty," error, and a kind of divine overreaction, not sin and corresponding chastisement. Rightly intuiting that Samson should "let another hand, not thine, exact / Thy penal forfeit from thyself" (507–8), Manoa nonetheless addresses only the misery, not the sin: "Thou must not in the meanwhile here forgot / Lie in this miserable loathsome plight / Neglected" (479–81).

Samson alone comes to recognize the sin behind the spectacle of misery. In response to Manoa, Samson posits a correspondence between offense and punishment: "if aught seem vile, / As vile hath been my folly" (376–77). But he still sees his punishment as self-induced, if representational. Such is not a jeremiad vision. As Manoa intuits, Samson still mistakenly thinks that the hand which punishes him must be his own:

> let me here,
> As I deserve, pay on my punishment;
> And expiate, if possible, my crime,
> Shameful garrulity.
>
> (488–91)

In his encounter with Manoa, Samson rejects the lesser temptation not to repent fully, but he struggles with pride and the related state of despair.[22]

Samson's sense of his sin is initially too extreme, showing a continuing overconcern with self:

> To have reveal'd
> Secrets of men, the secrets of a friend,
> How heinous had the fact been, how deserving
> Contempt, and scorn of all, to be excluded
> All friendship, and avoided as a blab,
> The mark of fool set on his front? But I
> God's counsel have not kept, his holy secret
> Presumptuously have publish'd, impiously,
> Weakly at least, and shamefully: A sin
> That Gentiles in thir Parables condemn
> To thir abyss and horrid pains confin'd.
> (491–501)



Samson's speech, despite his earlier claim to be concerned with God's dishonor, is focused on his own shame, the contempt and scorn he has brought upon himself. His reference to the "mark of fool" significantly recalls the mark of Cain, and shows the danger that, like Cain, Samson may fall into remorse, not true repentance.[23] Samson's sense that his sin goes beyond Cain and that of the classical myths is an exaggeration based on pride and leading to despair. Self-indicted, self-punishing, Samson shows not jeremiad repentance but pride.

Paradoxically, Samson falls into despair because of, not despite, his renewed assurance that God will get along without him. He feels deserted, cast off by a God who can fend for himself. Samson torments himself with thoughts of the difference between past and present:

> My griefs not only pain me
> As a ling'ring disease,
> But finding no redress, ferment and rage,
> Nor less than wounds immedicable
> Rankle, and fester, and gangrene,
> To black mortification.
> (617–22)

In the jeremiad mode, the speakers argue that external punishment represents internal sin and urge their listeners to search for the "plague within." Samson much more problematically exacerbates both punishment and the disease with his own thoughts.

Samson's self-punishment is more remorse than repentance, despair as an ongoing form of pride:

Thoughts my Tormentors arm'd with deadly stings
Mangle my apprehensive tenderest parts;
Exasperate, exulcerate, and raise
Dire inflammation which no cooling herb
Or med'cinal liquor can assauge.

(623–27)

Samson's words indicate that he is still obsessed with his miseries, punishing himself. Susan Snyder writes that "pride is the root and beginning of all sin; despair is its end product. Yet the pendulum can swing quickly from one to the other."[24] Samson's earlier pride is not yet overcome but has shifted to the despair that is its dark twin: "Thence faintings, swoonings of despair, / And sense of Heav'n's desertion" (631–32). For Samson, the worst state is to be given over by God. And he has only one remaining prayer: "no long petition, speedy death, / The close of all my miseries, and the balm" (650–51).

But Samson's fellow Israelites see only his misery and not his sin. While they intuit the hand of God, they puzzle over its arbitrariness:

God of our Fathers, what is man!
That thou towards him with hand so various,
Or might I say contrarious,
Temper'st thy providence through his short course.

(667–70)

The words of the Chorus strikingly reverse the humility of the psalmic lament they echo. While the stance of the psalmist is that of humility, "What is man, that thou art mindful of him" (Psalm 8.4), the Chorus complains that God does not appreciate this man enough. They do not understand why Samson and other great men should be punished:

Yet toward these, thus dignifi'd, thou oft,
Amidst thir height of noon,
Changest thy count'nance and thy hand, with no regard
Of highest favors past
From thee on them, or them to thee of service.

(682–86)

To the Chorus it seems patently unfair that "Just or unjust, alike seem miserable, / For oft alike, both come to evil end" (703–4). Struggling and puzzling, the Chorus here evinces a pride that, as I will later argue, marks and limits its reactions to the end.

Shamed and driven into despair by the appearance of the Hebrews whom he has apparently not seen since his days of glory, Samson is jolted out of such despair by his encounter with Dalila.[25] Dalila sees only human actions, her own hand in his fallen state. But Samson knows better (although he is not telling her) and he begins to think again about his relationship with God, albeit in negative terms:

> God sent her to debase me,
> And aggravate my folly who committed
> To such a viper his most sacred trust
> Of secrecy, my safety, and my life.
> (999–1002)

This insight, however flawed, is an absolutely crucial move away from "despair / And sense of Heav'n's desertion" toward knowledge that the hand of God is still upon him.

In the exchange with Harapha, Samson finally recognizes not only the justice but the mercy of the hand of God. When Harapha reiterates Samson's own earlier belief that God has "delivered [him] up / Into [his] Enemies' hand" (1158–59), Samson now asserts that the hand upon him is in fact divine:

> All these indignities, for such they are
> From thine, these evils I deserve and more,
> Acknowledge them from God inflicted on me
> Justly, yet despair not of his final pardon
> Whose ear is ever open; and his eye
> Gracious to re-admit the suppliant.
> (1168–73)

In this crucial turning point, Samson achieves the jeremiad vision of the afflicting hand of God acting not in vengeance but in mercy.

Samson does not, as has sometimes been argued, reach an unambiguous state of patience and humility.[26] Rather, for complex and very human motives—including a kind of pride that returns when he can compare himself favorably against Dalila and Harapha—he suddenly recognizes that his punishment might be, in fact, divine chastisement, sign of election and continuing favor. This insight, as we have seen, is a distinctive and crucial jeremiad revision of external signs of misery and indignity. Samson's new internalization of jeremiad vision allows him to embrace the "indignities" he had earlier rejected and to act once again as an instrument of the divine.

We recall that the jeremiads over plague and fire evinced precisely this sense of divine chastisement as election pointing toward pardon. Hence, Rege Sincera writes in *Observations Both Historical and Moral* (1667): "But courage, o thou that art now my country, thou art fallen into the hands of God, and not of men; he that chastiseth thee is thy father, and if he hath a rod to punish thee, he hath also a staff to comfort thee; turn to him, and he will turn to thee, for he is merciful and long-suffering; not willing that any should perish, but that all should come to repentance."[27] Samson's punishment, or his recognition of that punishment, turns out to be his saving grace. He moves from a debilitating sense of "Heaven's desertion" to seeing the signs of heaven in his very misery.



While Samson to the end shows traces of continuing pride or despair, his sense of God's forgiveness and favor in his very punishment allows him to act at last. He alludes to "Favor renew'd" (1356) and will not agree

> to displease
> God for fear of Man, and Man prefer,
> Set God behind: which in his jealousy
> Shall never, unrepented, find forgiveness.
> (1373–76)

Samson does not choose to go to the Temple only to be humiliated, to be, as Arnold Stein argues, "the Fool of God."[28] But neither does he go off in pride or despair.[29] Rather, he reaches a kind of calm midpoint between the two alternatives with which he has been struggling: "If there be aught of presage in the mind, / This day will be remarkable in my life / By some great act, or of my days the last" (1387–89). The state of mind Samson sustains at the end is not revealed to the audience. But the spectacle with which the drama ends tends to confirm that he acts by "rousing motions" that are genuinely inspired. God's hand upon Samson in chastisement and against the Philistines in wrath implies that there is yet hope for the chosen nation—of Israel and of England.

## III

The Chorus, however, fails to recognize what has happened. Because the Chorus does not acknowledge Samson's guilt—or their own—they do not see the jeremiad process through which Samson has progressed. The current debate between regenerationists and revisionists on *Samson Agonistes* has obscured the point that the true tragic figure in the drama—as in the book of Judges—is the nation of Israel, marked by pride and failing to acknowledge the merciful but chastising hand of an offended God.[30] In their responses to Samson's plight, the Chorus continually finds ways to deflect introspection, self-searching, and lament for sin. Unlike Samson, the Chorus does not even haltingly achieve the jeremiad vision.

The Chorus can always find someone else to blame. When Samson rebukes Israel as a nation that has chosen "Bondage with ease than strenuous liberty" (271), the Chorus deflects the rebuke into the past, adducing the unfaithfulness of the earlier Israelites who "contemn'd / The matchless *Gideon*" (279–80) and "how ingrateful *Ephraim* / Had dealt with *Jephtha*" (282–83). When Samson urges that they "add mee to the roll" (290) of neglected deliverers, the Chorus again finds a target over which they can feel superior:

> Just are the ways of God
> And justifiable to Men
> Unless there be who think not God at all:
> If any be, they walk obscure;
> For of such Doctrine never was there School,
> But the heart of the Fool,
> And no man therein Doctor but himself.
> (293–99)



Far worse than the chosen nation that neglects its leader is the fool who does not believe in God at all, and the Chorus finds comfort in the comparison.

Similarly, the Chorus exaggerates Samson's own sense of superiority over Dalila, as they feel superior to all women:

> Is it for that such outward ornament
> Was lavish't on thir Sex, that inward gifts
> Were left for haste unfinish't, judgment scant,
> Capacity not rais'd to apprehend
> Or value what is best
> In choice, but oftest to affect the wrong?
> Or was too much of self-love mixt,
> Of constancy no root infixt,
> That either they love nothing, or not long?
> (1025–33)

But these very words could be describing Old Testament Israel. The Judges account depicts an ever-straying nation, "oftest to affect the wrong," notably without "constancy." We find, in Judges 2.17, for instance: "They went a whoring after other gods, and bowed themselves unto them: they turned quickly out of the way which their fathers walked in, obeying the commandments of the Lord."

The irony is that the Chorus correctly recognizes the pride of the Philistines. For the Chorus, Dalila is like a ship of Tarshish, symbol of pride. Harapha approaches, "his look / Haughty as is his pile high-built and proud" (1068–69). And the drunken, rejoicing Philistines are marked by pride and idolatry:

So fond are mortal men
Fall'n into wrath divine,
As thir own ruin on themselves to invite
Insensate left, or to sense reprobate,
And with blindness internal struck.
(1682–86)



The Israelites in their struggles for understanding cannot be equated with the Philistines, but they do share their characteristic vice of pride, thinking better of themselves than circumstances would warrant. They do not recognize Samson's guilt or their own because they can always find someone else to blame.

In the 1660s, with the plague and fire of London, both dissenting and established clergy stressed the people's own sins. Yet many of the people seemed to blame the calamity of fire not on their own sins, however specified, but on their religious and national enemies—the Dutch, the French, and especially the papists.[31] In blaming the Catholics for setting the fire, the London mobs threatened disorder, even anarchy. William Taswell writes that "the ignorant and deluded mob, who upon the occasion were hurried away with a kind of phrenzy, vented forth their rage against the Roman Catholics and Frenchmen; imagining these incendiaries (as they thought) had thrown red-hot balls into the houses."[32] Such blame caused disorder, even mass hysteria, as Taswell writes: "A report on a sudden prevailed that four thousand French and Papists were in arms, intending to carry with them death and destruction, and increase the conflagration. Upon which every person, both in city and suburbs, having procured some sort of weapon or other, instantly almost collected themselves together to oppose this chimerical army."[33]

While civic officials in fact produced and punished a self-proclaimed Catholic arsonist (and probable lunatic), Robert Hubert, ecclesiastical and civil discourses strove to turn the people's view from natural causes to the hand of God, which afflicts them for their sins.[34] Samuel Rolle writes in *The Burning of London in the Year 1666:* "Disown Providence in this, and you will disown it everywhere. If there were something of the hand of man in it, doubtless, there was more of the hand of God."[35] Similarly, Thomas Vincent argues in *God's Terrible Voice:* "Whoever were the Instruments God was the author of this evil, which hath come upon us; there being no evil in the City (that is, evil of punishment) which the Lord as righteous and the supream Judge doth not inflict. And surely more of the extraordinary Hand of God, than of any men, did appear in the burning of the City of *London*" (48). The jeremiads did not deny the role of the Catholics, but deployed the papist threat to urge that the people discipline themselves.

Papists remained papists, demonized and threatening, but the hand of God behind the threat called for self-discipline. The true threat was within.

In relation to these jeremiad motifs, the limitations of the Chorus in *Samson Agonistes* are clear. The Hebrews at the end see only the punishment of an enemy nation. Their response to the spectacular destruction of the Philistine temple does not include looking inward to see why the punishment falls on Samson as well. They do not turn to lamentation and repentance in the face of divine spectacle:



> Come, come, no time for lamentation now
> Nor much more cause: *Samson* hath quit himself
> Like *Samson*, and heroicly hath finish'd
> A life Heroic, on his Enemies
> Fully reveng'd hath left them years of mourning,
> And lamentation to the Sons of *Caphtor*
> Through all *Philistian* bounds.
>
> (1708–14)

While the Philistines have cause to mourn, Israel does not: "Nothing is here for tears" (1721). Manoa envisions the virgins who come to the tomb, "only bewailing / His lot unfortunate in nuptial choice, / From whence captivity and loss of eyes" (1741–43). In the closing words of the Chorus, there is nothing about sin and repentance, nothing about divine grace and mercy. God simply "unexpectedly returns" (1750), having been away behind a cloud. The Chorus rejoices over the punishment of the Philistines, failing to see God's chastising hand upon Samson or to recognize that their own lack of punishment may be the greatest punishment of all.

## IV

Published two years after *Samson Agonistes*, Milton's *Of True Religion* shares its concern with the chosen nation, which through pride shifts all blame to a defining other—whether papist or Philistine. Although ostensibly against an external danger, *Of True Religion* uses the threat of popery to discipline and reform a Protestant audience, to exorcise popery in its various guises not only without but also within. In concluding *Of True Religion*, Milton deploys the stance and ideology of the jeremiad to explain and comment upon the contemporary political and social scene. But he also takes a crucial step beyond the jeremiad to envision lack of punishment and hardness of heart.

*Of True Religion* concludes with a lament over the sins of the nation. "The last means to avoid Popery," Milton writes, "is to amend our lives," and he goes on to denounce the manifold sins of the nation: "It is a general complaint that this Nation of late years, is grown more numerously and excessively vitious than heretofore; Pride, Luxury, Drunkenness, Whoredom, Cursing, Swearing, bold and open Atheism every where abounding: Where these grow, no wonder if Popery also grow apace" (*CPW* 7:439). But now it is the absence of punishment that elicits Milton's exhortation and warning. He goes on to warn that continued sinning and lack of repentance may lead God to stop punishing them, paradoxically the greatest punishment of all: "For God, when men sin outragiously, and will not be admonisht, gives over chastizing them, perhaps by Pestilence, Fire, Sword, or Famin, which may all turn to their good, and takes up his severest punishments, hardness, besottedness of heart, and Idolatry, to their final perdition" (*CPW* 7:439). As in the jeremiads of the 1660s, Milton interprets the plague and fire as divine punishment, but now in the context of their having been ominously removed.[36]



In his exhortation to the nation, Milton moves beyond the warning of divine chastisement and the need to repent, to envision the destruction of a reprobate people, given over to idolatry. *Of True Religion* makes specific and political the tragic dilemma that remains paradigmatic in *Samson Agonistes.* The assurances of the jeremiad mode—that punishment attests to elect status and continuing divine regard—may not continue to hold. God may give the English, like the heathen, over to idolatry:

> And Isaiah 44.16. Speaking of Idolaters, *They have not known nor understood, for he hath shut their Eyes that they cannot see, and their hearts that they cannot understand.* Let us therefore . . . amend our lives with all speed; least through impenitency we run into that stupidly, which we now seek all means so warily to avoid, the worst of superstitions, and the heaviest of all Gods Judgements, Popery. (*CPW* 7:440)

The tract uses antipopery to point to the people's own sins, which have made them vulnerable. In warning against superstition, popery, and idolatry, Milton moves beyond the assurances of the jeremiad. Divine spectacle is no longer efficacious; they see but they do not understand, bringing popery on themselves. In *The Readie and Easie Way*, Milton's earlier jeremiad over the Restoration of the Stuart monarchy, he warned that the sin of return to kingship would be its own punishment. Now, in the 1670s, the very lack of punishment of the nation discloses that it may be under the threat of ultimate punishment, having been given over to idolatry and "the heaviest of all Gods Judgements, Popery."[37]

In warning against popery Milton does not explicitly impugn the increasingly Catholic court. But it may well be the case, as Christopher Hill suggests, that Milton took advantage of popular feeling against popery to attack Stuart absolutism indirectly.[38] Charles II had close connections with Louis XIV, the powerful Catholic king of France, and had, in fact, signed a secret agreement to reintroduce Catholicism into England in exchange for French support. The Court was widely seen as a center of Catholic conversion and intrigue. Milton's final writings can be situated in relation to the antipopery sentiment of the 1670s, enhanced by Titus Oates's revelation of a Popish plot to kill Charles II and by the crisis triggered by the prospect of a Catholic heir to the throne. I would like to trace the way in which this antipopery was evinced in spectacle, culminating the development of spectacle we have traced from 1649 onward, and finally to look at how Milton's posthumous voice remained both relevant and distinct.



## V

In the 1670s pope burnings demonized Catholicism and created an external threat against which the people could be united.[39] The pope burnings deployed the images of the grotesque and demonic that had earlier played a role in Restoration celebrations and triumphs to demonize the enemies of the king. But now the spectacle was organized by those also wishing to limit royal prerogative and heighten opposition to James as Catholic heir to the throne. Unlike the positive spectacles of state that induced admiration, the horrors of public execution, or the divine displays evoking repentance, this spectacle seemed pure demonization, instilling hatred and fear.

Contemporary observer Charles Hatton describes a pope burning in 1673, after James made an unpopular marriage to a Catholic princess: "The pope and his cardinals were, in Cheapside and other places, hung up and burned in their effigies. One told me he counted two hundred bonfires between Temple Bar and Aldgate."[40] A procession in 1677 was much more grotesque and frightening: "Mighty bonfires and the burning of a most costly pope, carried by four persons in divers habits, and the effigies of two devils whispering in his ears, his belly filled full of live cats who squawled most hideously as soon as they felt the fire: the common people saying all the while it was the language of the pope and the Devil in a dialogue betwixt them."[41] The pope burnings of the 1670s show another turn in the nature and use of spectacles we have been tracing, from the tragic and sublime to the grotesque.

After 1678, when Titus Oates made his revelation of a popish plot to kill Charles, and after Sir Edmund Berry Godfrey, the judge to whom depositions had been given, was found mysteriously murdered, antipopery hysteria intensified.[42] An extravagant procession in the autumn of 1679 evinced a central strategy of demonization through the use of the grotesque body, parody, and the sacrilegious. A broadsheet, *The Solemn Mock Procession of the*

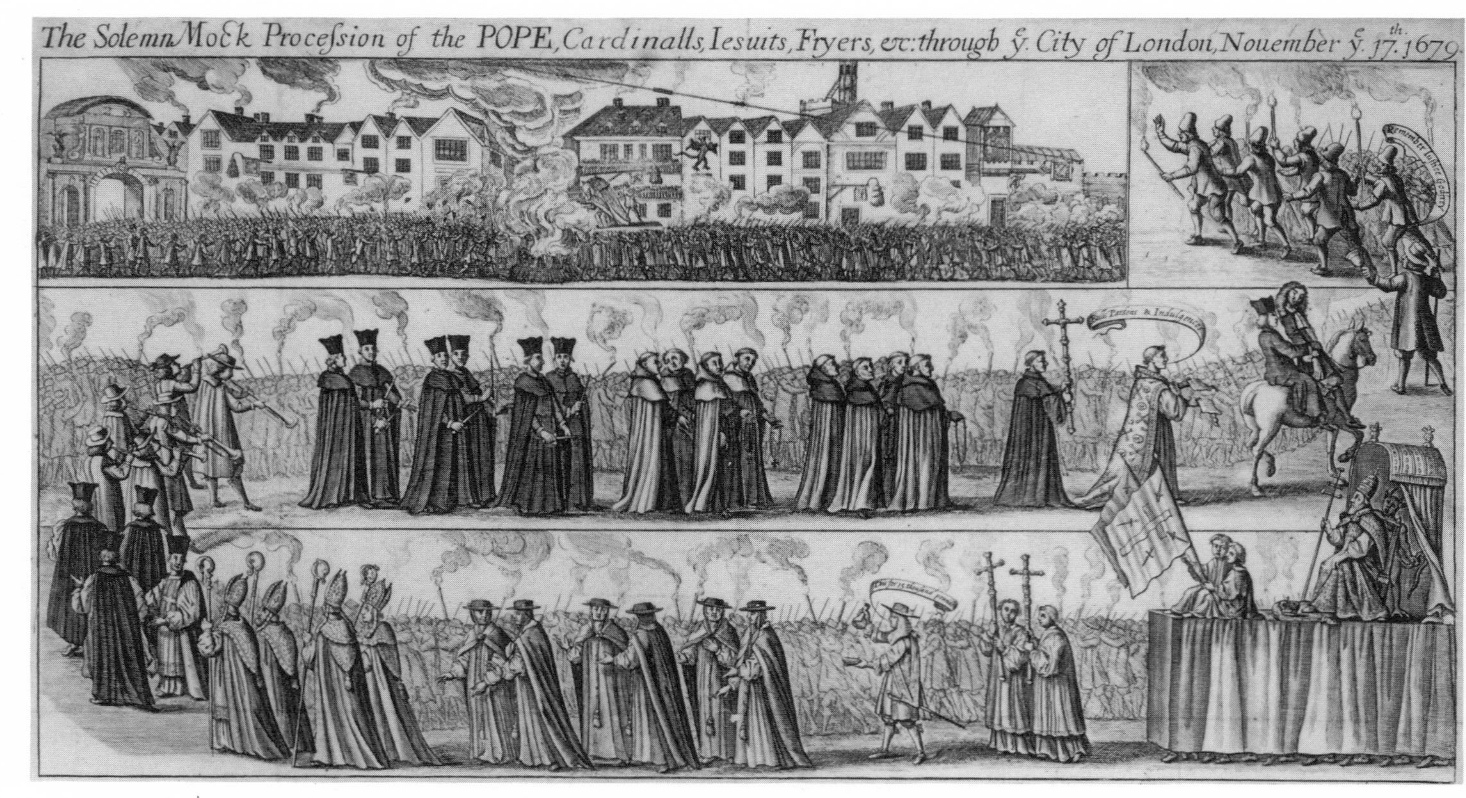


FIGURE 20 Pope-burning procession, from *The Solemn Mock Procession of the Pope, Cardinals, Jesuits, Fryers, &c* (1679). *By permission of the Trustees of the British Museum.*

*Pope, Cardinalls, Jesuits, Fryers, &c* (1679), includes an illustration (Fig. 20) of the spectacle, a kind of carnivalesque anti-triumph. Prominently featured was a dead body representing the murdered judge Edmund Berry Godfrey: "In the Habit he usually wore, the Cravat wherewith he was murdered about his Neck, with spots of Blood on his Wrists, Shirt and white Gloves that were on his hands, his Face pale and wan, riding on a White Horse, one of his Murderers behind him to keep him from falling." In addition to the grisly corpse, the procession included other images of the grotesque body such as "the Popes Chief Physitian with *Jesuites Powder* in one hand and an *Urinal* in the other." The threat of violence was displayed through "a Priest in a Surplice, with a cope Embroidered with Dead mens Bones, Skeletons, Skuls, &c. giving pardons very freely to those who would murder *Protestants* and proclaiming it Meritorious" and "Six *Jesuits* with Bloody Daggers."



Finally, the Pope appeared "in a lofty Glorious Pageant" accompanied by his counselor, the Devil, "frequently caressing, hugging, and whispering, and oft-times instructing him aloud, to destroy His Majesty, to forge a *Protestant*-Plot, and to fire the City again." The entire display, which culminated when the pope was "tumbled from all his grandeur into the Impartial flames," parodied the royal procession: "Never were the *Balconies*, Windows and Houses more numerously filled, nor the Streets closer throng'd with multitudes of People, all expressing their abhorrence of *Popery* with continual Shouts and Acclamations."

It is significant in the context of spectacles and power which we have been tracing that the most memorable spectacles of the 1670s were staged to challenge the monarchy by the newly emergent Whigs. The pope burnings incorporated the demonization we have seen in the executions and exhumings of the regicides, parodied the glory of the monarchical progress, and evoked public rage, even hysteria, against popery and (ostensibly) in support of the monarchy. If in 1661 the coronation triumph idealized Charles II in the classical Roman mode, the grotesque body was used in the pope burnings to demonize the king's opponents and to limit his power.

It would be, of course, an overstatement to argue that the Whigs came into power in 1688 because they successfully harnessed and deployed the power of spectacle with which the Cromwellian government had struggled. Indeed, the immediate goal of passing the Exclusion bill was unsuccessful and the pope burnings did not continue beyond the defeat of Shaftesbury in 1682. Yet the lasting changes came in the monarchy not in 1649 but in 1688, and antipopery, stirred up by the pope burnings, played a crucial role. Nonetheless, in the demonization of Catholicism that marked these spectacles, Milton's iconoclastic voice remains distinct. For Milton, to demonize popery is a swerve away from the real problems. Plagued with Philistines—or papists—Israel is nonetheless always her own worst enemy.

# AFTERWORD

IN THE late eighteenth century, a story circulated about Milton that encapsulates the ironies and ambivalences we have seen in the contested sites of power and punishment, human and divine. The account tells how the Duke of York, the future James II, one day "told the king his brother, that he had heard so much of old Milton, that he had a great desire to see him." With Charles's permission, James went privately to visit Milton, and the subject of conversation not surprisingly turned to politics:

> The Duke asked Milton, whether he did not think the loss of his sight was a judgment upon him for what he had written against the late King his father? Milton's reply was to this effect: "If your Highness thinks that the calamities which befall us here are indications of the wrath of Heaven, in what manner are we to account for the fate of the King your father? The displeasure of Heaven must, upon this supposition, have been much greater against him, than against me: for I only lost my eyes, but he lost his head. (*LR* 4:390)

The Milton of the polemical prose had not lost his touch for the ironic riposte.

But Milton did not have the last word. James returned to the court and complained to his brother, insisting that he have "that old rogue Milton hanged." But the king, ascertaining from James that Milton was old, poor, and "blind as a beetle," replied: "Why then you are a fool, James, to want to have him hanged as a punishment: to hang him will be doing him a service: it will be taking him out of his miseries. No, if he is old, and poor, and blind, he is miserable enough in all conscience: let him live" (*LR* 4:390).

However dubious the authenticity of the story, this view of the blind and miserable Milton who writes despite his defeat, hearkening back to the 1640s or finding solace in inner spirituality, has become a canonical article of faith. But in tracing the spectacles of punishment and power in Restoration England, I have argued that Milton's emotional investments lie in the Restoration, that his major poems and late prose respond pointedly and defiantly to royalist spectacles of the 1660s and 1670s. Milton not only challenges the royalist mode but reconstitutes spectacle as true witness before a divine audience.



We have seen that the years from 1649 to 1679 evinced a remarkable number of contested, interrelated, and powerful spectacles in England: the execution of Charles I, the executions of the regicides and fifth monarchists, the exhuming of Cromwell, the Restoration celebrations and triumphs, the pope burnings, and even the plague and fire viewed as divine display. The ambivalences of Milton's Restoration poetry reflect the fissures and ambivalences of the political context, as he undertakes to further "Puritan" reform through counterspectacle, a kind of iconoclastic art against art.

Far from anachronistic, Milton's poetry evinces the ongoing struggle of dissent against state and church authorities for whom spectacle was a crucial mode of power. Milton's iconoclastic art incorporates the same paradox seen on January 30, 1649, when the Independents determined in an act both iconoclastic and spectacular to cut off the head of their king.

While the joke in the story recounted above seems finally to be on Milton, we should recall that in 1688, Milton's much-lauded *Paradise Lost* appeared in a handsome folio edition and his prose was being reprinted and circulated as part of Whig propaganda. And in that same year, James II kept his eyes and his head, but lost his entire kingdom.

# NOTES

## Introduction

1. On the spectacles of kingship see Roy Strong, *Splendor at Court*, revised and expanded as *Art and Power*. More specifically on representations of Charles II, Nicholas Jose, *Ideas of the Restoration*, traces the distinctive classicism of the coronation; Gerard Reedy, "Mystical Politics," delineates the range of imagery used in the coronation panegyric; Harold Weber, "Representations of the King," shows how narratives of Charles's escape after his defeat at Worcester mediate and legitimate his power; and M. L. Donnelly, "Caroline Royalist Panegyric," posits the breakdown of the panegyric mode during and after the civil war and Interregnum. In my discussion of the power of display and the display of power, I am generally indebted to recent new historicist critics, whom I discuss below. Jean Howard, "The New Historicism in Renaissance Studies," Louis Montrose, "Renaissance Literary Studies and the Subject of History," and Alan Liu, "The Power of Formalism: The New Historicism," provide cogent introductions to the new historicism.

2. Austin Woolrych, "The Good Old Cause," discusses the chaotic events leading up to the Restoration. Detailed accounts of the early Restoration are given in Woolrych, "Introduction," *CPW*, vol. 7; Ronald Hutton, *The Restoration;* Godfrey Davies, *The Restoration of Charles II;* J. R. Jones, *Country and Court;* and Tim Harris, *London Crowds in the Reign of Charles II*, 36–61. Christopher Hill, *Some Intellectual Consequences*, 7–15, dissents from the usual view that the enthusiasm for the restored monarchy was widespread and genuine. In response to Hill, Harris (36–37) argues that support for the Restoration was widespread but conditional upon the resolution of specific economic, constitutional, and religious grievances.

3. In tracing spectacles from 1649 into the 1670s, I find continuities and ambivalences that weigh against clear-cut ideological opposition and absolute changes. In this regard, my position accords with revisionist historians who have questioned the causes, nature, and scope of the "Puritan revolution" as posited by both Whig and Marxist histories. A good introduction to the debate is "After Revisionism" in Richard Cust and Ann Hughes, eds., *Conflict in Early Stuart England*, 1–46.

Christopher Hill's *The English Revolution* is a classic Marxist articulation of a bourgeois revolution. The revisionist position, which questions whether there was a revolution at all, is variously set out in Conrad Russell, ed., *Origins of the English Civil War;* Mark Kishlansky, "The Emergence of Adversary Politics," and John Morrill, *The Revolt of the Provinces.* I will return to the impact of this debate on the problematic terms, Puritan and Puritanism. I am continuing to use these terms, although with qualifications.



4. Michel Foucault, *Discipline and Punish,* 1–69.

5. James Holstun, "Ranting at the New Historicism," and Frank Lentricchia, "Reading Foucault (Punishment, Labor, Resistance)," make similar points in critiquing Foucault from a Marxist perspective.

6. Stephen Orgel, *The Illusion of Power.* Although Orgel's analysis is not explicitly Foucauldian, he posits a similarly effective, monolithic display. David Norbrook, "The Reformation of the Masque," argues that the masque could critique the king through its very silences.

7. Stephen Greenblatt, *Shakespearean Negotiations,* 62–65.

8. Greenblatt, *Renaissance Self-Fashioning,* 11–33.

9. Louis Montrose, "Eliza, Queene of Shepheardes" and "Shaping Fantasies."

10. Jonathan Goldberg, *James I and the Politics of Literature.*

11. Leonard Tennenhouse, *Power on Display.*

12. There are, of course, exceptions. In a rich study of the literal production of treason through executions and the display of body parts, Curtis Breight, "Treason doth never prosper," situates *The Tempest* within "a sphere of oppositional discourse that arose against official discourse in this period." Karen Cunningham, "Renaissance Execution and Marlovian Elocution," demonstrates how the staged violence of Marlowe's plays subversively exposes the ambivalence and artifice of Tudor executions.

13. Deborah Shuger, *Habits of Thought,* finds in recent new historicism "the almost total neglect of society's religious aspects in favor of political ones" (5). James Holstun, "Ranting at the New Historicism," points to radical oppositional voices in the ranters. Caroline Porter, "Are We Being Historical Yet?," charges that Greenblatt "frames the discursive field in such a way that sites of potential or actual resistance are either excluded from that field, or incorporated within it in terms that confirm the tautology's rule [apparent resistance ultimately serves power]" (769). Like Shuger, David Baker, "Wildehirissheman," points to heterogeneity within the dominant mode: "Discursive heterogeneity . . . is what characterizes the imperial discourse of English power and not the consolidation of every voice into a 'monological' whole" (61).

14. Orgel, *The Illusion of Power,* 43–44.

15. In a 1992 essay, William Kerrigan points out that new historicism "can claim scant impact on Milton studies" ("Seventeenth-Century Studies," 73).

16. Sir Walter Raleigh, *Milton,* 88.

17. M. H. Abrams, *The Norton Anthology,* 4th ed., 1722.

18. Abrams, *The Norton Anthology,* 5th ed., 1769.

19. Martin Price, "The Restoration and the Eighteenth Century," in Frank Ker-

mode and John Hollander, eds., *The Oxford Anthology of English Literature*, 1553. For further critique of these literary histories, see Nigel Keeble, *The Literary Culture of Nonconformity*, 20–22.

20. Tucker Brooke, "The Renaissance, 1500–1660," in Albert Baugh, ed., *A Literary History*, 689.

21. Douglas Bush, *English Literature in the Earlier Seventeenth Century*, 402. *The Cambridge History*, ed. A. W. Ward and A. R. Waller, similarly places Milton in an earlier volume under "Cavalier and Puritan," rather than in "The Age of Dryden."

22. Margaret Drabble, ed., *The Oxford Companion to English Literature*.

23. On the ideological construct of the author more generally, see Foucault, "What is an Author?"

24. David Masson, *The Life of John Milton;* Arthur Barker, *Milton and the Puritan Dilemma;* and Don Wolfe, *Milton in the Puritan Revolution*. As their titles indicate, Barker and Wolfe work with a Whiggish historiography that aligns Milton with a progressive and radical Puritan ideology and revolution. But the long-vexed terms "Puritan" and especially "Puritanism" have recently been further challenged by revisionists, who variously see Puritanism as part of an extremist and elitist group not necessarily opposed to monarchy (Christopher Haigh, "The Church of England, the Catholics, and the People") or as part of a broadstream Calvinist Protestantism reacting against popish-looking Arminianism (N. R. N. Tyacke, "Puritanism, Arminianism, and Counter-Revolution"). Literary studies reflect various "Puritan" Miltons. Boyd Berry, *Process of Speech*, locates Milton "at the radical end of a liberal-reformist-radical continuum" (270), arguing that some of the apparent oddities of Milton as Puritan, including his oxymoronic "Puritan epic," are actually the furthest working out of the radical Protestant tradition. Most recently, Richard Hardin, *Civil Idolatry*, focuses on Milton the Puritan as iconoclast, arguing that "the most crucial issues of the Puritan-Anglican conflict" were "the Protestant demythologizing of liturgy" (164).

25. Bush, *English Literature in the Earlier Seventeenth Century*, 402. Although Bush is a prominent spokesman for the humanist Milton, he here articulates the collapse of Milton's political aims.

26. James Holly Hanford, *John Milton: Poet and Humanist*, 183.

27. Humanism, like Puritanism, is a vexed and problematic term. Although there is broad agreement on humanism in England as curricular reform based on the study and ideals of Greek and Latin literature, the nature, range, and political scope of the movement is disputed. Alistair Fox, "Facts and Fallacies: Interpreting English Humanism," 9–33, gives a lucid account of competing views. While classic studies present humanism as an aristocratic mode championing individualism, Mary Thomas Crane, *Framing Authority*, has compellingly argued for a humanism that fostered "a socially constituted subject, common ownership of texts and ideas, and a collective model of authorship" (6). The humanist Milton still dominates Milton criticism. Most recently, Joan Bennett, *Reviving Liberty*, projects Milton's humanism as a reflection of his libertarian political sensibility.

28. David Daiches, *A Critical History of English Literature*, 457.

29. See Bernard Sharratt, "The Appropriation of Milton." The separation of

the political from the aesthetic has been challenged by Kevin Sharpe and Steven Zwicker, "Introduction," in *Politics of Discourse*, 1–20, and in David Loewenstein and James Turner, eds., *Politics, Poetics, and Hermeneutics in Milton's Prose*, a collection of essays that foreground the literary qualities of Milton's prose.

30. Hill, *Milton and the English Revolution* and *The Experience of Defeat*, 247–328.

31. Among the best recent studies linking Milton's prose and poetry, Jackie DiSalvo, "'The Lord's Battells': *Samson Agonistes* and the Puritan Revolution," sees in Samson the vocation and discipline of the New Model army. Joan Bennett, "God, Satan, and King Charles," links Milton's representation of Charles I's tyranny in *Eikonoklastes* with Satan in *Paradise Lost.* Stevie Davies, *Images of Kingship in "Paradise Lost,"* draws on Milton's prose polemics against Charles I to illumine the multifaceted depiction of monarchy in *Paradise Lost.* David Loewenstein, *Milton and the Drama of History*, argues that "Milton continues to grapple [in his poetry] with historical conflicts already registered in his revolutionary prose works" (6).



32. Keeble, *The Literary Culture of Nonconformity.*

33. Earl Miner, *The Restoration Mode*, 47.

34. Ibid., 288.

35. Steven Zwicker, "Lines of Authority," 249.

36. Sharpe and Zwicker, "Introduction," 9. In "England, Israel, and the Triumph of Roman Virtue," Zwicker similarly asserts that "in 1650, the central book of English culture was Scripture; by 1700 the texts men chose to talk about themselves were those of Roman history and Roman politics" (37).

37. Jose, *Ideas of the Restoration*, 142–63.

38. The regicide as an act of iconoclasm was underscored to me in conversation with Stephen Baskerville.

39. On iconoclasm, see John Phillips, *The Reformation of Images;* Margaret Aston, *England's Iconoclasts;* Ernest Gilman, *Iconoclasm and Poetry.*

40. Joseph Wittreich, *Interpreting "Samson Agonistes";* Clay Daniel, "Lust and Violence in *Samson Agonistes*"; Michael Wilding, *Dragon's Teeth*, 232–58; Andrew Milner, *John Milton and the English Revolution*, 138–94.

41. David Quint, "David's Census," 130.

42. On Milton in the Restoration, see Godfrey Davies, "Milton in 1660"; Masson, *The Life of John Milton* 6:162–217; William Riley Parker, *Milton: A Biography*, 567–89; and Woolrych, "Introduction," *CPW* 7:219–23.

43. *The Life of Mr. John Milton* by Edward Phillips (1694), in Helen Darbishire, *The Early Lives of Milton*, 74.

44. Ibid.

45. Annabel Patterson, *Censorship and Interpretation*, 3–23. Gary Hamilton, "*The History of Britain* and Its Restoration Audience," uses Patterson's hermeneutics of censorship to argue persuasively that Milton critiques kingship through the art of indirection in his 1670 prose history.

46. Keeble, *The Literary Culture of Nonconformity*, 22.

47. Nancy Maguire's valuable *Regicide and Restoration*, which appeared after my study was complete, strikingly corroborates in the drama the ongoing obsession

with Charles I (and Cromwell) that I trace in Restoration spectacle, occasional verse, and Milton's major poems.



### Chapter 1: *Paradise Regained* and Royal Martyrdom

1. For an account of Charles's life and death see C. V. Wedgwood, *A Coffin for King Charles*. On the civil war controversies see Merritt Hughes, "Introduction," in *CPW*, vol. 3.

2. *An Act of the Commons of England assembled in Parliament*, 1649.

3. Foucault, *Discipline and Punish*. Foucault's argument, however, does not account for what happens when the king himself is the subject of punishment.

4. John Cook, *King Charls, His Case, or An Appeal to all Rational Men*, 1649, 5.

5. Ibid.

6. *A Perfect Narrative of the whole Proceedings of the High Court of Justice*, in Thomas Bayly Howell, *State Trials* 4:998.

7. Foucault, *Discipline and Punish*, 46.

8. *A Perfect Narrative*, in Howell, *State Trials* 4:1138–41. Bruce Boehrer, "Elementary Structures of Kingship," 97–98, points astutely to the theatrical nature of Charles's execution.

9. Henry, *Diaries and Letters*, 12.

10. *Mercurius Elencticus* (London, 1649), reprinted in *A History of English Journalism*, App. A, 205.

11. Quoted in Introduction to *Eikon Basilike*, ed. Philip Knachel, xxxii. All *Eikon Basilike* quotations are from this edition. Valuable on the vexed question of authorship is F. F. Madan, *A New Bibliography of the Eikon Basilike.*

12. Foxe's *Acts and Monuments of these latter and perilous days*, popularly known as the "Book of Martyrs," was first published in English in 1563 and frequently reprinted; after 1570 a copy was placed with the Bible in every English church. On the enormous influence of Foxe, see William Haller, *Foxe's Book of Martyrs and the Elect Nation.*

13. Florence Sandler, "Icon and Iconoclast," 162, argues that the *Eikon Basilike* effectively represented Charles as the culmination of Foxe's tradition of martyrs. John Knott, Jr., "'Suffering for Truths Sake': Milton and Martyrdom," 159–62, nonetheless points out the ironies in using the Foxean model for a defender of the religious establishment. Janel Mueller, "Embodying Glory," 16, argues that the centrality of the whole social spectrum of suffering martyrs in Foxe's writings tends to dissociate him from the imperial tradition.

14. Lois Potter, *Secret Rites and Secret Writing*, 160–63, gives valuable details on the frontispiece, but argues unpersuasively that the emblem is (only) Davidic and not Christic. Roy Strong, *Van Dyck: Charles I on Horseback* (29–30), David Loewenstein, *Milton and the Drama of History* (52–53), and Thomas Corns, *Uncloistered Virtue* (90–91), argue for Christic resonances. Corns also makes the point that the violence was not represented.

15. See Helen Randall, "The Rise and Fall of a Martyrology," and Potter, *Secret Rites*, 184–93.

16. *An Elegie upon the Death of Our Dread Soveraign Lord King Charls the Martyr*, broadsheet.

17. Henry King, *A Deep Groane Fetch'd At the Funerall of that Incomparable and Glorious Monarch, Charles the First*, 3.

18. *A Hand-Kirchife for Loyall Mourners or a Cordiall for Drooping Spirits*, 5–6.

19. *The Scotch Souldiers Lamentation Upon the Death of the most Glorious and Illustrious Martyr, King Charles*, 18.

20. Bishop Juxon, *The Subjects Sorrow; Or, Lamentations Upon the Death of Britaines Josiah* (1649). The picture can also be found elsewhere.

21. Andrew Marvell, *An Horation Ode*, in *The Poems and Letters of Andrew Marvell*, ed. H. M. Margoliouth, 1:91–94. I should point out that the Ode was not published until 1681.

22. Critics have variously interpreted the strikingly dual focus. Warren Chernaik, *The Poet's Time*, 15, argues that "Charles I and Cromwell are seen as actors playing the roles allotted to them." Barbara Everett, "The Shooting of the Bears," 83, meditates on the poem's "peculiarly public" qualities. For Blair Worden, "Andrew Marvell, Oliver Cromwell, and the Horation Ode," Marvell imbues heated contemporary politics with "timelessness." But others find less balance and more polemics. David Norbrook, "Marvell's 'Horation Ode,'" argues that Marvell radically revises a royalist genre to praise Cromwell in distinctively republican terms; Wilding, *Dragon's Teeth*, 114–37, sees the poem as eliciting through signifying silences support for Cromwell's army; Corns, *Uncloistered Virtue*, 227–35, contends that Marvell may stir sentiment for the martyred king, but he effectively rules out Charles II as an option.

23. Corns, *Uncloistered Virtue*, 228, underscores the macabre and surreal details in Marvell's description of Charles's execution.

24. Annabel Patterson, *Marvell and the Civic Crown*, 68.

25. Lois Potter, *Secret Rites*, 182–84, sees Milton attacking Charles as an actor in three senses: as a hypocrite, a mere mouthpiece of rituals, and an effeminate puppet. Lana Cable, "Milton's Iconoclastic Truth," 143–45, comments that Milton attacks *Eikon Basilike* as a "self-witnessing idol" whose "spectacular shows demand worship, not applause." David Loewenstein, *Milton and the Drama of History*, 51–73, argues that Milton replaces the image of martyr with king as tyrant.

26. Dorothy Gardiner, ed., *The Oxinden and Peyton Letters, 1642–1670*, 214–15.

27. The Bishop of Down, *The Martyrdom of King Charls I*, 31.

28. Ibid., 32.

29. *The Great Memorial: Or, a List of the Names of those Pretended Judges who Sate*, broadsheet.

30. Charles Stuart, *By the King. A Proclamation for Observation of the Thirtieth day of January as a day of Fast and Humiliation*, broadsheet.

31. Arthur Brett, *The Restauration. Or, a Poem on the Return of the most Mighty and ever Glorious Prince*, 7.

32. Abraham Cowley, *Ode, Upon His Majesties Restoration and Return*, in *Poems*, 425.

33. *The Manner of the Solemnity of the Coronation of His Most Sacred Majesty King Charles*, broadsheet.
34. J. Ailmer, *Britannia Rediviva*, Sig $B3_r$.
35. Cowley, *Ode, Upon His Majesties Restoration*, in *Poems*, 428.
36. *Englands Triumph; A More Exact History of His Majesties Escape*, 107–8.
37. *To the King Upon His Majesties Happy Return*, 6.
38. Alexander Brome, *A Congratulatory Poem*, 5.
39. Henry Beeston and Henry Bold, *A Poem to his most Excellent Majesty Charles the Second*, 5.
40. Quoted in Randall, "The Rise and Fall of a Martyrology," 136.
41. Roger L'Estrange, *Treason Arraigned, In Answer to Plain English* (1660), in Parker, *Milton's Contemporary Reputation*, 100.
42. Richard Perrinchief, Introduction to *The Workes of King Charles the Martyr*, 94–95.
43. Recent critics have variously explored the political significance of *Paradise Regained.* Christopher Hill, *Milton and The English Revolution*, 413–27, sees Christ as rejecting those things that led the revolutionaries astray. Andrew Milner, *John Milton and the English Revolution*, 167–79, argues that Christ's rejection of Satan's political offers reflects Milton's own withdrawal from politics after the collapse of the Commonwealth. Michael Wilding, *Dragon's Teeth*, 249–53, also finds quietism in the poem. David Quint, "David's Census," argues that the poem challenges the Davidic claims of Charles I and Charles II.
44. See, respectively, John Carey, *Milton*, 137; Alan Fisher, "Why Is *Paradise Regained* So Cold?," 206; and Northrop Frye, "The Typology of *Paradise Regained*," 439.
45. For instance, Fisher, "Why Is *Paradise Regained* So Cold?"; challenging this view, Wayne Anderson, "Is *Paradise Regained* Really Cold?".
46. Barbara Lewalski, *Milton's Brief Epic*, reconstructs the history and form of brief epic.
47. Stanley Fish, in "The Temptation of Plot" and "Inaction and Silence," examines the antitheatricality of the poem. Jeffrey Morris, "Disorientation and Disruption," argues compellingly that "the poem's formal disorientation leads to a more theological orientation" (220).
48. Christ's reply to Pilate in the gospel of John is considerably different: "Thou sayest that I am a king. To this end was I born, and for this cause came I into the world, that I should bear witness unto the truth. Every one that is of the truth heareth my voice" (John 18.37). Interestingly enough, while Milton's Son of God seems to be closest to this Christ, the gospel of John has no temptation account. Milton welds the Christ of the gospel of John with the temptations found in the synoptic gospels.
49. John Knott, Jr., "'Suffering for Truths Sake,'" points out the link with *Eikon Basilike*, 167. Jeffrey Morris, "Disorientation and Disruption," shows how the stable, unmoved Son serves for the reader as "the only unifying point amidst diffuse and disorienting action" (234).

## Chapter 2: *Samson Agonistes* and the Regicides

1. Ronald Hutton, *The Restoration*, 132–35, and David Masson, *Life of John Milton*, 76–98, discuss the trials and punishments of the regicides. For primary sources, see *The Trial of Twenty-nine Regicides at old Bailey for High Treason* along with extracts from contemporary accounts of the scaffold speeches and behavior of the regicides, reprinted in Howell, *State Trials* 5:947–1364. J. A. Sharpe, "'Last Dying Speeches,'" describes the genre of scaffold confessions.

2. *Mercurius Publicus*, Thursday, October 11–Thursday, October 18, 1660, 672. Further references are to this issue unless otherwise noted.

3. *A True and Perfect Relation of the Grand Traytors Execution*, broadsheet.

4. *A Looking-Glasse for Traytors*, broadsheet.

5. *The Speeches and Prayers of Major General Harrison [et al] . . . The Times of their Deaths.* Further references to this martyrology will be parenthetical. See the trials of Dover, Brewster, and Brooks for "causing to be printed, publishing and uttering a seditious, scandalous, and malicious book," reprinted in Howell, *State Trials* 6:539–64. All were found guilty, fined, made to stand on the pillory, and sentenced to gaol.

6. *The Trials, Behaviour, and Dying Speeches of Colonel Okey, Col. Barkstead, and Miles Corbet, esq. April 1662*, in Howell, *State Trials* 5:1306.

7. Ibid., 1307.

8. *Observations Upon the Last Actions and Words of Maj. Gen Harrison Written by a Minister in a Letter to a Countrey Gentlewoman*, single page letter.

9. Quoted in Varley, *Cromwell's Latter End*, 43–44. Along with Varley, see the accounts of the disinterment given in Hutton, *The Restoration*, 134, and Antonia Fraser, *Cromwell: The Lord Protector*, 678–707. A number of contemporary accounts are reproduced in *Cromwelliana*.

10. Charles Stuart, *By the King. A Proclamation for Observation of the Thirtieth day of January as a day of Fast and Humiliation*, broadsheet.

11. *The Last Farewel of Three Bould Traytors*, broadsheet.

12. Quoted in Varley, *Cromwell's Latter End*, 55–56.

13. *A New Meeting of Ghosts at Tyburn*, Sig $A2_r$.

14. *T' Radt van Avontveren* (The Wheel of Fortune), 1661. The illustration is a detail, "Kromwel's Graf" (Cromwell's Grave). Dutch illustrations of the execution of Charles I were considerably more graphic than English prints; one showed Cromwell holding Charles's bleeding head by the hair.

15. See *A New Meeting of Ghosts at Tyburn* (1661) and *The Last Farewel of Three Bould Traytors* (1661).

16. Collonel Baker, *The Blazing-Star, or Noll's Nose* (1660). It is worth noting that the title page, "Wherin is set down, the Acts of all those / In *Pluto's* Black Court, that guarded *Nolls* Nose," includes Milton himself: "And next those Black Chaplains that preach'd up *Nolls* Nose, / *Goodwin*, *Milton* and *Peter's* in the close."

17. Bakhtin, *Rabelais and His World*.

18. Marchamont Nedham and Payne Fisher, *The Speeches of Oliver Cromwell, Henry Ireton, and John Bradshaw* (1661).

19. Jonathan Richardson, *The Life of Milton and a Discourse on Paradise Lost* (1734), in Darbishire, *The Early Lives of Milton*, 276.

20. I am following the traditional assumption of a post-Restoration date for the writing of *Samson Agonistes.* William Parker argues for an earlier date in *Milton: A Biography* 2:903–17. But Mary Ann Radzinowicz makes a definitive defense of the later date in *Toward "Samson Agonistes,"* 387–407. The links between *Samson Agonistes* and the punishments of the regicides should strengthen the argument that the work is a later, more political drama, not the private drama of the 1640s that Parker envisions.

21. Radzinowicz, *Toward "Samson Agonistes,"* 87–108, 167–79.

22. Hill, *Milton and the English Revolution*, 442–43, and *The Experience of Defeat*, 310–19. Robert Wilcher, "*Samson Agonistes* and the Problem of History," concludes, much like Hill, that Milton writes "to demonstrate that God does not abandon his 'faithful champion' and to strengthen the spirits of the few who remained true to their election, so that they—like Samson—would be ready if the time should come" (129).

23. DiSalvo, " 'The Lord's Battells.' "

24. Jose, *Ideas of the Restoration*, 142–99.

25. Irene Samuel, "*Samson Agonistes* as Tragedy"; Wittreich, *Interpreting "Samson Agonistes,"* 364–85.

26. Loewenstein, *Milton and the Drama of History*, 126–51.

27. T. S. K. Scott-Craig, "Concerning Milton's Samson," states unequivocally that "Samson Agonistes is really Christus Agonistes" (46). More recently, D. M. Rosenberg, "*Samson Agonistes:* 'Proverb'd for a Fool,' " argues that Milton "develops the ritual pattern of Samson's death and rebirth, presenting him as a prototype of the risen Christ" (77). Links with the suffering, crucified Christ are often drawn upon or assumed in arguments for a regenerated Samson, as in Anthony Low, *The Blaze of Noon.*

28. Derek Wood, " 'Exil'd from Light,' " 253–56, astutely delineates the contrasts between Samson and Christ in *Paradise Regained.*

29. Stanley Fish, "Spectacle and Evidence in *Samson Agonistes,*" posits radical ambiguity: "God and Samson unite only in being inaccessible, objects alike of an interpretive activity that finds no corroboration in the visible world" (586).

30. Merritt Hughes, in Milton, *Complete Poems*, 568, identifies the allusion.

31. Jose, *Ideas of the Restoration*, 162–63, connects Dalila as a naval creature not only with Dagon but also with the Restoration regime.

32. Ibid., 156.

33. Several earlier critics have linked Samson's violence with the wrath of the apocalypse. Anna Nardo, " 'Sung and Proverb'd for a Fool,' " cogently notes that Samson shows "the wrath of the apocalypse more than the forgiveness of the passion" (9). Barbara Lewalski, "*Samson Agonistes* and the 'Tragedy' of the Apocalypse," sees Samson as a type of the elect saints' participation in Christ's final judgment.

34. Perhaps the first critic of the violence was Irene Samuel, "*Samson Agonistes* as Tragedy," who argues that, although no pacifist, Milton links vengeance and

violence with the tyrannical and diabolical rather than with the divine. Joseph Wittreich, *Interpreting "Samson Agonistes,"* points to the violence in his argument for a deeply flawed, unregenerate, and self-destructive Samson. Clay Daniel, "Lust and Violence in *Samson Agonistes,*" similarly argues that Samson's vices result in his death and damnation. Jose, *Images of the Restoration* (142–63), Ernest Gilman, *Iconoclasm and Poetry* (149–77), and Loewenstein, *Milton and the Drama of History* (126–51), defend Samson's violence as iconoclasm.

35. Franklin Baruch, "Time, Body, and Spirit at the Close of *Samson Agonistes,*" describes this veneration as the "saint's life without the actual sanctity" (325). Helen Damico, "Duality in Dramatic Vision," views the Israelites as behaving like Philistine idolators (108).

36. Northrop Frye, *Spiritus Mundi*, 222.

37. Richard Hardin, *Civil Idolatry*, 20–22, 164–201.

38. *The True Manner of the most Magnificent Conveyance of his Highness Effigies*, 11.

39. Edmund Ludlow, *Memoirs* 2:260.

40. Abraham Cowley, *A Discourse By way of Vision*, in *Essays, Plays and Sundry Verses*, 342.

41. Edward Burrough, *A Testimony against a great Idolatry Committed*, 2.

42. Sir Edward Nicholas writes on June 13, 1659, that Richard "dare not stirr out of Whitehall for feare of arrest [for debt]," *The Nicholas Papers*, 154.

43. Thomas Burton, *The Diary* 2: App. 7.

44. Woolrych, "Milton and Cromwell."

## Chapter 3: *Paradise Lost* and the Politics of Joy

1. Christopher Hill, *Some Intellectual Consequences*, 7–15, and *The World Turned Upside Down*, 41, 351, argues that the celebrations were shows sponsored by the elite. My reading goes against the liberation that Bakhtin, *Rabelais and His World*, sees in the carnivalesque festivals.

2. Graham Parry, *The Golden Age Restor'd*, discusses early Stuart golden age typology. Harry Levin shows both the prominence of the golden age motif and its linkage with the Christian Eden in *The Myth of the Golden Age in the Renaissance.*

3. Raymond Williams, *Marxism and Literature*, 128.

4. Leah Marcus, *The Politics of Mirth*, 1–23, and "Herrick's *Hesperides* and the 'Proclamation Made for May.'" Lois Potter, *Secret Rites, Secret Writing*, 137–48, persuasively argues that the drinking often mentioned in cavalier verse of the 1640s and 1650s was not a sign of degeneracy in defeat, but a kind of secret rite evincing loyalty to the king and hostility to the Puritan sects.

5. *Mercurius Publicus*, Thursday, May 27–Thursday, May 31, 1661, 344.

6. Ibid., 344–45.

7. *England's Triumph. A More Exact History*, 91.

8. James Heath, *The Glories and Magnificent Triumphs*, 102.

9. Ibid., 111.

10. John Ogilby, *The Entertainment of His Most Excellent Majestie Charles II*, 1.

11. *Festa Georgiana, or the Gentries & Countries Joy for the Coronation*, 5. Further references parenthetical.

12. Albert Cacicedo, "Seeing the King," traces the ways in which the biblical imagery limits the classical, arguing that the two are not simply interchangeable.

13. Ogilby, *The Entertainment*, 135.

14. *The Jubilee, or The Coronation Day*, in MacKay, *Cavalier Songs*, 246.

15. Aurelian Cook, *Titus Britannicus*, "The Epistle Dedicatory," Sig. $B3_r$.

16. *The Parliamentary Intelligencer*, Monday, May 21–Monday, May 28, 1660, 339.

17. Ibid.

18. Samuel Pordage, *Heroick Stanzas on His Majesties Coronation*, 7.

19. Rachel Jevon, *Exultationis Carmen to the Kings Most Excellent Majesty*, 2.

20. *The Claret Drinker's Song, or The Good Fellow's Design*, in MacKay, *Cavalier Songs*, 233.

21. *Anglia Rediviva*, 2.

22. Henry, *Diaries and Letters*, 84.

23. Stuart, *By the King. A Proclamation Against Vicious, Debauch'd, and Prophane Persons.*

24. *Depositions from the Castle of York*, 83.

25. Ibid., 99.

26. Marcia Landy, "'Bounds Prescrib'd,'" astutely construes Satanic psychology.

27. In early classic studies of Milton's hell, Merritt Hughes, "'Myself Am Hell,'" and Ernest Schanzer, "Milton's Hell Revisited," show how Satan's mind replicates the macrocosm of Hell. Much more recently, Robert Myers, "'God shall be all in all,'" makes a striking case for the replacement of hell by discipline.

28. John Carey, "Satan," and Kenneth Gross, "Milton's Satan," astutely trace the ambivalences of Milton's Satan, including this soliloquy.

29. Robin Jarvis, "Love between Milton and Wordsworth," and (with more focus on economics) Knoppers, "Rewriting the Protestant Ethic," link obedience with love in *Paradise Lost.*

30. Janet Halley, "Female Autonomy in Milton's Sexual Poetics," 250–53, and Mary Nyquist, "The Genesis of Gendered Subjectivity," 119–24, persuasively argue that Eve's subjectivity is precisely what is required of her.

31. Diane McColley, *Milton's Eve*, 43–48, explains that while the Genesis help-meet passage was traditionally taken to mean help in procreation, Puritan writers stressed companionship.

32. See, for example, Wilding's powerful discussion of Milton's blindness in this context, *Dragon's Teeth*, 232–58.

33. Steven Zwicker, "Lines of Authority," cogently notes the cultural authority Milton gains through the figure of Orpheus here: "Exile and humiliation are turned to mythic triumph" (253). But I am arguing for the simultaneous poignant registering of danger.

34. Milton, *Complete Poems*, 84.

35. J. Martin Evans, "Lycidas," 41.

36. Leah Marcus, *The Politics of Mirth*, 169–212, analyzes *Comus* as an "anti-Laudian masque."

## Chapter 4: Milton and the Roman Triumph



1. The fullest treatments of the coronation triumph are Eric Halfpenny, "Cities Loyalty Display'd"; Jose, *Ideas of the Restoration*, which demonstrates that "Romanness is established as a characteristic glory of Charles' Restoration" (121–22); and Ronald Knowles's scholarly introduction to his edition of John Ogilby, *The Entertainment of His Most Excellent Majestie.*

2. For the Roman background, see Max Cary, *A History of Rome*, and H. T. Peck, ed., *Harper's Dictionary of Classical Literature and Antiquities*, 1609–11. On Renaissance triumphs, see Roy Strong, *Art and Power*, and Alastair Fowler, *Triumphal Forms.*

3. Jonathan Goldberg, *James I and the Politics of Literature;* Stephen Orgel, *The Illusion of Power.* See also David Bergeron, *English Civic Pageantry, 1558–1642.*

4. Ruth Nevo, *Dial of Virtue*, 138–56, characterizes the pageantry as "baroque heroic" that evinced material splendor.

5. Henry Beeston and Henry Bold, *A Poem to His Most Excellent Majesty, Charles II*, 7.

6. James Heath, *The Glories and Magnificent Triumphs*, 183; 208 (mispag. 160).

7. Ogilby, *The Entertainment of His Most Excellent Majestie Charles II* (1662). The year before Ogilby published a less ambitious volume, *The Relation of His Majesties Entertainment* (1661). All quotes are from the 1662 volume and will be given parenthetically.

8. My stress on the incorporation of the shameful within the panegyric differs from Ruth Nevo, *Dial of Virtue*, who points to iconoclasm, scurrility, and satire as later responses.

9. Samuel Pordage, *Heroick Stanzas on His Majesties Coronation*, 6.

10. *To the King, Upon His Majesties Happy Return*, 5.

11. Howard Erskine-Hill, *The Augustan Idea in English Literature*, 221–27, traces disillusionment in the 1670s with the hyperbolic Augustan model of 1660–61, and a contrasting Antonian mode seemingly more suited to Charles II. I am pointing to tensions already in the 1660–61 panegyric. Alastair Fowler, *Triumphal Forms*, 27–28, notes the ongoing uneasiness with human glory celebrated in the triumph. Howard Weinbrot, *Augustus Caesar in "Augustan" England*, is the fullest account of the historical and ideological ambivalences of the Roman mode.

12. *To the King, Upon His Majesties Happy Return*, 6.

13. Thomas Higgins, *A Panegyrick to the King*, 7.

14. Harold Weber, "Representations of the King," perceptively treats escape narratives of Charles II as fictions that reconstitute royal power in the face of just these ambiguities.

15. Samuel Pordage, *Heroick Stanzas*, 9.

16. S. W., *Epinicia Carolina*, 12.

17. Richard Perrinchief, *The Syracusan Tyrant or the Life of Agathocles.* The illustration is a reproduction of a 1653 print.

18. J. Nalson, *A True Copy of the Journal of the High Court of Justice* (1684).

19. *To the King, Upon His Majesties Happy Return,* 1.

20. Higgins, *A Panegyrick to the King,* 8.

21. Pordage, *Heroick Stanzas,* 5.

22. Martin Llevelyn, *To the King's Most Excellent Majestie.*

23. Potter, *Secret Rites,* 173.

24. Aurelian Cook, *Titus Britannicus* (1685), Sig B2$_r$–B3$_v$.

25. My discussion of the triumphs in *Paradise Lost* draws upon and extends into Restoration politics two valuable studies, Stevie Davies's *Images of Kingship* (89–126), which elucidates Milton's epic triumphs in relation to their classical origins and Milton's own polemical prose, and John Demaray's *Milton's Theatrical Epic,* which links Milton's triumphs with Caroline masques. In my discussion of glory of these triumphs, I have also benefited from John Rumrich, *Matter of Glory,* which provides a thorough grounding for glory in *Paradise Lost* in Hebrew, Roman, Christian, Homeric, and Virgilian traditions. Steven Zwicker, "Lines of Authority," 246–58, argues broadly for the cultural authority Milton appropriates through his use of the classics.

26. John Rumrich, *Matter of Glory,* 83–98, discusses the nature and implications of Satan's "withered glory."

27. Both Davies, *Images of Kingship,* 92–126, and Demaray, *Milton's Theatrical Epic,* 57–72, discuss Satan's return to hell as an attempted triumph. See also Lewalski, *"Paradise Lost" and the Rhetoric of Literary Forms,* 107–9.

28. Rumrich, *Matter of Glory,* 14–25, discusses divine glory in *Paradise Lost* as Hebrew *kabod,* meaning both substantial essence and ensuing fame.

29. Ibid., 173.

30. Davies, *Images of Kingship,* 122–24, and Demaray, *Milton's Theatrical Epic,* 85–101, discuss this heavenly triumph.

31. Michael Lieb, "'The Chariot of Paternal Deitie,'" 21–23, and *Poetics of the Holy.*

32. Lieb, "'The Chariot of Paternal Deitie,'" 22, and *Poetics of the Holy,* 121–27.

33. Wilding, *Dragon's Teeth,* 241–42, explores the political implications of Marvell's tribute.

34. Howard Erskine-Hill, *The Augustan Idea,* 224, discusses *Paradise Regained* as part of the disillusionment with the Augustan mode. David Quint, "David's Census," also points to the poem's anti-Augustan setting. Malcolm Kelsall, "The Historicity of *Paradise Regained,*" puts the poem in a Roman historical setting but without any comment on the significance for "Augustan" England.

35. It is noteworthy that the Son gains his martyr's glory not through suffering but through constancy; the revisions of the martyrdom discussed in chapter 1 also apply to the question of the martyr's glory in *Paradise Regained.*

36. Jose, *Ideas of the Restoration,* 156–60.

37. See Cromwell, *Writings and Speeches.*

38. Andrew Marvell, *An Horation Ode*, in *Poems* 1:94.

39. Thomas Sprat, *To the Happie Memory of the Most Renowned Prince, Oliver* (1659), 21.

40. Payne Fisher, *Veni, Vidi, Vici*, Sig. $B4_v$.

41. Sprat, *To the Happie Memory*, 22.

42. Fisher, *Veni, Vidi, Vici*, 10, 11.

43. Milton, *Complete Poems*, 160.

44. Ibid.

45. Ruth Nevo, *Dial of Virtue*, 74–137, compellingly traces in Cromwellian panegyric an ideological tension between heroic virtue and providentialism, a tension she sees successfully resolved in Milton.

46. J. D. Durnovariae, *Short Meditations on . . . the Life and Death of Oliver Cromwell*, 7. It is worth recalling that the displays of the Cromwellian state became increasingly lavish and that accounts of his lying-in-state refer to the model of Rome.

47. *Justa Sive Inferiae Regicidarum*, broadsheet.



## Chapter 5: *Paradise Regained* and Venner's Uprising

1. Detailed historical accounts of Venner's uprising can be found in C. Burrage, "The Fifth Monarchy Insurrections," 739–45; Michael McKeon, *Politics and Poetry in Restoration England*, 84–87; Richard L. Greaves, *Deliver Us from Evil*, 49–57; and Philip George Rogers, *The Fifth Monarchy Men*, 110–22.

2. James Heath, *A Brief Chronicle* (1662), 56, misprint for 66. See also Clarendon, *The Life*, 477.

3. Ecclesiastical histories of the Restoration period include Gerald Cragg, *Puritanism in the Period of the Great Persecution* and "The Collapse of Militant Puritanism," Douglas Lacey, *Dissent and Parliamentary Politics in England*, and more recently, Nigel Keeble, *The Literary Culture of Nonconformity.*

4. On fifth monarchism see B. S. Capp, *The Fifth Monarchy Men*, and Tai Liu, *Discord in Zion.* While millenarianism was most pronounced among fifth monarchists, distinctive in their advocacy of violence to bring in the kingdom, it was by no means confined to them, even after the Restoration. See William Lamont, *Richard Baxter and the Millennium;* Keeble, *The Literary Culture of Nonconformity.* A classic treatment of millenarianism is Norman Cohn, *The Pursuit of the Millennium.*

5. George Fox, *Journal*, 12.

6. Ephraim Paggitt, *Heresiography*, 282–83.

7. Ibid., 283.

8. William Aspinwall, *A Brief Description of the Fifth Monarchy*, 2.

9. Ibid., 14.

10. Lewalski, "Milton: Political Beliefs and Polemical Methods," 200–201.

11. Venner's earlier attempt is detailed in John Thurloe, *A Collection of the State Papers* 6:184–85. Burrage, "The Fifth Monarchy Insurrections," reprints a journal record of the insurrection plans, 725–39.

12. On the pretended plots, see Ludlow, *Memoirs* 2:329–30, and McKeon, *Politics and Poetry in Restoration England*, 84.
13. Venner, *A Door of Hope*, 1, 4.
14. *Mercurius Publicus*, Thursday, January 17–Thursday, January 24, 1660, 34, 37.
15. Clarendon, *The Life*, 477.
16. Venner, *The Last Speech and Prayer*, 4. Further references parenthetical.
17. *Londons Glory*, 4–5.
18. *The Last Farewel to the Rebellious Crew of Fifth Monarchy Men*, 8.
19. *An Advertisment as touching the Fanaticks late Conspiracy*, 4–5.
20. *Mercurius Publicus*, Thursday, January 10–Thursday, January 17, 1661, 17.
21. *An Impartial Narrative of the Late Rebellious Insurrection*, in *The Kingdomes Intelligencer*, Monday, January 7–Monday, January 14, 1661. Further references parenthetical.
22. *A Renuntiation and Declaration of the Ministers of the Congregational Churches*, 4–5. Greaves, *Deliver Us from Evil*, 49–57, gives a detailed account of the nonconformists' responses to Venner.
23. *The Humble Apology of some commonly called Anabaptists.*
24. Thomas Ellwood, *The History of the Life*, ed. C. G. Crump, 55.
25. George Fox et al., *A Declaration from the Harmles & Innocent People of God.*
26. Henry, *Diaries and Letters*, 75.
27. On ecclesiastical history see chapter 5, n. 3.
28. Andrew Milner, *John Milton and the English Revolution*, 167–79.
29. Wilding, *Dragon's Teeth*, 249.
30. Joan S. Bennett, *Reviving Liberty*, 198–202.
31. Hill, *Milton and the English Revolution*, 421.
32. Michael Fixler, *Milton and the Kingdoms of God*, 248.
33. Edward LeComte, "Satan's Heresies in *Paradise Regained*," 257–58, points out the heresy of the military Messiah.
34. Hill, *Milton and the English Revolution*, 417.
35. Lewalski, *Milton's Brief Epic*, 210–14.
36. Ibid., 268–70.
37. John Clarke, *The Plotters Unmasked*, 2.
38. Ibid., 3.
39. My essay, "Milton's *The Readie and Easie Way* and the English Jeremiad," 225, locates this precise but previously unrecognized context through the use of the term "idol queen."

## Chapter 6: Plague, Fire, Jeremiad, and *Samson Agonistes*

1. Early and richly detailed studies of plague and fire are Walter Besant, *London in the Time of the Stuarts;* Walter Bell, *The Great Plague in London in 1665* and *The Great Fire of London in 1666.* Good recent accounts are Hutton, *The Restoration*, 248–50, and Paul Slack, *The Impact of Plague in Tudor and Stuart England.*
2. Sacvan Bercovitch, *The American Jeremiad*, gives the classic formulation of

the jeremiad, although he posits the genre as distinctively American. Arguing for English jeremiads are James Egan, "'This is a Lamentation and shall be for a Lamentation'" and Knoppers, "Milton's *The Readie and Easie Way.*"

3. Nathaniel Hodge, *Loimologia*, 108–9.

4. Thomas Gumble, *The Life of General Monck, Duke of Albemarle*, 415.

5. Matthew Mead, *Solomon's Prescription*, Preface to the Reader, Sig $A3_r$. Further references parenthetical.

6. *London's Plague-Sore Discovered*, 4–5.

7. Thomas Vincent, *God's Terrible Voice in the City* (1671), 28. This is the thirteenth edition of Vincent's widely circulated sermon. Further references parenthetical.

8. John Tabor, *Seasonable Thoughts in Sad Times*, 2.

9. Samuel Rolle [Rolls], *The Burning of London*, 81–82.

10. *The Plague Checkt*, 62, 63. Further references parenthetical.

11. Stuart, *A Proclamation For a General Fast through England and Wales*, broadsheet. I would like to thank Paul Youngquist for help in procuring this proclamation from the British Library.

12. William Sancroft, *Lex Ignea*, 26.

13. Ibid., 28.

14. Edward Stillingfleet, *A Sermon Preached before the Honourable House of Commons*, 32–33.

15. John Bell, *London's Remembrancer*, Sig [$D3_r$].

16. Letter in *London Burning* (1667), in James P. Malcolm, *Londinium Redivivum* 4:80.

17. Ibid.

18. I am arguing that the distinctive stance, themes, and concerns of the jeremiad mode shape Milton's use of Greek tragedy. The classic treatment of *Samson Agonistes* as tragedy is William Riley Parker, *Milton's Debt to Greek Tragedy.* More recently, critics have perceived a complex generic mixture in the poem. Most relevant for my concerns are John Ulreich, "Beyond the Fifth Act," who views *Samson Agonistes* as tragicomedy modeled on Amos and Jonah, and John Wall, "The Contrarious Hand of God," who argues that Milton incorporates the biblical laments drawn from Job, Psalms, and other Old Testament writings.

19. See Robert Boling, *Judges.*

20. I have discussed this controversy in chapter 2. While regenerationists see Samson's pride as replaced with patience and humility, revisionists point to ongoing pride, with lust and violence, as signs of a second fall.

21. Stanley Fish, "Spectacle and Evidence," 557–59, points out that the Chorus continually averts its gaze from the spectacle of Samson's misery, evincing an "unwillingness to behold."

22. Susan Snyder, "The Left Hand of God."

23. Dayton Haskin suggested to me this possible allusion to the mark of Cain. In *Christian Doctrine* 1:17, Milton writes: "Penitence is common to the regenerate and unregenerate. Cain, Esau, Pharoah, Saul, Ahab, and Judas are all examples of the unregenerate; and there are many others" (*CPW* 6:458).

24. Snyder, "The Left Hand of God," 46.

25. Interpretations of Dalila differ dramatically. Relevant here, Charles Mitchell, "Dalila's Return," and Laurie Morrow, "The 'Meet and Happy Conversation,'" specifically discuss Dalila as a model of false repentance. But even Samson's rejection of Dalila may involve pride. Knoppers, "'Sung and Proverb'd for a Fool,'" shows how Samson demonizes Dalila as the "strange woman" of Proverbs.



26. Arnold Stein, *Heroic Knowledge*, argues for Samson's "total victory of patience" (196). For the view that Samson continues to show impatience, see Mason Tung, "Samson Impatiens."

27. Rege Sincera, *Observations Both Historical and Moral*, 331–32.

28. Stein, *Heroic Knowledge*, 196. But Anna Nardo, "'Sung and Proverb'd for a Fool,'" points out that "Samson abases himself as festival fool . . . to mock his revilers and to obliterate the defamers of Yahweh" (9).

29. Wittreich, *Interpreting "Samson Agonistes"* (80), and Helen Damico, "Duality in Dramatic Vision" (110), see Samson going off in pride.

30. Earlier critics, of course, have seen certain limits in the Chorus. For John Huntley, "A Reevaluation of the Chorus' Role," the Chorus represents "the vast ambivalent mass of mankind which neither knows what it feels nor feels what it knows" (139). Franklin Baruch, "Time, Body, and Spirit at the Close of *Samson Agonistes*," views the Chorus as sharing to some extent the "blindness internal" of the Philistines. Joan Bennett, "Liberty under the Law," contrasts the Chorus's pietistic and irrational view with Samson's more rational understanding of God.

31. John Miller, *Popery and Politics*, provides an excellent account of Restoration anti-Catholicism. Miller discusses the Great Fire, 103–5. On anti-Catholicism and the Great Fire, see also McKeon, *Politics and Poetry*, 132–47, and Bell, *The Great Fire*, 196–209. Contemporaries on the anti-Catholicism and near hysterical xenophobia include Evelyn, *Diary* 3:461–62, and Clarendon, *The Life* 2:282–89. On the atrocities against foreigners, see *A Foreign Visitor's Account. A True and Faithful Account of the Informations exhibited to the Committee* (1667) reproduces the colorful but highly dubious depositions against Catholics. The Middlesex Court indicted a number of suspected incendiaries (*MCR* 3:384–87).

32. William Taswell, *Autobiography and Anecdotes*, 11.

33. Ibid., 11–12.

34. See the account of Hubert in Howell, *State Trials* 6:807–66.

35. Rolle, *The Burning of London*, 77.

36. In the Yale prose edition, Keith Stavely points out that "the London Plague of 1665, the London fire of 1666, and the defeats suffered in the Dutch Wars were often cited as divine judgments, visited on England for reasons that varied with the grievance of the writer" (*CPW* 7:439 n. 91).

37. In *Of True Religion*, Milton specifically attacks Catholicism as idolatrous (*CPW* 7:430–31). Similar charges of the idolatry of Catholicism can be found in plague and fire jeremiads, e.g. Matthew Mead, *Solomon's Prescription*, 40–41.

38. Hill, *Milton and the English Revolution*, 225.

39. See K. H. D. Haley, "'No Popery' in the Reign of Charles II," and O. W. Furley, "The Pope-Burning Processions."

40. Charles Hatton, *Correspondence* 1:119.

41. Ibid., 157.

42. On the popish plot and the exclusion crisis, see Miller, *Popery and Politics*, 154–88.

# WORKS CITED

## Primary Sources

*An Act of the Commons of England assembled in Parliament for erecting a High Court of Justice for the Trying and Judging of Charles Steward King of England.* London, 1649.

*An Advertisment as touching the Fanaticks late Conspiracy and Outrage Attempted and Acted Partly in the City.* London, 1661.

Ailmer, J. *Britannia Rediviva.* London, 1660.

*Anglia Rediviva: A Poem on His Majesties Most Joyfull Reception into England.* London, 1660.

Aspinwall, William. *A Brief Description of the Fifth Monarchy, or Kingdome. That shortly is to come into the World.* London, 1653.

Baker, Collonel [pseud.]. *The Blazing-Star, or Noll's Nose, Newly Revived, and Taken out of his Tomb.* London, 1660.

Beeston, Henry, and Henry Bold. *A Poem to his Most Excellent Majesty Charles the Second.* London, 1660.

Bell, John. *London's Remembrancer: Or, a true Accompt of every particular weeks Christnings and Mortality in all the Years of Pestilence.* London, 1665.

The Bishop of Down. *The Martyrdom of King Charls I. Or, his Conformity with Christ in his Sufferings. In a Sermon preached at Bredah, Before his Sacred Majesty King Charls the Second.* The Hague, 1649; Rev. London, 1660.

Bold, Henry. *St. Georges Day Sacred to the Corōnation of His Most Excellent Majesty Charles the II.* London, 1661.

Brett, Arthur. *The Restauration. Or, a Poem on the Return of the most Mighty and ever Glorious Prince, Charles the II To His Kingdoms.* London, 1660.

Brome, Alex[ander]. *A Congratulatory Poem on the Miraculous and Glorious Return of that unparallel'd King Charls the II.* London, 1660.

Burnet, Gilbert. *Bishop Burnet's History of His Own Time.* New ed. London: W. S. Orr & Co., 1850.

Burrough, Edward. *A Testimony against a great Idolatry Committed and a True Mourning of the Lords Servant Upon the Many Considerations of his heart upon the 23 day of the ninth month.* London, 1658.

Burton, Thomas. *The Diary of Thomas Burton.* 4 vols. London: J. T. Rutt, 1828.

*Calendar of State Papers, Domestic Series, of the Reign of Charles II.* Edited by Mary Anne Everett Green. 28 vols. London: Longman, Green, Longman, & Roberts, 1860–1968.

*Calendar of State Papers, Venetian, and Manuscripts Relating to English Affairs, existing in the Archives and Collections of Venice.* Edited by Allen B. Hinds. 30 vols. London: His Majesty's Stationery Office, 1864–1870.

Clarendon, Edward Hyde, Earl of. *The Life of Edward Earl of Clarendon.* 2 vols. Oxford: Oxford University Press, 1827.

Clarke, John. *The Plotters Unmasked, Murderers No Saints. Or, a Word in Season to all those that were Concerned in the Late Rebellion against the Peace of their King and Country.* London, 1661.

Cobbett, William. *Parliamentary History of England.* 36 vols. London: R. Bagshaw, 1806–20.

Cook, Aurelian. *Titus Britannicus: An Essay of History Royal in the Life and Reign of His Late Sacred Majesty, Charles II.* London, 1685.

Cook, John. *King Charls, His Case, or An Appeal to all Rational Men, Concerning His Tryal at the High Court of Justice.* London, 1649.

Cowley, Abraham. *Essays, Plays, and Sundry Verses.* Edited by A. R. Waller. Cambridge: Cambridge University Press, 1906.

———. *Poems.* Edited by A. R. Waller. Cambridge: Cambridge University Press, 1905.

Cromwell, Oliver. *Cromwelliana: A Chronological Detail of Events in which Oliver Cromwell was engaged from the Year 1642 to his death, 1658.* Westminster, 1810.

———. *The Writings and Speeches of Oliver Cromwell.* Edited by W. C. Abbott. 4 vols. Cambridge, Mass.: Harvard University Press, 1937–47.

Darbishire, Helen, ed. *The Early Lives of Milton.* London: Constable & Co., 1932.

*Depositions from the Castle of York: Relating to Offences Committed in the Northern Counties in the Seventeenth Century.* London: Blackwood and Sons, 1861.

Dolittle, Thomas. *Rebukes for Sin by God's Burning Anger by the Burning of London by the Burning of the Wicked in Hell Fire.* London, 1667.

Dryden, John. *The Works of John Dryden.* Edited by Edward Niles Hooker and H. T. Swedenberg, Jr. 20 vols. Berkeley and Los Angeles: University of California Press, 1956–.

Durnovariae, J. D. [pseud.]. *Short Meditations on, with a briefe Description of the Life and Death of Oliver Cromwell.* London, 1661.

*Eikon Basilike, The Portraiture of His Sacred Majesty in His Solitudes and Sufferings. 1649.* Edited by Philip A. Knachel. Ithaca, N.Y.: Cornell University Press, 1966.

*An Elegie upon the Death of Our Dread Soveraign Lord King Charls the Martyr.* London, 1649.

Ellwood, Thomas. *The History of the Life of Thomas Ellwood.* Edited by C. G. Crump. London: Methuen, 1900.

*Englands Triumph. A More Exact History of His Majesties Escape After the Battle of Worcester . . . till His return into England, with the most Remarkable Memorials since, to this present September, 1660*. London, 1660.
Evelyn, John. *The Diary of John Evelyn*. Edited by E. S. de Beer. 6 vols. Oxford: Clarendon Press, 1955.
*Festa Georgiana, or the Gentries & Countries Joy for the Coronation of the King, on St. George's Day*. London, 1661.
Fisher, Payne. *Veni, Vidi, Vici: The Triumphs of the Most Excellent & Illustrious Oliver Cromwell*. London, 1652.
*A Foreign Visitor's Account of the Great Fire, 1666*. Edited and translated by P. P. A. Harvey. In *Transactions of the London and Middlesex Archaeological Society*. London, 1959, 76–87.
Fox, George. *The Journal of George Fox*. Edited by Norman Penney. Cambridge: Cambridge University Press, 1911.
[———] et al. *A Declaration from the Harmles & Innocent People of God, called Quakers. Against all Plotters and Fighters in the World*. London, 1661.
Foxe, John. *Actes and Monuments of these latter and perilous days, touching matters of the church . . . from the year of Our Lord a thousand to the time now present*. London, 1641.
French, J. Milton. *The Life Records of John Milton*. 5 vols. New Brunswick, N.J.: Rutgers University Press, 1949–58.
Gardiner, Dorothy, ed. *The Oxinden and Peyton Letters, 1642–1670*. London: The Sheldon Press, 1937.
*The Great Memorial: Or, a List of the Names of those Pretended Judges who Sate, and Sentenced our late Soveraign King Charles the First, in the Place which they called the High Court of Justice, January 27, 1648*. London, 1660.
Gumble, Thomas. *The Life of General Monck, Duke of Albemarle*. London, 1671.
*A Hand-Kirchife for Loyall Mourners or a Cordiall for Drooping Spirits, Groaning for the bloody murther, and heavy losse of our Gracious King*. London, 1649.
Hardy, Nathaniel. *A Loud Call to great Mourning in a Sermon Preached on the 30th of January, 1661, being the Anniversary Fast for the Execrable Murther of Our Late Soveraign Lord King Charles the First*. London, 1662.
*Hatton Correspondence. Correspondence of the Family of Hatton*, A.D. 1601–1704. Edited by Edward M. Thompson. 2 vols. Camden Society n.s. 22–23. London: The Camden Society, 1878.
Heath, James. *A Brief Chronicle of the Civil Wars of England, Scotland, and Ireland*. London, 1662.
———. *The Glories and Magnificent Triumphs of the Blessed Restitution of His Sacred Majesty K. Charles II*. London, 1662.
Henry, Philip. *Diaries and Letters of Philip Henry*. Edited by Matthew Henry Lee. London: Kegan, Paul, Trench & Co., 1882.
Higgins, Thomas. *A Panegyrick to the King*. London, 1660.
Hodge, Nathaniel. *Loimologia: Or, An Historical Account of the Plague in London in 1665*. Translated by John Quincy. In *Historical Sources of Defoe's Journal of the Plague Year*, edited by Watson Nicholson. Boston: The Stratford Co., 1919.

Howell, Thomas Bayly, ed. *A Complete Collection of State Trials.* 33 vols. London: T. C. Hansard, 1816–26.

*The Humble Apology of some commonly called Anabaptists with their Protestation against the late wicked Insurrection.* London, 1661.

Jevon, Rachel. *Exultationis Carmen to the Kings Most Excellent Majesty upon His Most Desired Return.* London, 1660.

*Justa Sive Inferiae Regicidarum: or Tyburns Revels Presented before Protector Cromwell, Lord President Bradshaw, Lord Deputy Ireton.* London, 1661.

[Juxon, Bishop]. *The Subjects Sorrow; Or, Lamentations Upon the Death of Britaines Josiah, King Charles, Most unjustly and cruelly put to Death by His owne People.* London, 1649.

[King, Bishop Henry]. *A Deep Groane Fetch'd At the Funerall of that Incomparable and Glorious Monarch, Charles the First.* London, 1649.

*The Kingdomes Intelligencer, of the Affairs now in agitation in England, Scotland, and Ireland.* 1660–61.

*The Last Farewel of Three Bould Traytors.* London, 1661.

*The Last Farewel to the Rebellious Crew of Fifth Monarchy Men.* London, 1661.

Llevelyn, Martin. *To the King's Most Excellent Majestie.* London, 1661.

*London's Glory, Or, The Riot and Ruine of the Fifth Monarchy Men, and all their Adherents.* London, 1661.

*London's Plague-Sore Discovered: Or, Some Serious Notes and Suitable Considerations upon the present Visitation at London.* London, 1665.

*A Looking-Glasse for Traytors, being the Manner of the Triall of those Barbarous wretches at Justice-Hall in the Old Baily . . . With an account of their severall Arraignments, Conviction, Condemnation, and Execution.* London, 1660.

Ludlow, Edmund. *The Memoirs of Edmund Ludlow, 1625–72.* Edited by C. H. Firth. 2 vols. Oxford: Clarendon Press, 1894.

MacKay, Charles, ed. *The Cavalier Songs and Ballads of England from 1642 to 1684.* London: Griffin Bohn and Co., 1863.

Malcolm, James P. *Londinium Redivivum; or, An Ancient History and Modern Description of London.* Vol. 4. London: J. Nichols & Son, 1807.

*The Manner of the Solemnity of the Coronation of His most Sacred Majesty King Charles.* London, 1661.

Marvell, Andrew. *The Poems and Letters of Andrew Marvell, Vol. 1.* Edited by H. M. Margoliouth. 3rd ed. Revised by Pierre Legouis with E. E. Duncan-Jones. Oxford: Clarendon Press, 1971.

Mead, Matthew. *Solomon's Prescription for the Removal of the Pestilence: Or, the Discovery of the Plague of our Hearts, in order to the Healing of that in our Flesh.* London, 1665.

*Mercurius Elencticus.* 1649. Reprinted in *A History of English Journalism to the Foundation of the Gazette.* Edited by J. G. Muddiman. London, 1908.

*Mercurius Publicus, comprising the Sum of all Affairs now in Agitation in England, Scotland, and Ireland.* 1660–61.

*Middlesex County Records.* Old Series. Edited by John Cordy Jeaffreson. 4 vols. Middlesex, 1886.

Milton, John. *Complete Poems and Major Prose of John Milton.* Edited by Merritt Hughes. Indianapolis: The Odyssey Press, 1957.

———. *Complete Prose Works of John Milton.* Edited by Don M. Wolfe. 8 vols. New Haven: Yale University Press, 1953–82.

Mundy, Peter. *The Travels of Peter Mundy in Europe and Asia, Vol. V.* Edited by Richard C. Temple and Lavinia Mary Anstey. London: The Hakluyt Society, 1936.

Nalson, John. *A True Copy of the Journal of the High Court of Justice for the Tryal of K. Charles I.* London, 1684.

Nedham, Marchamont, and Payne Fisher. *The Speeches of Oliver Cromwell, Henry Ireton, and John Bradshaw, Intended to Have been spoken at their Execution at Tyburne, Jan 30. 1660. But for many weightie Reasons omitted.* London, 1661.

*A New Meeting of Ghosts at Tyburn.* London, 1661.

Nicholas, Sir Edward. *The Nicholas Papers: Correspondence of Sir Edward Nicholas, Secretary of State.* Edited by Sir George Warner. Camden Third Series, Vol. 31. London: Camden Society, 1920.

*Observations Upon the Last Actions and Words of Maj. Gen. Harrison Written by a Minister in a Letter to a Countrey Gentlewoman.* London, 1660.

Ogilby, John. *The Entertainment of His Most Excellent Majestie Charles II in His Passage through the City of London to his Coronation. With a description of the triumphal Arches and Solemnity. 1662.* Facsimile edited by Ronald Knowles. Binghamton: Medieval and Renaissance Texts and Studies, 1988.

———. *The Relation of His Majesties Entertainment.* London, 1661.

Paggitt, Ephraim. *Heresiography, Or a Description and History of the Hereticks and Sectaries Sprang up in these latter times.* 6th ed. London, 1662.

Parker, William Riley, ed. *Milton's Contemporary Reputation.* Columbus: Ohio State University Press, 1940.

*The Parliamentary Intelligencer.* 1659–1660.

Pepys, Samuel. *The Diary of Samuel Pepys.* Edited by Robert Latham and William Matthews. 11 vols. Berkeley and Los Angeles: University of California Press, 1970–83.

Perrinchief, Richard. *The Syracusan Tyrant or the Life of Agathocles.* London, 1661.

———. *The Workes of King Charles the Martyr.* London, 1662.

*The Plague Checkt; Or, Piety will either Prevent or Alter the Property of the Plague.* London: 1665.

*A Poem to his most Excellent Majesty Charles the Second.* London, 1660.

Pordage, Samuel. *Heroick Stanzas on His Majesties Coronation.* London, 1661.

*A Renuntiation and Declaration of the Ministers of the Congregational Churches and Publick Preachers of the same Judgment, Living in, and about the City of London: Against the late Horrid Insurrection and Rebellion.* London, 1661.

Reynell, Carew. *The Fortunate Change. Being a Panegyrick to his Sacred Majesty, King Charles the Second, Immediately on his Coronation.* London, 1661.

Rolle [Rolls], Samuel. *The Burning of London in the Year 1666.* London, 1667.

Rugg, Thomas. *The Diurnal of Thomas Rugg, 1659–1661.* Edited by William L. Sachse. Camden Third Series, Vol. 91. London: Royal Historical Society, 1961.

Sancroft, William. *Lex Ignea: Or, The School of Righteousness. A Sermon Preach'd before the King, Octob. 10. 1666. At the Solemn Fast appointed For the late Fire in London.* London, 1666.

*The Scotch Souldiers Lamentation Upon the Death of the most Glorious and Illustrious Martyr, King Charles.* London, 1649.

Sincera, Rege [pseud.]. *Observations Both Historical and Moral Upon the Burning of London, 1666.* London, 1667.

*The Solemn Mock Procession of the Pope, Cardinalls, Jesuits, Fryers, &c Through the City of London, November 17th, 1679.* London, 1679.

*The Speeches and Prayers of Major General Harrison [et al.] . . . The Times of their Deaths. Together with Severall occasionall Speeches and Passages in their Imprisonment till they came to the place of Execution.* London, 1660.

Sprat, Thomas. *To the Happie Memory of the Most Renowned Prince, Oliver, Lord Protector.* London, 1659.

Stillingfleet, Edward. *A Sermon Preached before the Honourable House of Commons, at St. Margarets Westminster Octob. 10 being the Fast-day appointed for the late Dreadfull Fire in the City of London.* London, 1666.

[Stuart, Charles]. *By the King. A Proclamation Against Vicious, Debauch'd and Prophane Persons.* 1660.

———. *By the King. A Proclamation for Observation of the Thirtieth day of January as a day of Fast and Humiliation according to the late Act of Parliament for that Purpose.* 1660.

———. *A Proclamation For a General Fast through England and Wales, and the Town of Barwick upon Tweed, on Wednesday the tenth of October next.* 1666.

Tabor, John. *Seasonable Thoughts in Sad Times, being some Reflections on the Warre, the Pestilence, and the Burning of London, Considered in the Calamity, Cause, Cure.* London, 1667.

Taswell, William. *Autobiography and Anecdotes.* Translated by Henry Taswell. *The Camden Miscellany.* Vol. 2. Edited by George Perry Elliott. London: The Camden Society, 1853.

Thurloe, John. *A Collection of the State Papers of John Thurloe . . . containing Authentic Memorials of the English Affairs from the year 1638 to the Restoration of King Charles II.* Vol. 6. Edited by Thomas Birch. London, 1742.

*To the King, Upon His Majesties Happy Return. By a Person of Honour.* London, 1660.

*A Triumphant Panegyrick in Honour and Memory of King Charles the Second his Coronation.* London, 1661.

*A True and Faithful Account of the Informations exhibited to the Committee Appointed to Inquire into the Late Burning of the City of London, 1667.* London, 1660.

*A True and Perfect Relation of the Grand Traytors Execution, as at severall times they were drawn, Hang'd, and Quartered at Charing-crosse, and at Tiburne.* London, 1660.

*The True Manner of the most Magnificent Conveyance of his Highness Effigies from Sommerset-house to Westminster on Tuesday November 23, 1658.* London, 1658.

[Venner, Thomas.] *A Door of Hope: or, A Call and Declaration for the Gathering Together of the first ripe Fruits unto the Standard of Our Lord King Jesus.* London, 1661.

[———.] *The Last Speech and Prayer with other Passages of Thomas Venner, The Chief Incourager and Promoter of the late Horrid Rebellion, immediately before his Execution*. London, 1661.

Vincent, Thomas. *God's Terrible Voice in the City*. 1667. 13th ed. London, 1671.

W., S. *Epinicia Carolina, or An Essay upon the Return of His Sacred Majesty Charles the Second*. London, 1660.

Willes, Samuel. *To the Kings Most Sacred Majestie upon his Happy and Glorious Return*. London, 1660.

## Secondary Sources

Abrams, M. H., ed. *The Norton Anthology of English Literature*. 4th ed. New York: Norton, 1979.

———. *The Norton Anthology of English Literature*. 5th ed. New York: Norton, 1986.

Anderson, Wayne. "Is *Paradise Regained* Really Cold?" *Christianity and Literature* 34 (1983): 15–23.

Aston, Margaret. *England's Iconoclasts: Volume I, Laws against Images*. Oxford: Clarendon Press, 1988.

Baker, David. "'Wildehirissheman': Colonialist Representation in Shakespeare's *Henry V*." *English Literary Renaissance* 22 (1992): 37–61.

Bakhtin, Mikhail. *Rabelais and His World*. Translated by Helene Iswolsky. Cambridge: MIT Press, 1968.

Barker, Arthur E. *Milton and the Puritan Dilemma, 1641–1660*. Toronto: University of Toronto Press, 1942.

Baruch, Franklin. "Time, Body, and Spirit at the Close of *Samson Agonistes*." *ELH* 36 (1969): 319–39.

Baugh, Albert, ed. *A Literary History of England*. New York: Appleton-Century-Crofts, 1948.

Bell, Walter. *The Great Fire of London in 1666*. London: John Lane, 1920.

———. *The Great Plague in London in 1665*. London: John Lane, 1924.

Bennett, Joan S. "God, Satan, and King Charles: Milton's Royal Portraits." *PMLA* 92 (1977): 441–57.

———. "Liberty under the Law: The Chorus and the Meaning of *Samson Agonistes*." *Milton Studies* 12 (1978): 141–64.

———. *Reviving Liberty: Radical Christian Humanism in Milton's Great Poems*. Cambridge, Mass.: Harvard University Press, 1989.

Bercovitch, Sacvan. *The American Jeremiad*. Madison: University of Wisconsin Press, 1978.

Bergeron, David. *English Civic Pageantry, 1558–1642*. Columbia: University of South Carolina Press, 1971.

Berry, Boyd M. *Process of Speech: Puritan Religious Writing and "Paradise Lost."* Baltimore: Johns Hopkins University Press, 1976.

Besant, Sir Walter. *London in the Time of the Stuarts*. Vol. 5 of *The Survey of London*. London: Adam & Charles Back, 1903.

Boehrer, Bruce. "Elementary Structures of Kingship: Milton, Regicide, and the Family." *Milton Studies* 23 (1987): 97–118.
Boling, Robert. *Judges*. Vol. 6 of *The Anchor Bible Commentary*. New York: Doubleday, 1975.
Breight, Curtis. " 'Treason doth never Prosper': *The Tempest* and the Discourse of Treason." *Shakespeare Quarterly* 41 (1990): 1–28.
Burrage, Champlin. "The Fifth Monarchy Insurrections." *The English Historical Review* 25 (1910): 722–47.
Bush, Douglas. *English Literature in the Earlier Seventeenth Century, 1600–1660*. Vol. 5 of *The Oxford History of English Literature*. 2nd ed. Oxford: Clarendon Press, 1962.
Cable, Lana. "Milton's Iconoclastic Truth." In Loewenstein and Turner, *Politics, Poetics, and Hermeneutics*, 135–51.
Cacicedo, Alberto. "Seeing the King: Biblical and Classical Texts in *Astrea Redux*." *Studies in English Literature* 32 (1992): 407–27.
Capp, B. S. *The Fifth Monarchy Men: A Study in Seventeenth-Century English Millenarianism*. Totowa, N.J.: Rowman and Littlefield, 1972.
Carey, John. *Milton*. London, 1969.
———. "Satan." In Danielson, *The Cambridge Companion to Milton*, 131–46.
Cary, Max. *A History of Rome Down to the Reign of Constantine*. 3d ed. London: Macmillan, 1975.
Chernaik, Warren L. *The Poet's Time: Politics and Religion in the Work of Andrew Marvell*. Cambridge: Cambridge University Press, 1983.
Cohn, Norman. *The Pursuit of the Millennium: Revolutionary Millenarians and Mystical Anarchists of the Middle Ages*. Revised ed. New York: Oxford University Press, 1970.
Corns, Thomas. " 'Some Rousing Motions': The Plurality of Miltonic Ideology." In Healy and Sawday, *Literature and the English Civil War*, 110–26.
———. *Uncloistered Virtue: English Political Literature, 1640–1660*. Oxford: Clarendon Press, 1992.
Cragg, Gerald R. "The Collapse of Militant Puritanism." In *Essays in Modern Church History in Memory of Norman Sykes*, edited by G. V. Bennett and J. D. Walsh, 76–103. New York: Oxford University Press, 1966.
———. *Puritanism in the Period of the Great Persecution, 1660–1688*. 1957. Reprint. New York: Russell & Russell, 1971.
Crane, Mary Thomas. *Framing Authority: Sayings, Self, and Society in Sixteenth-Century England*. Princeton, N.J.: Princeton University Press, 1993.
Cunningham, Karen. "Renaissance Execution and Marlovian Elocution: The Drama of Death." *PMLA* 105 (1990): 209–22.
Cust, Richard, and Ann Hughes, eds. *Conflict in Early Stuart England: Studies in Religion and Politics, 1603–1642*. London: Longman, 1989.
Daiches, David. *A Critical History of English Literature. Vol I*. 2d ed. New York: Ronald Press, 1970.
Damico, Helen. "Duality in Dramatic Vision: A Structural Analysis of *Samson Agonistes*." *Milton Studies* 12 (1978): 91–116.

Daniel, Clay. "Lust and Violence in *Samson Agonistes.*" *South Central Review* 6 (1989): 6–31.
Danielson, Dennis, ed. *The Cambridge Companion to Milton.* Cambridge: Cambridge University Press, 1989.
Davies, Godfrey. "Milton in 1660." *Huntington Library Quarterly* 18 (1955): 351–63.
———. *The Restoration of Charles II, 1658–60.* San Marino, Cal.: Huntington Library, 1955.
Davies, Stevie. *Images of Kingship in "Paradise Lost": Milton's Politics and Christian Liberty.* Columbia: University of Missouri Press, 1983.
Demaray, John G. *Milton's Theatrical Epic: The Invention and Design of "Paradise Lost."* Cambridge, Mass.: Harvard University Press, 1980.
DiSalvo, Jackie. "'The Lord's Battells': *Samson Agonistes* and the Puritan Revolution." *Milton Studies* 4 (1973): 39–62.
Donnelly, M. L. "Caroline Royalist Panegyric and the Disintegration of a Symbolic Mode." In *"The Muses Common-weale": Poetry and Politics in the Seventeenth Century*, edited by Claude J. Summers and Ted-Larry Pebworth, 163–76. Columbia: University of Missouri Press, 1988.
Drabble, Margaret, ed. *The Oxford Companion to English Literature.* Oxford: Oxford University Press, 1985.
Egan, James. "'This is a Lamentation and shall be for a Lamentation': Nathaniel Ward and the Rhetoric of the Jeremiad." *Proceedings of the American Philosophical Society* 122 (1978): 400–410.
Erskine-Hill, Howard. *The Augustan Idea in English Literature.* London: Edward Arnold, 1983.
Evans, J. Martin. "Lycidas." In Danielson, *Cambridge Companion*, 35–50.
Everett, Barbara. "The Shooting of the Bears: Poetry and Politics in Andrew Marvell." In *Andrew Marvell: Essays on the Tercentenary of His Death*, edited by R. L. Brett, 62–103. Oxford: Oxford University Press, 1979.
Fish, Stanley. "Inaction and Silence: The Reader in *Paradise Regained.*" In Wittreich, *Calm of Mind*, 25–47.
———. "Spectacle and Evidence in *Samson Agonistes.*" *Critical Inquiry* 15 (1989): 556–86.
———. "The Temptation of Plot in *Paradise Regained.*" *Milton Studies* 17 (1983): 163–85.
Fisher, Alan. "Why Is *Paradise Regained* So Cold?" *Milton Studies* 14 (1980): 195–217.
Fixler, Michael. *Milton and the Kingdoms of God.* Evanston, Ill.: Northwestern University Press, 1964.
Foucault, Michel. *Discipline and Punish: The Birth of the Prison.* Translated by Alan Sheridan. New York: Pantheon Books, 1977.
———. *The History of Sexuality. Volume 1: An Introduction.* New York: Pantheon Books, 1980.
———. *Power/Knowledge: Selected Interviews and Other Writings, 1972–77.* Edited by Colin Gordon. Translated by Colin Gordon et al. New York: Pantheon Books, 1980.
———. "What Is an Author?" In *Language, Counter-Memory, Practice*, edited by

Donald F. Bouchard, 113–38. Ithaca, N.Y.: Cornell University Press, 1977.

Fowler, Alastair. *Triumphal Forms: Structural Patterns in Elizabethan Poetry*. Cambridge: Cambridge University Press, 1970.

Fox, Alistair. "Facts and Fallacies: Interpreting English Humanism." In *Reassessing the Henrician Age: Humanism, Politics, and Reform, 1500–1555*, edited by Alistair Fox and John Guy, 9–33. Oxford: Blackwell, 1986.

Fraser, Antonia. *Cromwell: The Lord Protector*. New York: Knopf, 1973.

Frye, Northrop. *Spiritus Mundi: Essays on Literature, Myth, and Society*. Bloomington: Indiana University Press, 1976.

———. "The Typology of *Paradise Regained*." In *Milton: Modern Essays in Criticism*, edited by Arthur E. Barker, 429–46. New York: Oxford University Press, 1965.

Furley, O. W. "The Pope-Burning Processions of the Late Seventeenth-Century." *History* 44 (1959): 16–23.

Gilman, Ernest. *Iconoclasm and Poetry in the English Reformation: Down Went Dagon*. Chicago: University of Chicago Press, 1986.

Goldberg, Jonathan. *James I and the Politics of Literature*. Baltimore: Johns Hopkins University Press, 1983.

Greaves, Richard. *Deliver Us from Evil: The Radical Underground in Britain, 1660–1663*. New York: Oxford University Press, 1986.

Greenblatt, Stephen. *Renaissance Self-Fashioning: From More to Shakespeare*. Chicago: University of Chicago Press, 1980.

———. *Shakespearean Negotiations: The Circulation of Social Energy in Renaissance England*. Berkeley and Los Angeles: University of California Press, 1988.

Gross, Kenneth. "Milton's Satan." In Nyquist and Ferguson, *Re-membering Milton*, 318–41.

Haigh, Christopher. "The Church of England, the Catholics, and the People." In *The Reign of Elizabeth I*, edited by Christopher Haigh, 195–219. Athens: University of Georgia Press, 1985.

Haley, K. H. D. " 'No Popery' in the Reign of Charles II." In *Britain and the Netherlands*, edited by J. S. Bromley and E. H. Kossman, 102–19. The Hague, 1975.

Halfpenny, Eric. "Cities Loyalty Display'd: A Literary and Documentary Causerie of Charles II's Coronation 'Entertainment.' " *The Guildhall Miscellany* 1 (1952): 19–36.

Haller, William. *Foxe's Book of Martyrs and the Elect Nation*. London: J. Cape, 1963.

———. *The Rise of Puritanism*. New York: Columbia University Press, 1938.

Halley, Janet. "Female Autonomy in Milton's Sexual Poetics." In *Milton and the Idea of Woman*, edited by Julia M. Walker, 230–53. Urbana: University of Illinois Press, 1988.

Hamilton, Gary. "*The History of Britain* and Its Restoration Audience." In Loewenstein and Turner, *Politics, Poetics, and Hermeneutics*, 241–56.

Hanford, James Holly. *John Milton: Poet and Humanist*. Cleveland: The Press of Case Western Reserve University, 1966.

Hardin, Richard F. *Civil Idolatry: Desacralizing and Monarchy in Spenser, Shakespeare, and Milton*. Newark: University of Delaware Press, 1992.

Harris, Tim. *London Crowds in the Reign of Charles II: Propaganda and Politics from the Restoration until the Exclusion Crisis.* Cambridge: Cambridge University Press, 1987.

Healy, Thomas, and Jonathan Sawday, eds. *Literature and the English Civil War.* Cambridge: Cambridge University Press, 1990.

Hill, Christopher. *The Experience of Defeat: Milton and Some Contemporaries.* New York: Viking, 1984.

———. *God's Englishman: Oliver Cromwell and the English Revolution.* New York: Dial Press, 1970.

———. *Milton and the English Revolution.* New York: Viking, 1978.

———. *Some Intellectual Consequences of the English Revolution.* Madison: University of Wisconsin Press, 1980.

———. *The World Turned Upside Down: Radical Ideas during the English Revolution.* New York: Viking, 1972.

———, ed. *The English Revolution, 1640: Three Essays.* London: Lawrence & Wishart, 1941.

Holstun, James. "Ranting at the New Historicism." *English Literary Renaissance* 19 (1989): 189–225.

Howard, Jean. "The New Historicism in Renaissance Studies." *English Literary Renaissance* 16 (1986): 13–43.

Hughes, Merritt. " 'Myself am Hell.' " *Modern Philology* 54 (1956): 80–94.

Huntley, John. "A Reevaluation of the Chorus' Role in Milton's *Samson Agonistes.*" *Modern Philology* 64 (1966): 132–45.

Hutton, Ronald. *Charles II, King of England, Scotland, and Ireland.* Oxford: Clarendon Press, 1989.

———. *The Restoration: A Political and Religious History of England and Wales, 1658–1667.* Oxford: Clarendon Press, 1985.

Jarvis, Robin. "Love between Milton and Wordsworth." In Nyquist and Ferguson, *Re-membering Milton*, 301–17.

Jones, J. R. *Country and Court: England, 1658–1714.* Cambridge, Mass.: Harvard University Press, 1978.

Jose, Nicholas. *Ideas of the Restoration in English Literature 1660–1671.* Cambridge, Mass.: Harvard University Press, 1984.

Keeble, Nigel. *The Literary Culture of Nonconformity in Later Seventeenth-Century England.* Leicester: Leicester University Press, 1987.

Kelsall, Malcolm. "The Historicity of *Paradise Regained.*" *Milton Studies* 12 (1978): 235–51.

Kermode, Frank, and John Hollander, eds. *The Oxford Anthology of English Literature*, Vol. 1. New York and London: Oxford University Press, 1973.

Kerrigan, William. "Seventeenth-Century Studies." In *Redrawing the Boundaries*, edited by Stephen Greenblatt and Giles Gunn, 64–79. New York: Modern Language Association, 1992.

Kishlansky, Mark. "The Emergence of Adversary Politics in the Long Parliament." *Journal of Modern History* 49 (1977): 617–40.

Knoppers, Laura Lunger. "Milton's *The Readie and Easie Way* and the English Jeremiad." In Loewenstein and Turner, *Politics, Poetics, and Hermeneutics*, 213–25.

———. "Rewriting the Protestant Ethic: Discipline and Love in *Paradise Lost*." *ELH* 58 (1991): 545–59.

———. " 'Sung and Proverb'd for a Fool': *Samson Agonistes* and Solomon's Harlot." *Milton Studies* 26 (1990): 239–51.

Knott, John, Jr. " 'Suffering for Truths Sake': Milton and Martyrdom." In Loewenstein and Turner, *Politics, Poetics, and Hermeneutics*, 153–170.

Lacey, Douglas. *Dissent and Parliamentary Politics in England, 1661–1689*. New Brunswick, N.J.: Rutgers University Press, 1969.

Lamont, William. *Richard Baxter and the Millennium*. London: Croom Helm, 1979.

Landy, Marcia. " 'Bounds Prescrib'd': Milton's Satan and the Politics of Deviance." *Milton Studies* 14 (1980): 117–34.

Lecomte, Edward. "Satan's Heresies in *Paradise Regained*." *Milton Studies* 12 (1978): 253–66.

Lentricchia, Frank. "Reading Foucault (Punishment, Labor, Resistance)." Parts 1, 2. *Raritan* (Spring, Summer 1982): 5–32, 41–70.

Levin, Harry. *The Myth of the Golden Age in the Renaissance*. Bloomington: Indiana University Press, 1969.

Lewalski, Barbara Kiefer. "Milton: Political Beliefs and Polemical Methods, 1659–1660." *PMLA* 74 (1959): 191–202.

———. *Milton's Brief Epic: The Genre, Meaning, and Art of "Paradise Regained."* Providence: Brown University Press, 1966.

———. *"Paradise Lost" and the Rhetoric of Literary Forms*. Princeton, N.J.: Princeton University Press, 1985.

———. "*Samson Agonistes* and the 'Tragedy' of the Apocalypse." *PMLA* 85 (1970): 1050–62.

Lieb, Michael. " 'The Chariot of Paternal Deitie.' " In *Milton's Legacy in the Arts*, edited by Albert Labriola and Edward Sichi, Jr., 21–58. University Park: Pennsylvania State University Press, 1988.

———. *Poetics of the Holy: A Reading of Paradise Lost*. Chapel Hill: University of North Carolina Press, 1981.

Lieb, Michael, and John Shawcross, eds. *Achievements of the Left Hand: Essays on the Prose of John Milton*. Amherst: University of Massachusetts Press, 1974.

Liu, Alan. "The Power of Formalism: The New Historicism." *ELH* 56 (1989): 721–71.

Liu, Tai. *Discord in Zion: The Puritan Divines and the Puritan Revolution, 1640–1660*. The Hague: Martinus Nijhoff, 1973.

Loewenstein, David. *Milton and the Drama of History: Historical Vision, Iconoclasm, and the Literary Imagination*. Cambridge: Cambridge University Press, 1990.

Loewenstein, David, and James Turner, eds. *Politics, Poetics, and Hermeneutics in Milton's Prose*. Cambridge: Cambridge University Press, 1990.

Low, Anthony. *The Blaze of Noon: A Reading of Samson Agonistes*. New York: Columbia University Press, 1974.

Madan, Francis F. *A New Bibliography of the Eikon Basilike of King Charles the First.* NS 3. Oxford: Oxford Bibliographical Society Publications, 1949.

Maguire, Nancy Klein. *Regicide and Restoration: English Tragicomedy, 1660–1671.* Cambridge: Cambridge University Press, 1992.

Marcus, Leah Sinanoglou. "Herrick's *Hesperides* and the 'Proclamation Made for May.'" *Studies in Philology* 76 (1979): 49–74.

———. *The Politics of Mirth: Jonson, Herrick, Milton, Marvell, and the Defense of Old Holiday Pastimes.* Chicago: University of Chicago Press, 1986.

Martz, Louis. "Chorus and Character in *Samson Agonistes.*" *Milton Studies* 1 (1969): 115–24.

Masson, David. *The Life of John Milton.* 7 vols. 1881–94. Reprint. New York: Peter Smith, 1965.

McColley, Diane. *Milton's Eve.* Urbana: University of Illinois Press, 1983.

McKeon, Michael. *Politics and Poetry in Restoration England: The Case of Dryden's "Annus Mirabilis."* Cambridge, Mass.: Harvard University Press, 1975.

Miller, John. *Popery and Politics in England, 1660–1688.* Cambridge: Cambridge University Press, 1973.

Milner, Andrew. *John Milton and the English Revolution.* Totowa, N.J.: Barnes & Noble, 1981.

Miner, Earl. *The Restoration Mode from Milton to Dryden.* Princeton, N.J.: Princeton University Press, 1974.

Mitchell, Charles. "Dalila's Return: The Importance of Pardon." *College English* 26 (1965): 614–20.

Montrose, Louis. "Eliza, Queene of Shepheardes, and the Pastoral of Power." *English Literary Renaissance* 10 (1980): 153–82.

———. "Renaissance Literary Studies and the Subject of History." *English Literary Renaissance* 16 (1986): 5–12.

———. "Shaping Fantasies: Figurations of Gender and Power in Elizabethan Culture." *Representations* 44 (1983): 61–94.

Morrill, John, ed. *Oliver Cromwell and the English Revolution.* London: Longman, 1992.

———. *The Revolt of the Provinces.* London: Allen and Unwin, 1976.

Morris, Jeffrey. "Disorientation and Disruption in *Paradise Regained.*" *Milton Studies* 26 (1990): 219–37.

Morrow, Laurie. "The 'Meet and Happy Conversation': Dalila's Role in *Samson Agonistes.*" *Milton Quarterly* 17 (1983): 38–42.

Mueller, Janel. "Embodying Glory: the Apocalyptic Strain in Milton's *Of Reformation.*" In Loewenstein and Turner, *Politics, Poetics, and Hermeneutics,* 9–40.

———. "On Genesis in Genre: Milton's Politicizing of the Sonnet in 'Captain or Colonel.'" In *Renaissance Genres,* edited by Barbara K. Lewalski, 213–40. Cambridge, Mass.: Harvard University Press, 1986.

Myers, Robert. "'God shall be all in all': The Erasure of Hell in *Paradise Lost.*" *The Seventeenth Century* 5 (1990): 43–53.

Nardo, Anna. "'Sung and Proverb'd for a Fool': Samson as Fool and Trickster." *Mosaic* 22 (1989): 1–16.

Nevo, Ruth. *The Dial of Virtue: A Study of Poems on Affairs of State in the Seventeenth Century.* Princeton, N.J.: Princeton University Press, 1963.

Norbrook, David. "Marvell's Horatian Ode and the Politics of Genre." In Healy and Sawday, *Literature and the English Civil War,* 147–69.

———. *Poetry and Politics in the English Renaissance.* London: Routledge & Kegan Paul, 1984.

———. "The Reformation of the Masque." In *The Court Masque,* edited by David Lindley, 94–110. Manchester: Manchester University Press, 1984.

Nyquist, Mary. "The Genesis of Gendered Subjectivity in the Divorce Tracts and in *Paradise Lost.*" In Nyquist and Ferguson, *Re-membering Milton,* 99–127.

Nyquist, Mary, and Margaret Ferguson, eds. *Re-membering Milton: Essays on the Texts and Traditions.* New York and London: Methuen, 1987.

O'Donnell, Michael. "The Idolatrous Eye: Iconoclasm, Antitheatricalism, and the Image of the Elizabethan Theater." *ELH* 52 (1985): 279–310.

Ogg, David. *England in the Reign of Charles II.* 2 vols. 2d ed. Oxford: Oxford University Press, 1956.

Orgel, Stephen. *The Illusion of Power: Political Theater in the English Renaissance.* Berkeley and Los Angeles: University of California Press, 1975.

Parker, William Riley. *Milton: A Biography.* 2 vols. Oxford: Clarendon Press, 1968.

———. *Milton's Debt to Greek Tragedy in "Samson Agonistes."* Baltimore: Johns Hopkins University Press, 1937.

Parry, Graham. *The Golden Age Restor'd: The Culture of the Stuart Court, 1603–1642.* Manchester: Manchester University Press, 1981.

Patterson, Annabel. *Censorship and Interpretation: The Conditions of Writing and Reading in Early Modern England.* Madison: University of Wisconsin Press, 1984.

———. *Marvell and the Civic Crown.* Princeton, N.J.: Princeton University Press, 1978.

Peck, H. T., ed. *Harper's Dictionary of Classical Literature and Antiquities.* New York: Harper & Row, 1962.

Phillips, John. *The Reformation of Images: Destruction of Art in England, 1535–1660.* Berkeley and Los Angeles: University of California Press, 1973.

Porter, Caroline. "Are We Being Historical Yet?" *The South Atlantic Quarterly* (1988): 743–86.

Potter, Lois. *Secret Rites and Secret Writing: Royalist Literature, 1641–1660.* Cambridge: Cambridge University Press, 1989.

Quint, David. "David's Census: Milton's Politics and *Paradise Regained.*" In Nyquist and Ferguson, *Re-membering Milton,* 128–47.

Radzinowicz, Mary Ann. *Toward "Samson Agonistes": The Growth of Milton's Mind.* Princeton, N.J.: Princeton University Press, 1978.

Raleigh, Sir Walter. *Milton.* London: E. Arnold, 1915.

Randall, Helen. "The Rise and Fall of a Martyrology: Sermons on Charles I." *Huntington Library Quarterly* 10 (1947): 135–67.

Reedy, Gerard. "Mystical Politics: The Imagery of Charles II's Coronation." In

*Studies in Change and Revolution: Aspects of English Intellectual History, 1640–1800*, edited by Paul Korshin, 21–33. Menston, Yorkshire: Scolar Press, 1972.

Rogers, Philip George. *The Fifth Monarchy Men*. London: Oxford University Press, 1966.

Rosenberg, D. M. "*Samson Agonistes:* 'Proverb'd for a Fool.'" *The Centennial Review* 32 (1988): 65–78.

Rumrich, John. *Matter of Glory: A New Preface to "Paradise Lost."* Pittsburgh: University of Pittsburgh Press, 1987.

Russell, Conrad, ed. *The Origins of the English Civil War*. New York: Barnes & Noble, 1973.

Samuel, Irene. "*Samson Agonistes* as Tragedy." In Wittreich, *Calm of Mind*, 237–57.

Sandler, Florence. "Icon and Iconoclast." In Lieb and Shawcross, *Achievements of the Left Hand*, 160–84.

Schanzer, Ernest. "Milton's Hell Revisited." *University of Toronto Quarterly* 24 (1955): 136–45.

Scott-Craig, T. S. K. "Concerning Milton's Samson." *Renaissance News* 5 (1952): 45–53.

Sensabaugh, George T. *That Grand Whig Milton*. Stanford University Series, Language & Literature, 11. Stanford: Stanford University Press, 1952.

Sharpe, J. A. "'Last Dying Speeches': Religion, Ideology and Public Execution in Seventeenth-Century England." *Past and Present* 107 (1985): 144–67.

Sharpe, Kevin, and Steven Zwicker, eds. *Politics of Discourse: The Literature and History of Seventeenth-Century England*. Berkeley and Los Angeles: University of California Press, 1987.

Sharratt, Bernard. "The Appropriation of Milton." In *Essays & Studies 1982: The Poet's Power*, edited by Suheil Bushrui, 30–44. London: English Association, 1982.

Shuger, Debora. *Habits of Thought in the English Renaissance: Religion, Politics, and the Dominant Culture*. Berkeley and Los Angeles: University of California Press, 1990.

Slack, Paul. *The Impact of Plague in Tudor and Stuart England*. London: Routledge, 1985.

Snyder, Susan. "The Left Hand of God: Despair in Medieval and Renaissance Tradition." *Studies in the Renaissance* 12 (1965): 18–59.

Stein, Arnold. *Heroic Knowledge: An Interpretation of "Paradise Regained" and "Samson Agonistes."* Minneapolis: University of Minnesota Press, 1957.

Strong, Roy. *Art and Power: Renaissance Festivals, 1450–1650*. Berkeley and Los Angeles: University of California Press, 1984.

———. *Splendor at Court: Renaissance Spectacle and the Theater of Power*. Boston: Houghton Mifflin, 1973.

———. *Van Dyck: Charles I on Horseback*. New York: Viking, 1972.

Tennenhouse, Leonard. *Power on Display: The Politics of Shakespeare's Genres*. New York: Methuen, 1986.

Tung, Mason. "Samson Impatiens: A Reinterpretation of Milton's *Samson Agonistes*." *Texas Studies in Language and Literature* 9 (1967–68): 475–92.

Tyacke, Nicholas R. "Puritanism, Arminianism, and Counter-Revolution." In Russell, *The Origins of the English Civil War*, 119–43.

Ulreich, John. "Beyond the Fifth Act: *Samson Agonistes* as Prophecy." *Milton Studies* 17 (1983): 281–318.

Underdown, David. *Revel, Riot, and Rebellion: Popular Politics and Culture in England, 1603–1660*. Oxford: Oxford University Press, 1985.

Varley, Frederick John. *Oliver Cromwell's Latter End*. London: Chapman & Hall, 1939.

Veeser, H. Aram, ed. *The New Historicism*. New York: Routledge, 1989.

Wall, John. " 'The Contrarious Hand of God': *Samson Agonistes* and the Biblical Lament." *Milton Studies* 12 (1978): 117–40.

Ward, A. W., and A. R. Waller, eds. *The Cambridge History of English Literature*. Cambridge: Cambridge University Press, 1911.

Weber, Harold. "Representations of the King: Charles II and His Escape from Worcester." *Studies in Philology* 85 (1988): 489–509.

Wedgwood, C. V. *A Coffin for King Charles*. New York: Macmillan, 1964.

Weinbrot, Howard. *Augustus Caesar in "Augustan" England: The Decline of a Classical Norm*. Princeton, N.J.: Princeton University Press, 1978.

Wilcher, Robert. "*Samson Agonistes* and the Problem of History." *Renaissance and Modern Studies* 26 (1982): 108–33.

Wilding, Michael. *Dragon's Teeth: Literature in the English Revolution*. Oxford: Oxford University Press, 1987.

Williams, Raymond. *Marxism and Literature*. Oxford: Oxford University Press, 1977.

Wittreich, Joseph. *Interpreting "Samson Agonistes."* Princeton, N.J.: Princeton University Press, 1986.

———, ed. *Calm of Mind: Tercentenary Essays on "Paradise Regained" and "Samson Agonistes" in Honor of John S. Diekhoff*. Cleveland: Press of Case Western Reserve University, 1971.

Wolfe, Don. *Milton in the Puritan Revolution*. New York: T. Nelson & Sons, 1941.

Wood, Derek. " 'Exil'd from Light': The Darkened Moral Consciousness of Milton's Hero of Faith." *University of Toronto Quarterly* 58 (1988–89): 244–62.

Woolrych, Austin. "The Good Old Cause and the Fall of the Protectorate." *Cambridge Historical Journal* 13 (1957): 133–61.

———. "Milton and Cromwell: 'A Short But Scandalous Night of Interruption?' " In Lieb and Shawcross, *Achievements of the Left Hand*, 185–218.

Worden, Blair. "Andrew Marvell, Oliver Cromwell, and the Horation Ode." In Sharpe and Zwicker, *Politics of Discourse*, 147–80.

Zwicker, Steven. "England, Israel, and the Triumph of Roman Virtue." In *Millenarianism and Messianism in English Literature and Thought, 1650–1800*, edited by Richard H. Popkin, 37–64. Leiden and New York: E. J. Brill, 1988.

———. "Lines of Authority: Politics and Literary Culture in the Restoration." In Sharpe and Zwicker, *Politics of Discourse*, 246–58.

# INDEX

Illustrations appear in bold.

Coláiste Mhuire Gan Smál
Luimneach